SPECIAL ISSUE
REVISITING RIGHTS

STUDIES IN LAW, POLITICS, AND SOCIETY

Series Editor: Austin Sarat

Recent Volumes:

Volumes 1–2:	Edited by Rita J. Simon
Volume 3:	Edited by Steven Spitzer
Volumes 4–9:	Edited by Steven Spitzer and Andrew S. Scull
Volumes 10–16:	Edited by Susan S. Sibey and Austin Sarat
Volumes 17–33:	Edited by Austin Sarat and Patricia Ewick
Volumes 34–48:	Edited by Austin Sarat

STUDIES IN LAW, POLITICS, AND SOCIETY   VOLUME 48

SPECIAL ISSUE REVISITING RIGHTS

EDITED BY

AUSTIN SARAT

*Department of Law, Jurisprudence & Social Thought and
Political Science, Amherst College, USA*

Emerald

United Kingdom – North America – Japan
India – Malaysia – China

PROPERTY OF WMU DISCARD
SOCIAL WORK LIBRARY

Emerald Group Publishing Limited
Howard House, Wagon Lane, Bingley BD16 1WA, UK

First edition 2009

Copyright © 2009 Emerald Group Publishing Limited

Reprints and permission service
Contact: booksandseries@emeraldinsight.com

No part of this book may be reproduced, stored in a retrieval system, transmitted in any
form or by any means electronic, mechanical, photocopying, recording or otherwise
without either the prior written permission of the publisher or a licence permitting
restricted copying issued in the UK by The Copyright Licensing Agency and in the USA
by The Copyright Clearance Center. No responsibility is accepted for the accuracy of
information contained in the text, illustrations or advertisements. The opinions expressed
in these chapters are not necessarily those of the Editor or the publisher.

British Library Cataloguing in Publication Data
A catalogue record for this book is available from the British Library

ISBN: 978-1-84855-930-1
ISSN: 1059-4337 (Series)

Awarded in recognition of
Emerald's production
department's adherence to
quality systems and processes
when preparing scholarly
journals for print

INVESTOR IN PEOPLE

CONTENTS

LIST OF CONTRIBUTORS

Jeb Barnes	Department of Political Science, University of Southern California, USA
Thomas F. Burke	Department of Political Science, Wellesley College, USA
Lisa Hajjar	Law and Society Program, University of California, USA
Thomas Hilbink	U.S. Programs, Open Society Institute, USA
Anna Kirkland	Departments of Women's Studies and Political Science, University of Michigan, USA
Ruth A. Miller	Department of History, University of Massachusetts, USA
Gerald N. Rosenberg	Department of Political Science, University of Chicago, USA

EDITORIAL BOARD

Gad Barzilai
*University of Washington, USA,
and Tel Aviv University, Israel*

Paul Berman
University of Connecticut, USA

Roger Cotterrell
University of London, UK

Jennifer Culbert
Johns Hopkins University, USA

Eve Darian-Smith
*University of Massachusetts,
USA*

David Delaney
Amherst College, USA

Florence Dore
Kent State University, USA

David Engel
*State University of New York
at Buffalo, USA*

Anthony Farley
Boston College, USA

David Garland
New York University, USA

Jonathan Goldberg-Hiller
University of Hawaii, USA

Laura Gomez
University of New Mexico, USA

Piyel Haldar
University of London, UK

Thomas Hilbink
*University of Massachusetts,
USA*

Desmond Manderson
McGill University, Canada

Jennifer Mnookin
*University of California, Los
Angeles, USA*

Laura Beth Nielsen
American Bar Foundation, USA

Paul Passavant
*Hobart and William Smith
College, USA*

Susan Schmeiser
University of Connecticut, USA

Jonathan Simon
University of California, USA

Marianna Valverde
University of Toronto, USA

Alison Young
University of Melbourne, Australia

MUCH ADO ABOUT NOTHING? THE EMPTINESS OF RIGHTS' CLAIMS IN THE TWENTY-FIRST CENTURY UNITED STATES

Gerald N. Rosenberg

ABSTRACT

What does it mean in practice to claim a right? Does claiming a right add to the persuasive power of political demands? Does it clothe political demands with a moral urgency, setting such claims apart from the ordinary class of interests? In examining these questions, I suggest that in practice rights' claims add little to political discourse. This is because Americans equate their policy preferences with rights. I find scant evidence for the belief that Americans have sufficient knowledge of rights to make them meaningful or that pronouncements of rights have persuasive power or imbue issues with heightened moral legitimacy.

INTRODUCTION

Since the mid-twentieth century, various groups in the United States have pressed political claims in the name of "rights." Whether one looks at the

Revisiting Rights
Studies in Law, Politics, and Society, Volume 48, 1–41
Copyright © 2009 by Emerald Group Publishing Limited
All rights of reproduction in any form reserved
ISSN: 1059-4337/doi:10.1108/S1059-4337(2009)0000048004

civil rights movement, the women's movement, gay rights, welfare rights, animal rights, etc., the language and symbols of "rights" permeates contemporary American politics.[1] "Not since the heady days of the American and French Revolutions," Waldron (1987, p. 1) suggests, "have rights been used so widely as touchstones of political evaluation or as an idiom for the expression of political demands." Not only are claims to these various rights made by lawyers pleading specific cases, but more interestingly, they are frequently invoked by non-lawyers operating solely in the political realm, and by ordinary citizens in everyday discourse.

In this chapter I ask, what does it mean in practice to claim a right? What effects do rights' claims produce? Does claiming a right add to the persuasive power of political demands? Does it clothe political demands with a moral urgency, setting such claims apart from the ordinary class of interests? Do pronouncements of rights by governmental institutions change citizens' views on the underlying substantive issue?

At first glance, one might think that asserting rights is a necessary element of progressive political change in any democratic system, particularly one like the United States, based on a written constitution in which certain "fundamental" rights are enshrined. Yet even American experience suggests this is not the case, for appeals to rights have not always been an important part of American movements for change. Furthermore, the European democratic experience suggests this view is false, too; the assertion of "rights" has not been a significant part of the political process in most European democracies.

Why are "rights" believed to be important politically? In the standard literature, the usual answer is that to assert a "right" is to make a special sort of moral, principled, claim, one of heightened legitimacy. In the United States, it is often argued that the language and symbolism of rights originates in the Constitution and has been reinforced by the courts, particularly in recent decades. If the United States is a nation of laws, then these rights must be respected, because if they are not, then political decisions will simply reflect the tyranny of majority preferences. In this view, decisions such as *Brown v. Board of Education* (1954), invoking the language of rights, greatly furthered the equality of African-Americans, and the explosion of 14th Amendment litigation after *Brown* expanded the freedoms of all Americans even further. Thus, judicial action is seen as the major source of rights-based political change, directly linked to the basic rights enshrined in the Constitution. The standard literature concludes that the unique role of the Constitution and courts in the American political system has brought the notion of rights to center stage and given rights-based claims heightened efficacy.

More recently, rights have been understood as providing the foundation for, and structuring, political movements (McCann, 1994; Scheingold, 2004). For example, McCann (1994, p. 6) argues that rights' discourse can be "*constitutive* of practical interactions among citizens." McCann suggests that rights' claims can mobilize individuals to organize and engage in social struggle, influence the substantive and rhetorical positions they take, and transform their self-understandings. Claims of rights can influence people to view existing arrangements in alternative ways. In his study of political mobilization for pay equity, for example, McCann argues that rights' claims led some women to see the wage structure as inequitable and to join the pay equity struggle. Claims of a right to better pay inspired these women. In contrast to a focus on rights as coming from courts, the importance of rights, then, can also be understood as bottom-up and de-centered, forged by ordinary citizens involved in political movements.

Both understandings of the importance of rights assert that rights' claims have an independent and measurable effect on actual political behavior. The court-centered literature has focused primarily on the rhetorical and philosophical side of legal theory and has assumed that providing legal sanction for rights ensures that rights will in fact be protected. But what if these rights are affirmed by courts but violated in practice? If so, then some of the attention that is normally paid to constitutional interpretation needs to be supplemented. Along with exploring the moral or philosophical justifications for particular rights, or their implications for constitutional theory, scholars ought also to be examining how and under what conditions the rights enshrined in the Constitution and invoked by the courts have greater or lesser impact on political life. This includes not merely substantive outcomes but also the way in which activists and the public alike use rights to organize, to evaluate, and to understand politics. This must also be the case with the bottom-up, de-centered, constitutive approach to understanding rights. In the simplest terms, when, if ever, and in what ways, do "rights" and rights' claims make a difference?

In the following pages, I offer a three-part response. First, I suggest that in practice rights' claims add little to political discourse. Rather than understanding them as claims of heightened normative power, or as constitutive of people's understandings of their relationships to authority structures, I wonder if they are little more than empty rhetoric. Could it be that Americans reflexively use the language of rights for anything and everything they want? That claims of rights are little more than a reflexive and empty rhetoric, the "um" and "uh" of modern American discourse? Second, I examine Americans' knowledge and views of political and constitutional rights. Third, I canvass public opinion literature to examine how judicially generated rights influence the views of Americans on the underlying substantive issues. I find scant evidence for the belief that Americans have sufficient knowledge of rights to make them meaningful or that pronouncements of rights have persuasive power or imbue issues with heightened moral legitimacy. What I offer in the rest of the chapter is not an attack on rights but a question about whether in contemporary American culture they have become politically meaningless.

THE VARYING HISTORICAL USE OF RIGHTS

To understand the allure of rights, it is important to know something historically about their political use. Although notions of rights date back to ancient times, they have varied enormously in their political importance. Notions of natural rights were used in Europe in the seventeenth and eighteenth centuries to challenge theories of political absolutism (Waldron, 1987, p. 7). They reached a highpoint in the language of the French Revolution but then were mostly replaced in the nineteenth century by theories of class and nation.[2] In the United States, although the American Revolution raised rights issues, as did the issue of slavery, until comparatively recent times their salience was low. In the rest of the world, general neglect until recent times is a fair characterization. Even the League of Nations, founded in the wake of World War I's devastation, had no provisions in its charter protecting human rights except, perhaps, a virtually meaningless provision for the "just treatment of the native inhabitants of territories" under the control of member states (quoted in Waldron, 1987, p. 154).

In the United States, notions of rights have not consistently been an important part of political discourse, nor always been taken seriously. The treatment of the Bill of Rights provides a good example. After ratification in 1791, Rakove (1991, p. 98) writes, the Bill of Rights "quickly passed into legal and political irrelevance." As Ely and Bodenhamer (1993, p. vii) note, "throughout much of our constitutional history the Bill of Rights played a secondary role in shaping individual liberties." Lacey and Haakonssen (1991, p.4) concur, finding that "through most of American history the Bill of Rights played little if any role in the broader scheme of national development." The sustained prevalence of rights' claims in the second half of the twentieth and early twenty-first centuries in the United States is a new phenomenon.

The political use of rights' claims has varied as well. Starting in Europe as a challenge to absolutism, and culminating in the French Revolution, calls to rights were made by those challenging monarchical power. That quickly changed and rights became the bulwark, both in Europe and the United States, of the defense of the status quo. In the United States, from the late-nineteenth century until 1937, notions of substantive due process and liberty of contract were successful rights-based legal defenses to government attempts at economic regulation and worker protection and welfare. Indeed the U.S. Supreme Court became a great proponent of rights-based defenses of inequality. "Throughout most of American history," Ely (1993, p. 87) notes, "the Supreme Court functioned as a guardian of property and economic rights against legislative encroachments." The political alignment in Europe was similar: "In all of Europe as well, from the time of the French Revolution, the party of reform identified its cause with popular sovereignty while identifying all 'higher law' arguments either with a discredited Catholic natural law philosophy or with efforts to endow the remnants of privilege left over from the Old Order with an undeserved fundamentality" (Horwitz, 1988b, p. 396).

This political alignment may be difficult for modern readers to understand. But both historically and well into the twentieth century, rights have most often served conservative aims of protecting the unequal status quo distribution of power and privilege. As Scheingold (2004, p. xxxiii) notes, "rights have historically had more to do with the protection of property and privilege than with their redistribution." Indeed, "for most of American constitutional history, rights theories have been associated with protection of property against a more just distribution of wealth and privilege" (Horwitz, 1988b, p. 405). Bartholomew and Hunt (1990, p. 2) note the "conspicuous role that 'rights-talk' has played in the political discourse of the traditional conservative...parties in modern Europe and North America." This led social reformers to attack rights as impeding progressive change. There is a good deal of writing by self-professed leftists that is hostile to rights. Horwitz (1988b, pp. 396, 395), for example, notes that in the United States "attacks by social reformers on the very concept of rights was a familiar pattern by the 1900s" and, by the early twentieth century, "Progressive legal opinion was overwhelmingly hostile to rights discourse." As late as 1937 Horwitz (1988a, p. 1034) finds that "virtually all progressive legal thinkers were hostile to the idea of rights." This leads him to conclude that "when the New Deal majority triumphed in 1937, one would surely have said the era of rights was over" (Horwitz, 1988a, p. 1035).

World War II appeared to revive rights as a force for progressive change. As Glendon (1991, p. 7) reminds us, in the wake of Hitler's genocide, "human rights were enshrined in a variety of covenants and declarations, notably the United Nations' Universal Declaration of Human Rights of 1948." In the United States, the post–World War II period saw a "marked increase in the assertion of rights-based claims, beginning with the civil rights movement of the 1950s and 1960s…" (Glendon, 1991, p. 4). In the "Rights Revolution" that followed, group after group, and interest after interest, used the language of rights to press for progressive change. And that language remains popular today.

The varying historical use of rights suggests two main points for understanding the political use of rights' claims in modern America. First, demands for political reform have not historically depended on rights' claims. Second, historically, rights' claims have predominantly been used by those defending the status quo distribution of resources. Understanding the political use of rights requires careful examination.

TO CLAIM A RIGHT – POSSIBLE MEANINGS

What is meant by rights? What are their salient characteristics? Definitions, distinctions, and characteristics abound. For the purposes of this chapter, however, I am interested less in the philosophical foundations and meanings of rights' claims and more in what is meant in current American politics and culture by those making rights' claims, and in what efficacy they have. This still requires noting possible variations in meanings. A classic distinction is between negative and positive rights, with the former being claims that government must not do certain things (e.g., prohibit speech critical of the government), whereas the latter is a claim that the government must in fact take positive action (e.g., provide all citizens with adequate food, housing, medical care). Most modern rights' claims are claims of positive rights, entitlement claims, claims that the government take positive action.[3]

A second and crucial aspect of rights' claims is that they involve a moral dimension. Haskell (1987, p. 984; emphasis in original) puts it this way: "When I say I have a *right* to do something…I am not merely saying that I want to do it and hope that others will let me; I am saying that they *ought* to let me, have a *duty* to let me, and will be guilty of an injustice, a transgression against moral standards, if they fail to do so." A claim of rights is a call to principle. It implies a duty in those to whom the claim is addressed. There is no duty to grant someone or some group that which they claim if it is a mere preference, something they merely want. It might be good to do so because it is good policy, or it makes sense, but there is no moral requirement to act. If, however, it is a right that is being claimed, a duty lies.

A third feature of rights is that they are universal, applicable to all persons who are similarly situated. For example, the right to criticize the government is available to all critics regardless of whether their criticisms come from the left or the right of the political spectrum. In contrast, the claim that I have a right to criticize the government but you don't is a claim of interest, not right. Similarly, a right to religious freedom may be claimed by all persons, not just those who follow a particular religion, and it cannot be denied to those who hold no religious beliefs.

A fourth important aspect of rights is the distinction between rights and statutory entitlements on the one hand and interests on the other hand. The distinction is based on the difference between a legally and/or constitutionally settled right and an interest in creating such a right. For example, under Title VII of the 1964 Civil Rights Act, a job applicant has the legal right not to have race negatively taken into account in her application for a job. However, in the early twenty-first century, the claim by a gay man or a lesbian not to have his or her sexual preference taken into account remains an interest; it has yet to be given statutory or constitutional protection. These two meanings are often confused in political discourse "The language of 'rights'," Westen (1986, p. 1009) concludes, "tends to mask the difference between entitlements and interests."

This distinction is crucial for understanding the political use of rights. An example may help clarify the distinction. As noted, under Title VII of the 1964 Civil Rights Act, an individual has a right not to be discriminated against in hiring and employment on the grounds of race, color, religion, sex, or national origin. However, in the United States, no individual has a legal or constitutional right to a job. A person claiming a "right" to a job may desperately need a job but that does not make the demand a right. It is an interest, or a preference. In contrast, a demand for non-discriminatory treatment in employment, or a complaint that such discrimination has occurred, is a demand for the enforcement of an existing legally protected right. Similarly, although an insurance company or a hospital cannot deny health care coverage or health care to an individual based on her race, there is no right to either health insurance or health care. Claims based on the "right to health care" are statements of interests or preferences, not legally recognized rights.

Finally, there is the issue of the state. The rights' claims that predominate in American politics are those that involve an attempt to induce government action. The kind of rights' claims that are involved here are distinct from those made in disputes between individuals where the state is not directly involved. Responding to those sorts of claims usually does not require redistributing power and resources on behalf of a group or class. The rights' claims that I examine in this chapter are addressed to the state and call for state action in their support.

Bringing these distinctions, definitions, and characteristics together, I understand the general notion of a rights' claim in modern American politics and culture to be a claim for positive action by the state to further the interests of the rights' claimer and all those similarly situated.[4]

THE PREVALENCE OF RIGHTS' CLAIMS

Rights' claims are everywhere in American society. "For better or worse," writes Mary Ann Glendon (1992, p. 532), Americans "take rights very seriously." What she means is that the discourse of rights is pervasive in American society. Her 1991 book, *Rights Talk*, is based on the observation that "discourse about rights has become the principal language that we use in public settings to discuss weighty questions of right and wrong..." (Glendon, 1991, p. x). Writing in the early 1990s, Glendon (1991, p. 4) saw an "increasing tendency to speak of what it most important to us in terms of rights, and to frame nearly every social controversy as a clash of rights." She was concerned that this "romance of rights" (Glendon, 1991, p. 5) had detrimental effects on the broader society. Although not everyone shares her concerns, commentators do concur in the prevalence of rights talk. Silverstein (1996, p. 17) notes that "we live in a society in which people see themselves as rights-bearing beings and in which legal, political, and social relationships are commonly defined in terms of rights." In celebrating rights, Walker (1998, p. xi) notes that "our daily discourse is pervaded by 'rights talk,' the habit of automatically thinking in terms of individual rights."

The prevalence of rights' claims is generally understood as a reflection of their importance. Walker (1998, p. xi), for example, argues that our "daily lives are very different as a result of the explosive growth of a set of individual rights." From civil rights to women's rights to abortion rights to speech rights to criminal rights and so on, Walker and others claim that the assertion of rights has fundamentally changed American society.

As the preceding discussion suggests, since the mid-twentieth century claims of rights have been most famously asserted in the United States by those on the political left.[5] They have asserted rights on behalf of the relatively disadvantaged to win equal treatment, limit arbitrary governmental authority, and widen and deepen access to shared societal benefits. Much of my argument in this chapter questions the efficacy of these rights' claims on empirical grounds. In addition, there has been a debate among scholars that also questions their efficacy on historical and philosophical grounds. It requires brief discussion.

There is both a longstanding and a more recent critique of the political efficacy of rights from many on the political left. Various strands of left-wing thought have been and remain hostile to rights' claims. At least some of this hostility stems from Marx's critique of liberal rights as merely the rights of the individual, alienated, bourgeoisie. As such, they can play no role in the march toward revolution. On this view, the politics of rights is illusionary, incapable of bringing about more than token change, and diversionary. Some of the left's hostility can also be traced to the political right's reliance on rights. Historically, as I have suggested, claims of rights have traditionally been used against the forces of progressive change. This has led many on the left to critique rights (see, e.g., Appleby, 1987, p. 808; Bartholomew & Hunt 1990, p. 2; Horwitz, 1988b). Additionally, in the late-twentieth century, the Critical Legal Studies Movement (CLS) launched a major attack on rights. At its heart, the CLS concern was that rights' claims, even when successful, produced only token changes, not the kind of fundamental changes in society that equality and justice demand. In exploring why this is the case, Tushnet (1984, pp. 1363–1364) offers four critiques of rights from a CLS perspective: 1) rights are "unstable"; 2) a right produces "no determinate consequences"; 3) the "concept of rights falsely converts into an empty abstraction (reifies) real experiences..."; 4) the "use of rights in contemporary discourse impedes advances by progressive social forces...." This means that even successful rights' claims provide no guarantees of fundamental change in society. As Peter Gabel puts it, "exactly what people don't need is their *rights*" (Gabel & Kennedy, 1984, p. 33). The brunt of the CLS criticism appears to be that claims of rights are individual, general, and abstract when communal, specific, and particular changes are required.

There are others on the left, however, who either are deeply committed to the importance of rights for social change or have developed a more nuanced and subtle understanding of them. One emotionally powerful defense of rights has come from some minority scholars who essentially argue that the critique of rights (particularly the CLS critique) undervalues the experience of people of color. Matsuda (1987, pp. 331, 324), for example, argues that the "standard critique" is too abstract and needs a "bottom-up perspective" because "those who have experienced discrimination speak with a special voice to which we should listen." Writing with that voice is Williams (1987, p. 416):

> For the historically disempowered, the conferring of rights is symbolic of all the denied aspects of humanity: rights imply a respect which places one within the referential range of self and others, which elevates one's status from human body to social being. For blacks, then, the attainment of rights signifies the due, the respectful behavior, the collective responsibility properly owed by a society to one of its own.

Delgado concurs: "Rights do, at times, give pause to those who would otherwise oppress us..." (quoted in Fisher, 1991, p. 317). Statements like these lead Fisher (1991, p. 317) to conclude that "the impact of rights discourse on social psychology is likely, on balance, to be beneficial to minorities."

Much of the recent debate about the role of rights in American society has focused on social movements. In part in response to the CLS critique, some students of social movements argued that rights can make an important difference to the powerless as a protection against oppression, a tool for organizing, and a support for dignity. Often accepting much of the historical and CLS critique of the limited value of rights in producing change, these writers nonetheless argue that rights can and have been used by the less powerful to gain resources (see, e.g., Bartholomew & Hunt, 1990, p. 7; Horwitz, 1988b, p. 395; Sparer, 1984, p. 514; White, 1992, p. 74). This happens in a number of ways. Some have argued, for example, that rights consciousness can provide the central point of identity for social groups and can build community strength (Freeman, 1988, p. 335; Milner, 1989, p. 631; Schneider, 1986, p. 649; Thelen, 1987, p. 795). Others have claimed that rights talk can help mobilize people and build movements (Appleby, 1987, p. 808; Scheingold, 2004, especially chapter 12; Scheingold, 1989; Schneider, 1986, pp. 611, 650; Sparer, 1984, p. 560). As Peter Gabel puts it, "the struggle to increase the strength and energy of a movement can partially result from the acquisition of rights" (Gabel & Kennedy, 1984, p. 37). Still others have argued that rights' claims can transform individuals' beliefs about the world, transforming their consciousness of their lives and their possibilities. From Kennedy's claim (Gabel & Kennedy, 1984, p. 40) that "rights analysis is a way of imagining the world" to Schneider's insistence (Schneider, 1986, p. 625) that the "women's rights movement has had an important affirming and individuating effect on women's consciousness," the consciousness-raising potential of rights has been repeatedly asserted.[6] Finally, most of these scholars are aware, as Bartholomew and Hunt (1990, pp. 50, 41) put it, that rights are only a "potential resource" that may have "different consequences and functions for different groups" at different times and places.

More recent work supports these views. In their study of the Americans with Disabilities Act (ADA), Engel & Munger find several positive features of rights' claims. Rights, they find, can "transform the sense of self," "subtly shape the terms of discussion or the images and conceptual categories that are used in everyday interactions," and "enter social settings indirectly, by changing institutional practices although no one has explicitly voiced a complaint" (Engel & Munger, 2003, p. 11).

The work of Stuart Scheingold is exemplary of this view. Although a long-time critic of what he labeled the "myth of rights" as a tool to bring about change (Scheingold, 2004), Scheingold has repeatedly stressed the positive roles rights can play as a resource for change. In addition to "challenging repressive practices," rights can also "offer considerable cultural space for liberating activism" (Scheingold, 1989, p. 86). Scheingold (1989, p. 87) finds that "within obvious limits, then, the soft hegemony of constitutional rights offers opportunities for meaningful, if not funda-mental, social change." Reviewing the social movement literature in 2004, he again stresses the conditional nature of rights. Although they are a "distinctly qualified political resource," they can, under "appropriate conditions...be deployed to promote collective political mobilization on behalf of an egalitarian agenda" (Scheingold, 2004, p. xxxi).

Michael McCann's *Rights at Work* is, in the words of one reviewer, "the primary source of theorizing about the many complicated ways that law and rights can matter for social movements or reform efforts at different stages of conflicts" (Paris, 2006, p. 1007). In this rich and evocative study of the political battle for pay equity, McCann argues that rights' claims played an important role in mobilizing women and helping them develop new understandings of themselves and the broader society. "[P]erhaps *the single most important achievement* of the movement," McCann (1994, p. 230) was told by the activists he interviewed, "has been the transformations in many working women's understandings, commitments, and affiliations – i.e., in their hearts, minds, and social identities." McCann credits this to the importance of rights.

The problem with this analysis, and many other studies of social move-ments, is that researchers have not been able to disentangle the importance of rights' claims from the importance of the movement itself.[7] Throughout *Rights at Work*, for example, McCann notes the crucial importance of union organization to pay equity activity. He is unable to assess what independent role, if any, rights' claims played in the effects he found. McCann argues that success occurred principally, if not solely, in venues where there were pre-existing worker organizations. For example, he concludes that "most pay equity campaigns included in this study originated at grassroots levels among small preexisting solidaristic groups of clericals" (McCann, 1994, p. 114). Where such organizations did not exist, law did not help: "legal tactics and rights claims contributed to movement building *only* to the extent that they resonated with the experiences of various target groups already *well situated* for political activation" (McCann, 1994, p. 135, emphasis added). It is possible, perhaps likely, that it was the union organizing itself and not the rhetoric of rights that produced the positive effects he found. Rights' claims were present in the movement but whether they added persuasive power to it remains unproven. The feelings of empowerment and consciousness raising that McCann highlights may be the results of organized activity rather than the rhetoric of rights.

Overall, then, there is a debate about the efficacy of rights' claims to change behavior even among those most sympathetic to their power. Most of the work is not empirically based and that which is does not differentiate the efficacy of rights' claims from other influences and actions. This means that it is entirely possible that rights' claims add little or nothing to political debate.

THE EMPIRICAL CHALLENGE TO THE EFFICACY OF RIGHTS' CLAIMS

Although many of these claims of the efficacy of rights are stirring, and made with confidence, they do not, on their own, settle the issue. Evidence is needed that rights' claims do make the kind of difference that is asserted. Most of the writers who assert the importance of rights are law professors, often at elite institutions. The standard claim they make is that rights have been important to groups with which they have worked and in their own lives. But for them to claim that rights have been important in their work and lives is about as startling as librarians claiming that books have been important in their work and lives. Both statements are undoubtedly true, but neither statement tells us very much about the importance of rights or books to the larger society. Empirical studies are needed that examine claims of rights consciousness, of the instigating and mobilizing potential of rights talk. Without them, the debate will remain general and abstract, offering little hope for deepening our understanding.

There is very little work that has empirically examined the political efficacy of rights. Glendon (1991), for example, eschews systematic evidence for a number of insightful and provocative claims about its effect on political life. Virtually all of the social movement studies are based on single samples and in-depth interviews. Although there is a great deal that can be learned about social movements from such an approach, separating out the importance of rights' claims from other parts of the movement's activities is next-to-impossible.

RIGHTS AS PREFERENCES

There is another understanding of the way rights are used in American politics. It is that rights are no different from preferences. Preferences, unlike rights, carry no moral weight. They are independent of any notion of rights. A preference is a desire with no strong moral claim to legitimacy. If rights are understood as preferences, then to claim a right is merely to state a preference. On this understanding, claims of rights need not be consistent, universal, or general. My right to do X does not necessarily have anything to do with your right to do X. For example, my friends and I have a right to free speech because we want it. You and your friends do not have that right because we do not like what you are saying. Under the notion of rights as preferences, the claim of a right to free speech, for example, actually means protection for anyone who wishes to say what the one claiming the right wishes to say. Rights' claims resonate with others when they speak to their experiences, vision, and understanding of the world. They do not persuade but rather confirm. They have no persuasive power outside of those already committed to the substantive belief.

It follows from this definition of rights as preferences that arguing for or protecting certain practices by calling them rights will have no effect on the evaluation of the practice. Since rights are merely a label that adds nothing to the underlying claim, what matters is the substance of the claim, not how it is labeled. So, for example, Supreme Court decisions finding a constitutional right to something should make no appreciable difference in how Americans react to whatever practice has been constitutionalized. Or, to take McCann's example, the claim to a *right* to pay equity is no different than a *demand* for pay equity, a *preference* for pay equity, or a *desire* for pay equity. It was the substantive idea of being paid more money for their work that inspired the workers, not the claim that they had a right to it.

Two examples illustrate the point I am suggesting. The first involves a reaction to the Supreme Court's 1989 decision in *Texas v. Johnson* (1989) granting protection to flag-burning as a form of constitutionally protected speech. A spokesman for the American Legion, interviewed on the *Today* show the day after the decision, explained the Legion's disagreement with the decision. The Legion was opposed to the decision because, the spokesman said, the "flag is the symbol of our country, the land of the free and the home of the brave." When pushed to say "what exactly does it symbolize," he responded, "it stands for the fact that this is a country where we have the right to do what we want" (quotes from Glendon, 1991, p. 8). This response, of course, entirely justifies the actions of the flag-burner of which the Legion complained. Glendon understands it as a harried and exasperated response, one that mischaracterizes the Legion's position. But if rights are nothing more than preferences, then the response makes some sense. Clearly, the spokesman and the Legion do not believe in burning flags. One can assume that no member of the Legion would ever have an interest in burning a flag, and knows no one who would. If this is the case, then the statement "we have a right to do what we want" simply means that people who think the way we do, and share our beliefs, have the right to do whatever they want. People who think differently do not have that right. Rights, then, protect Legion members in their activities, allowing them to do what they want to do. On this interpretation, there is neither contradiction nor inconsistency in the spokesman's statement.

The second example is not directly tied to rights but illustrates the substantive evaluation of legal understanding. It involves interviews with several laid-off steel workers who were using their cars as taxis but were not reporting their income, paying no taxes. As the *Wall Street Journal* reported, "for the most part, they are intensely proud people who hang the American flag from their neat front porches on holidays and respect the law, believing strongly in right and wrong." In this case, however, they "don't see why they should" pay taxes on their income. As the story reports, "their changed circumstances have altered the way many of them think" (quoted in Ansberry, 1986). The tax laws in question appear to be evaluated on the basis of group preferences. I would be surprised, however, if these laid-off steel workers would defend African-American women on welfare who did not declare income. On this interpretation, that behavior would be wrong because none of the men are on welfare. What I am suggesting is that rights, like obedience to the tax law in question here, may be nothing more than preferences, claims that the law should allow individuals and groups to do what they wish.

My analysis of these two examples finds support in the literature more generally. Reviewing the empirical literature in 1977 Sarat (1977, p. 448) found that "Americans seem too willing to tolerate restrictions on the rights of those who are strange, different, or threatening even as they profess devotion to the principles from which those rights derive." Similarly, employing in-depth interviews to investigate how people think about rights and liberties, Chong found a preference-based understanding. He found that respondents "commonly give responses based on how they are personally affected by the issue or how they feel about the group that wishes to exercise its rights" (Chong, 1993, pp. 885–886). If they do not like a particular group then they do not support protecting its activities. Furthermore, if they are not personally affected, then they judge governmental activity accordingly. Describing one respondent, Chong (1993, p. 887) writes, "[s]o long as his well-being is not threatened, he is not particularly troubled by violations of individual rights. He would not be bothered if the police conducted a search of his car for narcotics because he does not use drugs." In my language, these are claims of preference that need not be principled nor apply to others. Rights as preferences make sense of these views.

To a perhaps surprising extent, one can find hints and suggestions of such an understanding in some of the rights literature, including some literature written by supporters of the standard definition. Any number of commentators have worried that the plethora of rights' claims in modern America trivializes the moral weight of a rights claim by allowing any claim to be labeled a right. "A rapidly expanding catalog of rights," Glendon (1991, p. xi) notes, "risks trivializing core democratic values." Horwitz (1988b, p. 399) sees "an ungrounded conception of rights that allows anyone to propose his or her favorite right." And Waldron (1987, p. 2) writes that "few of us want the language of rights to degenerate into a sort of lingua franca in which moral and political values of all or many kinds may be expressed." If rights are merely preferences, then these fears are well grounded.

This fear of a "right for all seasons" may stem from the fact that rights' claims seem to be generated by individual or group desires to achieve certain ends and not by general, universal, principled argument. On a general level, Glendon notes that if Americans want to protect something, rather than providing substantive arguments for it, they "try to get it characterized as a right." This means, Glendon (1991, pp. 31, 171) concludes, that "the new rhetoric of rights is less about human dignity and freedom than about insistent, un-ending desires." Olsen (1984, p. 430) admits as much by urging feminists to "stop trying to fit our goals into abstract rights arguments and instead call for what we really want." As that great believer in the moral distinctiveness of rights, Leo Durocher, put it, "I believe I have a right to test the rules by seeking how far they can be bent" (quoted in Macaulay, 1987, p. 204).[8]

On a specific level, there is some evidence to support this rights as preferences position. Examining rights in the mental health area, Milner (1989, p. 45) suggests that "attitudes toward individual rights appear to vary a great deal from issue to issue, according to how much an individual feels a right touches his or her life." When steelworkers in Youngstown and Pittsburgh developed the idea of a community right to industrial property, even their great defender and champion Staughton Lynd (1987, p. 953) realized that they were "motivated, not by a belief in the intrinsic virtue of public enterprise, but by their desperate need for jobs." This labeling of preferences as rights is not unique to the twentieth century. Tushnet notes that "opponents of the Civil Rights Act of 1875 and the Fourteenth Amendment pointed out that their adversaries could not offer a definition of civil or political rights that explained why women were not protected," and Dubois notes that the failure of the 14th Amendment to apply to women led some women to denounce it as a "desecration" (Tushnet, 1987, p. 887, n.12; Dubois, 1987, p. 848). Brigham, although writing about the specific instance of the reaction of the gay community to a perceived threat to the community's bath houses, captures this point: "In the end, the rights claim was more like a stance, a political position, than an appeal to reason" (Brigham, 1987, p. 309).

Jeremy Bentham was an ardent foe of rights. "The strength of this argument [for any given right]," he wrote, "is in proportion to the strength of lungs in those who use it" (quoted in Waldron, 1987, p. 73). He continued:

> When a man is bent on having things his own way and give no reason for it, he says: I have a right to have them so. When a man has a political caprice to gratify, and is determined to gratify it, if possible, at any price, when he feels an ardent desire to see it gratified but can give no reason why it should be gratified, when he finds it necessary to get the multitude to join with him, but either stoops not to enquire whether they would be the better or the happier for so doing, or feels himself at a loss to prove it, he sets up a cry of rights. (quoted in Waldron, 1987, pp. 73–74)

The notion of rights as preferences does seem to have some support.

The notion of rights as preferences receives support from a major study of American youth commissioned by People for the American Way. The study, done during the spring of 1989, interviewed a national, stratified sample of over 1,000 young people ages 15–24, and followed up with 100 in-depth interviews. The findings suggest that American young people are strongly committed to a notion of rights, but understood, in the words of one respondent, as "the freedom to do as we please when we please" (People for the American Way, 1989, p. 14). When asked, "if someone from another country asked you to explain what makes America special, what would you tell them?" the responses suggested a rights-as-preferences view. Nearly two-thirds (63%) of the responses related to "freedoms available to Americans," while 23% mentioned freedom of speech or the press (People for the American Way, 1989, p. 67). However, these "freedoms" were usually defined as preferences. Notably missing were the democratic nature of the political system, mentioned by only 7%, and "such fundamental privileges and liberties as the right to vote (5%), freedom of religion (5%), and women's rights (4%)" (People for the American Way, 1989, pp. 67, 28). This characterization was illustrated by many of the responses in the in-depth interviews to the question of what makes America special. Responses included the following: "The freedom to do anything you want in terms of fulfilling your dreams"; "Baseball, football with gear, wide open spaces…"; "Freedom. I'd like to show them a rock concert"; "Individualism, and the fact that it is a democracy and you can do whatever you want"; "That we really don't have any limits" (People for the American Way, 1989, pp. 68–69).[9] In one focus group, "when asked to name qualities that make this country special, the young people sat in silence until one young man offered, 'Cable TV'" (People for the American Way, 1989, p. 9). Furthermore, as Table 1 illustrates, commitment to fundamental political rights was weak. When asked which rights they would fight hardest to keep, barely one-third chose freedom of speech, while barely one in ten would fight hardest to keep the right to vote, and almost nobody (1 in a 100!) would fight hardest to keep a free press. Similarly, over one quarter would most willingly give up a free press, and 17% would most willingly give up the right to protest. Again, these data suggest an emphasis on "personal rights and freedoms" (People for the American Way, 1989, p. 70), rights as preferences.

Another example of treating preferences as rights is provided by the American Cancer Society, an organization dedicated to prevent cancer and help those suffering from the disease. In 2007 in acknowledgments of support on National Public Radio, and in print advertisements, it made the

Table 1.   Rights and Freedoms: Fight to Keep or Give Up?.

Category	Fight Hardest *to Keep* (%)	Most Willing to *Give Up* (%)
Freedom of speech	34	2
Freedom of religion	18	11
Freedom to choose career	14	11
Right to vote	12	8
Right to own private property	8	15
Right to protest	5	17
Freedom of the press	1	27
Other	8	9

Source: People for the American Way (1989, p. 154, Questions 6a, 6b).

following claim: "No one deserves to get cancer, but everyone deserves the right to fight it" (American Cancer Society, 2007). This is a noble thought, but what is meant by the "right" to fight cancer? Presumably everyone suffering from cancer wants to fight it and wants to survive. But are cancer patients being prevented from fighting their cancer? Is some right to fight the disease being denied them? Or is the use of rights language merely a shorthand for the claim that cancer patients want to get better?

In searching the American Cancer Society's website, I learned that the Society is concerned that tens of millions of Americans lack the necessary health insurance to pay the enormous expenses for medical care to fight cancer. The rights' claim, then, is likely a claim that all cancer patients should have access to medical care. But for better or worse there is no legal or constitutional right to health care in the United States. Many believe it would be a good thing if all Americans had access to health care, but that does not make it a right. Cancer is a frightening disease, and I do not mean to trivialize its devastating impact. My point is simply that the American Cancer Society selected the language of rights to make a claim about a policy preference.

An even more telling example of the use of rights' language to mean preference in modern American discourse is provided by the iconic, fast-food, hamburger chain, Burger King. The chain's long-time slogan, "Have It Your Way," promises consumers choice in how their hamburgers are prepared. In the early years of the twenty-first century, Burger King restaurants provided paper liners for their plastic trays. A copy of the text is produced in Table. 2. Entitled the "Burger King Bill of Rights," it contains 13 sentences all of which start, "You have the right...." The first sentence sets the tone, stating, "You have the right to have things your way."

Table 2. Burger King Bill of Rights.

You have the right to have things your way.
You have the right to hold the pickles and hold the lettuce.
You have the right to mix Coke and Sprite.
You have the right to a Whopper sandwich with extra tomato, extra onion and triple cheese.
You have the right to have that big meal sleepy feeling when you're finished.
You have the right to put a paper crown on your head and pretend you are ruler of "(your make believe kingdom here)."
You have the right to have your chicken fire grilled or fried.
You have the right to dip your fries in ketchup, mayonnaise, BBQ sauce or mustard or not.
You have the right to laugh until soda explodes from your nose.
You have the right to stand up and fight for what you believe in.
You have the right to sit down and do nothing.
You have the right to eat a hot and juicy fire-grilled burger prepared just the way you like.
You have the right to crumple this Bill of Rights into a ball and shoot hoops with it.
Have it Your Way

Source: Wansink and Peters (2007, p. 200).

These "rights" include everything from the right to "mix Coke and Sprite," to have a "Whopper sandwich with extra tomato, extra onion and triple cheese," to "put a paper crown on your head and pretend you're ruler of (your make believe kingdom here)," to "stand up and fight for what you believe in," to "crumple this Bill of Rights into a ball and shoot hoops with it."

The remarkable aspect of this tray liner is the equation of a preference for a hamburger prepared in a certain way with a fundamental right. By titling it the "Bill of Rights," Burger King references the first ten amendments to the U.S. Constitution, which contain guarantees of fundamental rights. Along with the "right to hold the pickles and hold the lettuce" (and the other "rights" dealing with hamburgers), the "Burger King Bill of Rights" includes the "right to stand up and fight for what you believe in." That's a genuine right, protected in large part by the constitutional guarantees of free speech, a free press, and the right of association. It has little to do with one's preferences for hamburgers. The "Burger King Bill of Rights" lists them together, at the very least implying that they are similar. I do not know how these tray liners affected sales. The point, however, is that a very successful, consumer-dependent, huge American corporation used the language of rights to sell hamburgers.

Cancer is a serious matter; hamburgers are not. But both the American Cancer Society and Burger King used the language of rights to further their preferences. I have argued in this section that much contemporary American rights' rhetoric can be understood as nothing more than assertions of preferences. "When we want to protect something," Glendon (1991, p. 31) notes, "we try to get it characterized as a right." An animal rights activist concurred, saying: "In a sense I think rights are nonsense...[But] as long as we keep talking about rights, as long as we are living in a society where the language is a language of rights, then I think it's important that we talk about rights" (quoted in Silverstein, 1996, p. 97). The contemporary claim of rights, then, may be little more than a statement of preferences.

RIGHTS AS CONTEXTUAL PREFERENCES

Another way in which preferences are equated with rights is that their use is deeply contextual. In principle, rights are universal. If I have a right to vote, it does not depend on which candidate I support or whether my preferred candidate is winning or losing. The right exists independently of my candidate preferences. Support for the *right* to vote cannot depend on context. But if rights are nothing more than preferences, then support for a right may vary depending on the context. What I mean is that belief in a right will ebb and flow depending on other preferences. For example, a right might be claimed for a particular group of people in a given set of circumstances and denied for similarly situated people in different circumstances. There is a good deal of evidence that this is exactly how Americans perceive rights. For example, in his study of rights' consciousness in American history, Rogers (1993, p. 9) points out that when working men claimed rights in the nineteenth century, their movement was "shot through with the surrounding racism. Many of the same political figures who championed the rights of white free labor succeeded in cutting down the civil freedoms of Northern black citizens and forcing them from the voting rolls." There was nothing universal about this claim of rights. It was an attempt by one group, white working men, to better their own conditions. Now that may have been a good thing, but it was little more than a contextual preference. Rights to free labor only applied to white men. The claim of a right was nothing more than a preference. As Sarat (1977, p. 444) concludes, "Americans do not perceive the interrelatedness of their own freedom and the freedom of others; they value their own freedom but not the freedom of others." Rights understood as contextual preferences explains why.

The contextual nature of rights' claims is highlighted by scholarship based on in-depth interviews. In their 1998 book, Ewick and Silbey rely on the stories people tell about law, legality and rights to explore popular legal consciousness. On the basis of in-depth interviews, Ewick and Silbey highlight the contextual nature of rights' claims. Among the "three stories" people tell about law and legality, they find one in which "legality is depicted as a game, a terrain for tactical encounters through which people marshal a variety of social resources to achieve strategic goals…" (Ewick & Silbey, 1998, p. 28). In other words, when rights resonate with experience, rights' claims may be asserted. But they worry that rights' claims may be too abstract, working to deny the experience of the potential rights-claimer: "by employing the language of rights to describe a relationship, we deny the complexity, ambiguity, and contradictions of social experience that are referenced by the term 'right'" (Ewick & Silbey, 1998, p. 232). In Ewick and Silbey's understanding, rights' claims are deeply contextual.

Similarly, in their interview-based study of the ADA, Engel and Munger highlight the contextual nature of rights claims. They explore the ways in which legal discourse such as rights is intertwined with individual needs and understandings. They find that not all people with disabilities claim rights, including individuals who are clearly entitled to them under the law. Indeed, they report that "none of the sixty interviewees used rights explicitly and confrontationally in situations of perceived injustice" (Engel & Munger, 2003, p. 252). The factors that emerged as the best predictor of when rights' claims were made were individual. Engel and Munger (2003, p. 240) find that "identity provides the key to understanding how and when rights become active." In other words, "perceptions of who one is and where one belongs play a critical role in determining whether rights are understood as relevant" (Engel & Munger, 2003, p. 142). And this contextual assertion of rights' claims occurs in a situation in which statutory rights exist and provide a clear basis for entitlements.

Much of the social movement literature suggests that rights' claims are contextual and contingent. For example, Milner (1989, p. 645), discussing the use of rights' claims by several mental health organizations, found that "attitudes toward individual rights appear to vary a great deal from issue to issue, according to how much an individual feels a right touches his or her life." If rights are contextual preferences, then Milner's finding that "rights discourse was appealing and open-ended enough to be used in a wide variety of ways by groups and individuals throughout the culture, *even by those who are critical of rights*," makes sense (Milner, 1989, p. 671; emphasis added). Writing more generally, Sparer (1984, p. 560) notes that "the meaning of a right or entitlement depends upon the way in which it intertwines with social movement." Nowhere is the conditional nature of rights' claims more clearly stated than in McCann's seminal work. McCann argues that for rights to help progressive forces there must be public and elite support, pre-existing groups and resources committed to the issue, a committed leadership, and a pre-disposed target audience. When all these conditions are present, rights can, but will not necessarily, make a difference:

> Even under the most propitious circumstances, moreover, the contributions of legal maneuvers to catalyzing defiant collective action will be partial, conditional, and volatile over time....effective legal mobilization depends on a rare combination of favorable opportunities and resources often in short supply among subordinate groups. (McCann, 1994, pp. 137, 305)

The social movement literature seems clear that the use and efficacy of rights' claims is deeply contextual.

Public opinion survey data also show that the belief in rights is heavily influenced by the context in which they are asserted. A clear example of the way in which preferences are equated with rights comes from the tragic events of September 11, 2001. Consider responses to a Gallup poll question asked repeatedly in the years since the terrorist attack of September 11, 2001. Gallup asked respondents which position came closer to their view: "the government should take all steps necessary to prevent additional acts of terrorism in the U.S. even if it means your *basic civil liberties* would be violated, (or) the government should take steps to prevent additional acts of terrorism but not if those steps would violate your basic civil liberties"? (emphasis added). If civil liberties are a basic right, then support for them should not vary by context. However, this is not the case. In January 2002, a little more than four months after the attack, the public was split, with 47% supporting taking all necessary steps even if that meant violating basic civil liberties. Americans were frightened and losing "basic civil liberties" evidently was seen as a small price to pay for safety (Gallup Poll, January 25–27, 2002).[10] However, as time passed without additional attacks, and fear presumably receded, Americans re-evaluated the tradeoff. A year after the attacks only 33% supported violating basic civil liberties, a drop of 14 percentage points. Similarly, there was an increase of 15 percentage points in support of taking steps to combat terrorism without violating basic civil liberties (Gallup Poll, September 2–4, 2002). By August 2003, nearly two years after the attacks, Americans supported the protection of basic rights by better than two to one (Gallup Poll, August 25–26, 2003). The responses to these survey questions suggest that the *right* to basic civil liberties was understood as a *preference* that varied according to circumstances.

A similar set of data comes from a question asked by the First Amendment Center each year from 1999–2007. After being read the First Amendment, respondents were asked whether it "goes too far in the rights it guarantees?" In 1999 and 2000, 28% and 22% respectively thought it did. However, in the summer of 2002, 49% agreed that the First Amendment went too far, compared to 47% who disagreed. But as with the protection of basic civil liberties, as Americans felt safer, they re-evaluated the First Amendment. By 2006 and 2007, only 18% and 25% of respondents respectively agreed that the First Amendment went too far, in the range of the pre–September 11 responses ("State of the First Amendment", 2007). There is nothing principled about a belief in constitutional rights if they are only supported sometimes.

A particularly telling and final example of the contextual nature of rights' claims comes from a 1992 Gallup question about abortion. In July of that year, Vice President Dan Quayle, an abortion opponent, told an interviewer that he would support his daughter if she become pregnant and chose to terminate the pregnancy. Gallup asked, "some think that there is no serious contradiction in these two statements, others think it shows he wants abortion rights for his own family but not for other women. Which comes closest to your view?" Responses pretty much split with nearly 43% finding no contradiction (Gallup Poll, July 23–24, 1992). If rights are nothing more than preferences, then Quayle's contradictory positions can be understood.

Overall, these data show that the majority of Americans equate rights with preferences. Rights are not trumps, principled and universal. Rather they are seen as contextual preferences to be balanced against competing preferences. To claim a right may be little more than a statement of preference under given conditions.

KNOWLEDGE OF RIGHTS

For rights to have persuasive power, people must have knowledge of them. Rights cannot be asserted if individuals do not know rights exist. In addition, rights must be seen as distinct from preferences. Otherwise, rights convey no heightened moral legitimacy. Decades of public opinion research present a consistent picture of widespread ignorance of even basic rights, and the equating of rights with desires and preferences. This section summarizes some of these findings.

To start on a somewhat humorous note, a 1986 national survey reported that nearly half of all Americans believe that the statement, "From each according to his ability, to each according to his need," is found in the U.S. Constitution (Survey by Hearst Corporation and Research & Forecasts, 1986). More Americans placed it in the Constitution than said it was not a part of America's founding document. It is found, of course, in *The Communist Manifesto*! On a no less incorrect note, a whopping 84% of respondents to a 1997 survey undertaken by the National Constitution Center agreed that the Constitution "states that all men are created equal" (Survey by National Constitution Center and Shepardson Stern & Kaminsky, 1997). That is a lovely thought but, alas, it is found in the Declaration of Independence, not the U.S. Constitution. This matters because the Declaration is not a binding legal document. Finally, a 2006 survey reported that 68% of respondents believe that the pursuit of happiness is a constitutional right ("Are Americans Right About Their Constitutional Rights?", 2006). Here, too, that "right" is found in the Declaration of Independence, not the Constitution. Support for these three noble thoughts may be seen as the equation of preferences with rights, in this case constitutional rights. Americans, at their best, would like each of us to give what we can, and have what we need, believe that all people are equal, and want happiness. Therefore, these must be constitutional rights!

In their 1996 book, Delli Carpini and Keeter examined Americans' knowledge of politics, including rights. Reviewing "nearly 3,700 individual survey questions," they found that "a number of answers took a form we call *projection*..." (Delli Carpini & Keeter, 1996, pp. 66–67, 98). Although they do not precisely define the term, they appear to mean imputing to the political system the preferences of respondents. To support "projection," they cite respondents' incorrect beliefs that there are constitutional rights to health care, jobs, and a high school education, among others (Delli Carpini & Keeter, 1996, pp. 98–99), what I call the equation of preferences with rights. Tellingly they write that projection "answers were most common...especially for questions dealing with rights and liberties" (Delli Carpini & Keeter, 1996, 98).

Substantial evidence supports these conclusions. For example, a 1986 poll found 42% agreeing that the "U.S. Constitution guarantees every citizen's right to adequate health care if he or she cannot pay" (Survey by Hearst Corporation and Research & Forecasts, 1986). The Constitution, of course, does no such thing. This stunningly high percentage suggests that Americans equate their preference for adequate health care with a constitutional right to it. In 1986 nearly a third of respondents (29%) said that the statement, "the U.S. Constitution does not guarantee a citizen's right to a job" was false, presumably meaning they thought the Constitution does offer such a guarantee (Survey by Hearst Corporation and Research & Forecasts, 1986). It does not. Furthermore, in 1986, 75% of respondents expressed the belief (incorrect) that the Constitution "guarantees every citizen's right to a free public education through high school" (Survey by Hearst Corporation and Research & Forecasts, 1986). Free public education through high school and jobs are outcomes Americans want; therefore, they equate them with rights.

The notion of rights as preferences also helps explain a whole host of data. Consider survey results about drugs, judicial appeals, and religion. Americans oppose the illegal use of drugs. Since they have a preference for making drugs illegal, it follows that 68% incorrectly believe that the Constitution prohibits a state legalizing marijuana within its borders and only 28% believed that the Constitution permits such state action (Survey by Hearst Corporation and Research & Forecasts, 1986). In terms of judicial appeals, Americans want to be able to appeal court decisions to a higher court. So, 85% incorrectly believe that "any important court case can be appealed from the state courts to the U.S. Supreme Court" (Survey by Hearst Corporation and Research & Forecasts, 1986). Religion provides a third and deeply disturbing example. Most Americans are Christians and consider themselves religious. If preferences are equated with rights, then Americans should believe that the United States is a Christian country. They do. In the 2007 Freedom Forum study, 65% of respondents agreed that the "nation's founders intended the United States to be a Christian nation" and 55% agreed that the Constitution "establishes a Christian nation..." (Survey by Freedom Forum and New England Survey Research Associates, 2007). Furthermore, 45% of respondents believed that states had the constitutional right to "declare an official state prayer" (Survey by Hearst Corporation and Research & Forecasts, 1986). So much for the First Amendment guarantee of the separation of church and state!

FIRST AMENDMENT

Americans' knowledge of the rights guaranteed to them by the First Amendment is uneven. The First Amendment Center has been polling virtually every year since 1997 and in each poll has asked respondents to name as many First Amendment rights as they can. In no year has a majority of respondents named more than one right, and in both 1997 and 1999, no right was named by even half of the respondents. In the other years, between 56% and 64% of respondents named free speech. The next most common response in every year was "don't know." After that, most responses are in the twenties and teens. For example, the percentage of respondents naming freedom of religion as a First Amendment right varied from 13% to 22%. Freedom of the press fared even less well, with a range of 11%–16% of respondents noting it as a First Amendment right. And the right of assembly and free association was noted by anywhere from 8% to 16% ("State of the First Amendment 2007", 2007).

In 2007 as part of its State of the First Amendment Survey, respondents were asked a number of questions about how important certain constitutional rights were. These included the right to "assemble, march, protest or petition the government," the right to "speak freely," to "practice the religion of your choice," to "practice no religion," to be "informed by a free press," and to have the "right to privacy." 74% of respondents said that the right to practice the religion of their choice was "essential," as did 67% of respondents about privacy. All of the other rights received less support. Only 60% thought that the right "assemble, march, protest or petition the government" was "essential," and only 62% said that about the "right to be informed by a free press." Consistent with the notion of rights as preferences, however, fewer respondents extended rights of religious freedom to those with whom they disagreed. Although nearly three-quarters of respondents ranked the right to practice the religion of their choice as essential, this did not include protecting the rights of atheists. When asked about the "right to practice no religion," only 57% ranked it as essential, a full 17 percentage points less than those ranking the right to practice the religion of their choice as essential ("State of the First Amendment 2007", 2007). Evidently, only a slight majority believes that the right to practice the religion of one's choice applies to those with whom they most strongly disagree (atheists).

A common response to these kind of data is to say, "so what?" What matters is that Americans know what rights they have, not where they originate or whether they are contained in the Constitution. This is a troublesome claim for two main reasons. First, rights contained in the Constitution are supposed to have heightened legitimacy; that is the whole point of a constitution! The Constitution is designed, in both theory and practice, to have more moral legitimacy than rent-seeking legislation enacted on behalf of a special interest group like the oil industry. If citizens do not know what rights the Constitution enshrines, or whether a particular right is contained in it, then the Constitution cannot serve that role. Second, lack of knowledge of rights makes it easier to equate preferences with rights, turning every desire for government action into a right. If all desires are rights, then rights are meaningless. The point is that lack of knowledge of rights combined with equating preferences with rights makes rights an empty category.

A remarkable set of survey findings that further demonstrate the equation of rights with preferences concerns respondent's views on whether various branches of government violate, or pose a threat to violate, constitutional rights. In August 1995, Gallup found that 31% of respondents believe that the Federal Government violates their "constitutional rights" either "very" or "quite" often. About 55% thought it did so "only occasionally," whereas only 12% responded "never" (Gallup Poll, August 11–14, 1995). Responses for state and local government were similar, with 21% and 19% choosing the "often" category and 60% and 56% responding "only occasionally," with only 17% and 24% selecting "never," respectively (Gallup Poll, August 11–14, 1995). A majority (56%) told Gallup that the Federal Government was violating their constitutional rights "these days" (Gallup Poll, August 11–14, 1995). A whopping 70% said that they expected the Federal government to violate their constitutional rights in the future (Gallup Poll, August 11–14, 1995).

On the surface, these are truly bizarre results. The United States was not involved in a major war at the time. Although the terrorist bombing of the federal building in Oklahoma City took place in April 1995, there were no mass arrests or other alleged violations of constitutional rights. Furthermore, Americans have many more interactions with state and local officials than with officials from the federal government. If rights are violated, the culprits are much more likely to be state and local than federal. It is possible that these survey results capture concern over the events at Waco, Texas, in the Spring of 1993 when federal agents attacked the Branch Davidians' compound, resulting in the death of 74 people. Although the event was a tragedy, it occurred more than two years before the survey and involved a group that did not engender a great deal of sympathy.

One way of understanding these results is to interpret them less literally. If Americans equate rights, even constitutional rights, with preferences, then the results make sense. They can be understood as Americans saying that they are not receiving the benefits they want from government, particularly the federal government. Evidence for this interpretation can be found in a Gallup Poll taken a year earlier, in June 1994. Respondents were asked how serious a threat there was to "Americans' *rights and freedoms*" from several activities. When asked about a "military threat from a foreign country," approximately 23% said it posed a "very" serious threat and 41% said a "moderate" threat. In contrast, nearly 47% responded that "Lack of economic opportunity" posed a "very" serious threat to Americans' rights and freedoms and an additional 38% said it posed a "moderate" threat (Gallup Poll, June 17–19, 1994). The differences in these two responses are stark, with 24 percentage points more respondents saying lack of economic opportunity posed a very serious threat to Americans' rights and freedoms than a military threat from a foreign country. If rights are understood as preferences, then these responses make sense. People want good paying jobs, and they equate their preference with rights and freedoms. Thus, if government economic policy does not provide for economic opportunity, then rights are being violated. Responses to an additional question also support this interpretation. 41% of respondents said that "government regulations" pose a "very" serious threat to Americans' rights and freedoms and 42% said they posed a "moderate" threat (Gallup Poll, June 17–19, 1994). Either Americans are all libertarians opposed to governmental regulation or they object to not being able to do as they please. If government regulations limit people's preferences, then they believe their rights are being violated.

The survey data discussed earlier, and many more that I have not discussed, show that Americans do not know a great deal about the rights contained in the Constitution. However, this lack of knowledge creates no obstacle to belief that the Constitution is important. In a 1997 survey for the National Constitution Center, 71% of respondents "strongly agreed" and an additional 20% "somewhat agreed" with the statement, "the United States Constitution is important to me" (Survey by National Constitution Center and Shepardson Stern & Kaminsky, 1997). How can a document about which Americans know little be so important to them? The answer I suggest is that the data also show that on many issues Americans simply project their preferences onto the Constitution. Americans want health care and education, so they believe that the Constitution guarantees them. They are afraid of terrorists, so basic rights can be abridged. They do not like certain groups or ideas, so those groups or ideas can be suppressed. They like Christianity, so they believe that the United States is a Christian nation. They like religion, so it should be present in schools. The list goes on and on. Rights as preferences offers an explanation for why.

RIGHTS AND PUBLIC OPINION

If rights carry the moral weight that most commentators believe them to, then people should react with more support to rights' claims than to other forms of political demands. Since data directly testing this claim are lacking, proxies must be used. One such proxy is the reaction of Americans to Supreme Court decisions announcing constitutional rights. If rights carry moral suasion, if rights are more than preferences, then such decisions should produce changes in public opinion more supportive of the right, especially where respondents are reminded that the Court upheld the right. If, however, it is merely preferences that are at stake, then little will change.

There is a great deal of public opinion data that reports on how Americans respond to Supreme Court decisions. Overall, it provides very little evidence for the claim that rights, even when pronounced by the Supreme Court of the United States, change Americans' views. In a 2008 compilation of the influence of Supreme Court decisions on the views of Americans in 14 substantive areas including desegregation, rights of the accused, school prayer, abortion, gay rights, and the war on terror and civil liberties, Persily, Citrin, and Egan (2008) find few effects. Writing in the introduction, Persily (2008, p. 8) summarizes the findings: "in the vast majority of the cases reviewed here, Supreme Court decisions had no effect on the overall distribution of public opinion." If rights carry normative weight, decades of public opinion research present a puzzle. If rights are nothing more than preferences, then the findings make perfect sense. A *very brief* review of some relevant data, organized by topic, follows.

CIVIL RIGHTS[11]

The Supreme Court's landmark 1954 desegregation decision found public school segregation on the basis of race unconstitutional. If rights differ from preferences, and carry moral weight, then *Brown*'s assertion of right should have changed opinions about segregation. The available evidence, scanty though it is, suggests that this was not the case. Polls charting the reaction to *Brown* by Southerners over time showed no difference in support for the decision throughout the 1950s. Among white Southerners, support for desegregation actually dropped in half (to 8%) by the late 1950s. Poll respondents were no more supportive in their views of attempts by blacks to exercise their rights as American citizens. In May 1961, of those respondents (63%) who had read or heard something about the freedom rides, nearly two-thirds (64%) disapproved, whereas only 24% approved. Most poignantly, in December 1958, when Gallup asked its usual question about the most admired men in the world, Governor Orval Faubus of Arkansas, who gained a national and international reputation by repeatedly defying court orders a year earlier to prevent the desegregation of Central High School in Little Rock, was among the ten most frequently mentioned. Rights understood as preferences offers a parsimonious explanation for these data and findings.

Among black Americans, research suggests that the announcement of a constitutional right did not have much of an impact (Rosenberg, 2008). It did not help in organizing the civil rights movement, or in propelling individuals to action. The evidence suggests that *Brown*'s major positive impact was limited to reinforcing the belief in a legal strategy for change of those already committed to it. It is not that black Americans did not deeply believe that the apartheid system under which they lived was wrong. Rather, it is that rights meant little while political, economic, and social power was held by hostile whites. Only when the civil rights movement broke that monopoly were large numbers of black citizens moved to join the fight.

ABORTION[12]

Abortion provides another good test of the rights as preferences notion. If rights carry the moral suasion that the standard definition suggests, then the Court's 1973 abortion decisions, holding that women had a virtually unfettered constitutional right to terminate pregnancies, at least in the first trimester, should have changed opinions. The evidence, however, suggests that this is not the case. The authoritative pronouncement of constitutional rights appears to have had a negligible effect on public opinion. There was clearly no rapid or large change in Americans' support of abortion choice after the Court's action. "None of our time series on public views regarding abortion indicates that the Supreme Court decisions had an important effect on opinion" (Blake, 1977, p. 57). This finding is consistent with the notion of rights as preferences.

Public opinion about the constitutional right to abortion remained pretty much unchanged until the Court's 1989 *Webster* decision allowing states greater authority to limit abortions. Apparently in response, public opinion became more pro-choice. In 1988, for example, before *Webster*, Gallup recorded 24% of respondents in support of legal abortions "under any circumstances." This was only an increase of 3 percentage points over the 1975 figure of 21%. However, Gallup polls taken after *Webster* show an increase of as much as 9 percentage points, with an average of slightly over 31% of respondents over five polls supporting legal abortions "under any circumstances" (Hugick & Saad, 1992, p. 6). Although these numbers suggest that the public did react to the Court's decision, the change in opinion ran counter to the claim that rights carry weight, at least when pronounced by the Court.

Overall, the story with abortion is of little change in public opinion. Reviewing the data for Gallup in 2004, Saad (2004) reported that "for most of the nearly 30 years Gallup has been tracking abortion attitudes, the majority has preferred to see abortion legal, but only under certain circumstances." In 2006, Saad (2006) noted that "division of opinion about the legality of abortion has been fairly stable for the past decade." As Luks and Salamone (2008, p. 101) summarize the data, in the years since *Roe v. Wade* (1973) "no decision of the Supreme Court seems to have directly affected the trajectory or structure of public opinion on abortion rights."

Finally, there is the issue of membership in pro-choice and women's groups. Did the pronouncement of a right to abortion have the kind of mobilizing effect that many argue rights' claims do? Although the data are hard to obtain, and confusing, the answer appears to be no. The pro-choice movement essentially retired in the wake of the Court's decision, leaving the field to the anti-abortion forces. In this case, rights were enervating, not inspirational.

SCHOOL PRAYER

Another area that illustrates the lack of persuasive power of the pronouncements of rights involves school prayer. Although the Court found school prayer to violate the first amendment in *Engel v. Vitale* (1962) and *Abington School Dist. v. Schempp* (1963), this constitutional right to be free of state-enforced religion has never met with majority approval. More than 20 years after the decisions, in 1985, NORC's General Social Survey reported 55.6% of respondents in support of *required* reading of the Lord's Prayer or Bible verses in school (Green & Guth, 1989, p. 41). Another 20-plus years later found 58% of 2007 respondents supporting prayers in public schools (Survey by Freedom Forum and New England Survey Research Associates, 2007). As Gash and Gonzales (2008, p. 77) summarize decades or survey data, "public opinion has remained solidly against the Court's landmark decisions declaring school prayer unconstitutional."

RIGHTS OF CRIMINAL DEFENDANTS

Despite a slew of Court decisions requiring rights for criminal defendants, the American public remains unpersuaded that criminal defendants and suspects ought to be treated in a constitutional manner. Indeed, over the past 40 years, public opinion has grown and remains hostile to the granting of constitutional rights to criminal defendants. The data are well known here. For example, when asked in 1989 whether they were more worried that "some criminals are being let off too easily or that the constitutional rights of some people accused of committing a crime are not being upheld," only 16% of AIPO respondents expressed concern about the abuse of constitutional rights, compared to 79% who worried that criminals are being let off too easily (Survey Research Consultants International, 1991, p. 26). By 2002, that percentage had hardly changed with only 18% concerned about constitutional rights (Lerman, 2008, p. 54). Americans, worried about personal safety, do not have a preference for constitutional rights. Paraphrasing former Attorney General Ed Meese, most Americans seem to believe that if you are not a criminal you do not need constitutional protections.

FREE SPEECH AND PRESS

Press

Despite generally supportive views of the press, when asked by Gallup in 1979 if the "present curbs placed on the press are too strict – or not strict enough?" more than twice as many respondents said the restrictions were not strict enough than said they were too strict (37% to 17%) ("First Amendment and the Press", 1980, p. 24). This represents considerable erosion in support for the press since a comparable 1958 question found that 21% would approve of placing greater restrictions on the press and 58% would disapprove ("First Amendment and the Press", 1980, p. 23). By 2007, the ratio had grown worse with close to three times as many respondents saying that the press has "too much freedom to do what it wants" rather than "too little freedom" ("State of the First Amendment 2007", 2007). In delving behind the aggregate numbers in the earlier survey, Gallup discovered that one of three main reasons respondents gave for wanting stricter curbs placed on the press was that newspapers publish information "that should not be made public because it is not in the best interests of the nation." This finding is supported by several surveys a decade apart. A survey undertaken for the American Bar Association in 1991 found that 46% of respondents believed that Congress should ban the press from reporting on any national security issue without prior governmental approval ("ABA Survey Reveals Americans Don't Know Their Rights", 1992, p. 5). In 2007, the First Amendment Center found that more than a third (37%) of respondents disagreed with the statement that "newspapers should be allowed to freely criticize the U.S. military about its strength and performance" ("State of the First Amendment 2007", 2007). As a 1992 survey of American attitudes toward free speech issues conducted by the American Society of Newspaper Editors concluded, "free expression is in very deep trouble" (quoted in "ABA Survey Reveals Americans Don't Know Their Rights", 1992, p. 5). Taken together, these and other surveys suggest that Americans view the right to a free press as meaning only the ability to publish what people prefer to read. If the American public does not like the content, then the press should not be able to publish it. This is a clear rights-as-preferences view.

Speech

Pollsters have asked Americans their views of fundamental democratic freedoms and political dissent for the past 50 years or so. Although the questions are often spotty, a good deal of evidence has been accumulated. Overall, it quite clearly shows that Americans are both deeply committed to free speech in the abstract *and* strongly opposed to free speech for unpopular groups. That is, there is a good deal of empirical support for the notion of rights as preferences.

Americans are almost uniformly supportive of free speech, at least in the abstract. For decades they have told respondents with near unanimity that they support it. For example, when national samples were asked in both 1938 and 1940, "Do you believe in freedom of speech?" 96% and 97% respectively responded in the affirmative (Erskine, 1970, p. 485, 486). As McClosky and Zaller (1984, p. 18) conclude, "no value in the American Ethos is more revered than freedom." At the same time that Americans were overwhelmingly supporting free speech in the abstract, they were denying it to specific groups whose speech they did not like. In the 1938 poll cited earlier in which 96% of respondents professed a belief in freedom of speech, only 38% of the free speech supporters responded affirmatively to the next question: "Do you believe in free speech to the extent of allowing radicals to hold meetings and express their views in this community?" Similarly, in the 1940 Gallup poll above to which 97% of respondents supported free speech, only 22% of them were willing to support it for "Fascists and Communists." Throughout the 1940s and 1950s, Americans held to this pattern. In 1953 and 1954, for example, Gallup and the Michigan Survey Research Center found that only 29% and 27% of respondents respectively would allow "a person known to favor Communism" or an "admitted Communist" to make a speech (cited in Erskine, 1970, p. 489). From 1953 to 1964, no more than 20% of respondents told NORC that Communists should be allowed to speak on the radio (cited in Erskine, 1970, p. 488). The ability simultaneously to be committed to free speech and to deny it to disliked groups is surely the mark of rights as preferences.[13]

In the later years of the twentieth century, surveys found that Americans' un-willingness to protect the "rights" of Communists had moderated (Nunn, Crockett, & Williams, 1978). However, the best explanation for this is that Communists were not longer as powerfully disliked as they once were. If Americans do not have strong feelings about Communists, perhaps they are willing to let them speak (i.e., give them their "rights"). This conclusion is supported by the trend in American's willingness to let Communist Party candidates and members speak on the radio. In 1940, 32% were willing. By the end of World War II, with the Soviet Union as an ally, nearly half of respondents (48%) were favorable. However, by 1954, at the height of the Cold War, only 14% were supportive (Mueller, 1988, p. 8). Data from 1985 show that a majority (57%) would allow a Communist to give a speech in the respondent's community and only a bare majority (51%) would fire a Communist teacher (Mueller, 1988, p. 4).

For other groups, however, which Americans do not like, suppression remains overwhelmingly popular. A survey by the American Society of Newspaper Editors in the early 1990s found Americans "quite willing to remove legal protection from forms of free expression that they merely disagreed with or found offensive" ("ABA Survey Reveals Americans Don't Know Their Rights", 1992, p. 5). In surveys in 1976 and 1978, Sullivan, Pierson, and Marcus (1979, p. 787) asked respondents what groups they most disliked and then asked them a series of questions about those groups. In a 1978 NORC survey they commissioned, they found, for example, that only 16% would *not* ban a member of the group they most disliked from being President, only 19% would allow a member to teach in public schools, and only 29% would *not* outlaw the group. All that has changed is that the salience of Communists as the focus of intolerance has waned to be replaced, in the 1970s, by groups like the Ku Klux Klan, the Symbionese

Liberation Army, and the Black Panthers. So, for example, over the 10-year period 1997–2007, the First Amendment Center has asked respondents whether they agree that people "should be allowed to say things in public that might be offensive to racial groups?" In every year more than half of respondents have disagreed ("State of the First Amendment 2007", 2007, p. 6). In surveys in 1997 and 1999, the First Amendment Center found 90% and 86% of respondents agreeing that "people should be allowed to express unpopular opinions" ("State of the First Amendment 1999", 1999, p. 18). This is in keeping with support for the concept of free speech in the abstract. However, that support drops somewhat when the question is whether "any group that wants should be allowed to hold a rally for a cause or issue even if it may be offensive to others in the community." In 1997, 72% support the right of such a group while in 1999 62% do ("State of the First Amendment 1999", 1999, p. 24). However, once an unpopular group is named, majority support vanishes. When asked in 1999 whether "militia groups, white supremacists, skinheads or Nazis [should] be allowed to protest in a community like yours?" a majority said no ("State of the First Amendment 1999", 1999, p. 20). Thus, despite the First Amendment and Americans' attachment to the abstract principle of free speech, when that principle conflicts with preferences, the preferences overwhelm the principle, in the name of free speech!

The data on public opinion strongly suggest that there is little or no content to the right to free speech. "It is difficult to avoid the suspicion," Mueller writes, that rights, what he calls the "principles of democracy," are "for many, just so many civics lesson platitudes, barren of tangible content." As he bitingly puts it, a "survey in an Orwellian world could be expected to find principles like 'slavery is freedom' as emptily and mechanically accepted" (Mueller, 1988, pp. 20–21). This is the case, Mueller suggests, because Americans simply do not think much about rights: "it may be far too grand and generous to believe that there is anything like a real, tangible 'attitude about' or 'commitment to' or 'hostility toward' civil liberties one way or the other" (Mueller, 1988, p. 22). The data suggest that Americans respond to and evaluate rights' claims as they respond to and evaluate any other political statement, on whether they agree with the substantive issue. Whether it is called a right or not, the data suggest, adds little to its evaluation.

CONCLUSION – A RIGHT FOR ALL SEASONS?

In a particularly insightful essay, Haskell (1987, p. 993) asks, "What is the difference between saying, 'I have a *right* to X,' and saying simply, 'I want

X'?" Pitting Leo Strauss against Nietzsche, the eternal truth of natural right against the will to power, Haskell tries to split the difference. Rights, he suggests, are rational conventions, more than preferences but decidedly less than eternal, universal truths (Haskell, 1987, pp. 1004–1005). However, the data presented in this chapter challenge even this more modest claim for the political use of rights' claims in modern America.

In practice is a rights' claim anything more than an assertion of preference? I have argued that there is a good deal of evidence that in practice the answer is no; there is no difference. From health care to hamburgers to hate speech, Americans equate what they want with a right to it. American discourse is "marked by an almost reflexive habit of defining all problems in terms of rights. The words, expressed as demands, fall quickly from our lips: 'I have a right to...'" (Walker, 1998, p. vii). If everything is a right, then nothing is a right. As McDowell (1993, p. 19) notes, "calling an ordinary policy preference a fundamental rights does not, because it cannot, make that preference a right in any meaningful, philosophical sense. It only confounds the idea of rights with the power of clever rhetoric." Furthermore, the data show that Americans are ignorant of even fundamental constitutional rights, equate their policy preferences with constitutional rights, and apply their understanding of rights mostly to those with whom they agree. Furthermore, pronouncements of rights from even the U.S. Supreme Court do not persuade people to change their opinions.

If rights' claims are as politically empty as I am suggesting, then why are they so prevalent? One possibility is that they have become simply the "um" and "uh" of American political discourse, just another word for wants. The meaning of words changes over time and although the concept of rights has a deep and rich history, perhaps its meaning has been altered. Conceptually, then, Americans need a new word to capture the old concept of a right and all the moral weight it contains.

There is, however, a more sinister possibility why Americans make such heavy use of rights' claims. If "rights talk is nothing but a puffed-up form of the will to power," Haskell (1987, p. 994) notes, then there is "nothing surprising in the persistence of such talk so long as it serves some manipulative purpose." Could the prevalence of rights' claims serve a less-than-noble purpose? Could it be that relying on rights' claims allows Americans to have their cake and eat it too? That is, does it allow them to celebrate being a nation of laws that respects rights and then happily accord them only to those with whom they agree? By supporting rights in the abstract and preferences in practice, Americans can feel good about themselves and get what they want at the same time. Given the historic use of rights to protect privilege, the prevalence of rights' claims may be cause for concern.

NOTES

1. For a list of court cases dealing with rights in these and other salient areas, see Horwitz (1988b, pp. 393–394 nn. 2–13).

2. Waldron (1987, p. 154) notes that the issue of national minorities which "afflicted European politics from 1815 to 1945" was "sometimes addressed" in rights terms.

3. In some cases, it is not clear how to categorize the claimed right. For example, is the claim that a woman has the right to choose to terminate her pregnancy a negative claim that the government cannot interfere with that choice or a positive claim that the government must act to protect that choice?

4. In principle, the definition applies to negative or positive rights' claims.

5. More recently, some conservatives have taken a rights-based approach to further their interests including protecting property interests, limiting governmental regulation, and limiting or invalidating social programs such as affirmative action. Their use of rights raises a different set of empirical questions that are not explored here.

6. Gabel and Kennedy (1984, p. 40), Schneider (1986, p. 625). See, also, the essays in Symposium (1987), particularly Hartog (1987, pp. 1014, 1015 n. 4) and Lynd (1987).

7. For a critique of this approach, see Rosenberg (1996).

8. Durocher was the manager of the New York Dodgers and the New York Giants professional baseball teams for many years.

9. Of the 24 quotations the study provides, only 8 (one-third), on a generous interpretation, make any mention of rights other than as individual preferences.

10. A shocking result that illustrates how frightened Americans were comes from a *Newsweek* poll conducted in late June, 2002. The poll asked whether Americans supported "giving government the power to detain American citizens suspected of crimes indefinitely, without review by a judge." A whopping 44% of respondents supported this assault on perhaps the most basic of citizen rights (Survey by Newsweek and Princeton Survey Research Associates, 2002).

11. For an in-depth examination of the role of the Court as a progressive force in the civil rights movement, see Rosenberg (2008, Chapter 4).

12. For an in-depth examination of the role of the Court and abortion, see Rosenberg (2008, Chapters 6, 8).

13. This contradiction is nicely illustrated by the *Fort Worth Star-Telegram's* editorial reaction to the Supreme Court's 1951 decision in *Dennis v. United States,* upholding the jailing of the leadership of the American Communist Party for their speeches and writings: "We cannot feel that the Supreme Court's decision endangers any of the fundamental American rights" (quoted in Lofton, 1980, p. 241).

REFERENCES

ABA survey reveals Americans don't know their rights. (1992). *Bar report*, December/January, p. 5 (Washington, DC: Bar Association).

Abington School Dist. v. Schempp, 374 U.S. 203 (1963).

American Cancer Society. (2007). Available at www.cancer.org/downloads/accesstocare/AccessToCare_Print_Ad_1.pdf

Ansberry, C. (1986). Survival strategy: Laid-off steelworkers find that tax evasion helps make ends meet. *The Wall Street Journal*, October 1, pp. 1, 28.

Appleby, J. (1987). The American heritage: The heirs and the disinherited. *Journal of American History, 74*, 798–813.

Are Americans Right About Their Constitutional Rights? (2006). Findlaw.com. Available at http://www.thomson.com/content/pr/tlr/tlr_legal/100832

Bartholomew, A., & Hunt, A. (1990). What's wrong with rights? *Law and Inequality, 9*, 1.

Blake, J. (1977). The supreme court's abortion decisions and public opinion in the United States. *Population and Development Review, 3*, 45–62.

Brigham, J. (1987). Right, rage, and remedy: Forms of law in political discourse. *Studies in American Political Development, 2*, 303–316.

Brown v. Board of Education, 347 U.S. 483 (1954).

Chong, D. (1993). How people think, reason, and feel about rights and liberties. *American Journal of Political Science, 37*, 867–899.

Delli Carpini, M. X., & Keeter, S. (1996). *What Americans know about politics and why it matters*. New Haven: Yale University Press.

Dennis v. United States, 341 U.S. 494 (1951).

DuBois, E. C. (1987). Outgrowing the compact of the fathers: Equal rights, women suffrage, and the United States constitution, 1820–1878. *Journal of American History, 74*, 836–862.

Ely, J. W., Jr. (1993). The enigmatic place of property rights in modern constitutional thought. In: D. J. Bodenhamer & J. W. Ely, Jr. (Eds), *The bill of rights in modern American after 200 years* (pp. 87–100). Bloomington and Indianapolis: Indiana University Press.

Ely, J. W., Jr., & Bodenhamer, D. J. (1993). Introduction. In: D. J. Bodenhamer & J. W. Ely, Jr. (Eds), *The bill of rights in modern American after 200 years* (pp. vii–x). Bloomington and Indianapolis: Indiana University Press.

Engel v. Vitale, 370 U.S. 421 (1962).

Engel, D. M., & Munger, F. W. (2003). *Rights of inclusion: Law and identity in the life stories of Americans with disabilities*. Chicago: University of Chicago Press.

Erskine, H. (1970). The polls: Freedom of speech. *Public Opinion Quarterly, 34*, 483–496.

Ewick, P., & Silbey, S. S. (1998). *The common place of law: Stories from everyday life*. Chicago: University of Chicago Press.

First Amendment and the Press. (1980). *Gallup Opinion Index* Report No. 174 (January), pp. 23–27.

Fisher, W., III. (1991). The development of modern American legal theory and the judicial interpretation of the bill of rights. In: M. J. Lacey & K. Haakonssen (Eds), *A culture of rights: The bill of rights in philosophy, politics, and law – 1791 and 1991* (pp. 266–365). New York: Cambridge University Press.

Freeman, A. (1988). Racism, rights and the quest for equality of opportunity: A critical legal essay. *Harv. C.R.-C.L. L. Rev., 23*, 295.

Gabel, P., & Kennedy, D. (1984). Roll over Beethoven. *Stan. L. Rev.*, *36*, 1.

Gash, A., & Gonzales, A. (2008). School prayer. In: N. Persily, J. Citrin & P. J. Egan (Eds), *Public Opinion and Constitutional Controversy* (pp. 62–79). New York: Oxford University Press.

Glendon, M. A. (1991). *Rights talk: The impoverishment of political discourse*. New York: Free Press.

Glendon, M. A. (1992). Rights in twentieth-century constitutions. In: G. R. Stone, R. A. Epstein & C. R. Sunstein (Eds), *The bill of rights in the modern state* (pp. 519–538). Chicago: University of Chicago Press.

Green, J. C., & Guth, J. L. (1989). The missing link: Political activists and support for school prayer. *Public Opinion Quarterly*, *53*, 41–57.

Hartog, H. (1987). The constitution of aspiration and 'the rights that belong to us all'. *Journal of American History*, *74*, 1013–1034.

Haskell, T. L. (1987). The curious persistence of rights talk in the 'age of interpretation'. *Journal of American History*, *74*, 984–1012.

Horwitz, M. J. (1988A). The Bork nomination and American constitutional history. *Syracuse L. Rev.*, *39*, 1029.

Horwitz, M. J. (1988B). Rights. *Harv. C.R.-C.L. L. Rev.*, *23*, 393.

Hugick, L., & Saad, L. (1992). *Gallup Poll Monthly* (January), 6–9.

Lacey, M. J., & Haakonssen, K. (1991). Introduction: History, historicism, and the culture of rights. In: M. J. Lacey & K. Haakonssen (Eds), *A culture of rights: The bill of rights in philosophy, politics, and law – 1791 and 1991* (pp. 1–18). New York: Cambridge University Press.

Lerman, A. E. (2008). Rights of the accused. In: N. Persily, J. Citrin & P. J. Egan (Eds), *Public opinion and constitutional controversy* (pp. 41–61). New York: Oxford University Press.

Lofton, J. (1980). *The press as guardians of the first amendment*. Columbia: University of South Carolina Press.

Luks, S., & Salamone, M. (2008). Abortion. In: N. Persily, J. Citrin & P. J. Egan (Eds), *Public opinion and constitutional controversy* (pp. 80–107). New York: Oxford University Press.

Lynd, S. (1987). The genesis of the idea of a community right to industrial property in Youngstown and Pittsburgh, 1977–1987. *Journal of American History*, *74*, 926–958.

Macaulay, S. (1987). Images of law in everyday life: The lessons of school, entertainment, and spectator sports. *Law & Society Review*, *21*, 185.

Matsuda, M. J. (1987). Looking to the bottom: Critical legal studies and reparations. *Harv. C.R.-C.L. L. Rev.*, *22*, 323.

McCann, M. (1994). *Rights at work. Pay equity reform and the politics of legal mobilization*. Chicago: University of Chicago Press.

McClosky, H., & Zaller, J. (1984). *The American ethos: Public attitudes toward capitalism and democracy*. Cambridge: Harvard University Press.

McDowell, G. L. (1993). The explosion and erosion of rights. In: D. J. Bodenhamer & J. W. Ely, Jr. (Eds), *The bill of rights in modern American after 200 years* (pp. 18–35). Bloomington and Indianapolis: Indiana University Press.

Milner, N. (1989). The denigration of rights and the persistence of rights talk: A cultural portrait. *Law & Social Inquiry*, *14*, 631.

Mueller, J. (1988). Trends in political tolerance. *Political Opinion Quarterly*, *52*, 1–25.

Nunn, C. Z., Crockett, H. J., Jr., & Williams, J. A., Jr. (1978). *Tolerance for nonconformity*. San Francisco: Jossey-Bass.

Olsen, F. (1984). Statutory rape: A feminist critique of rights. *Tex. L. Rev.*, *63*, 387.

Paris, M. (2006). The politics of rights: Then and now. *Law & Social Inquiry*, *31*, 999.

People for the American Way. (1989). *Democracy's next generation: A study of youth and teachers.* Washington, DC: People for the American Way.

Persily, N. (2008). Introduction. In: N. Persily, J. Citrin & P. J. Egan (Eds), *Public opinion and constitutional controversy* (pp. 3–17). New York: Oxford University Press.

Persily, N., Citrin, J., & Egan, P. J. (2008). *Public opinion and constitutional controversy.* New York: Oxford University Press.

Polls, G. (Various Years). Gallup brain. Available at http://institution.gallup.com

Rakove, J. N. (1991). Parchment barriers and the politics of rights. In: M. J. Lacey & K. Haakonssen (Eds), *A culture of rights: The bill of rights in philosophy, politics, and law – 1791 and 1991* (pp. 98–143). New York: Cambridge University Press.

Roe v. Wade. 410 U.S. 113 (1973).

Rogers, D. T. (1993). Rights consciousness in American history. In: D. J. Bodenhamer & J. W., Ely, Jr. (Eds), *The bill of rights in modern American after 200 years* (pp. 3–17). Bloomington and Indianapolis: Indiana University Press.

Rosenberg, G. N. (2008). *The hollow hope: Can courts bring about social change?* (2nd ed.). Chicago: University of Chicago Press.

Rosenberg, G. N. (1996). Positivism, interpretivism, and the study of law. *Law & Social Inquiry*, *21*, 435.

Saad, L. (2004). Abortion divides public; Not a top issue for voters. *Gallup News Service*, (April 23).

Saad, L. (2006). Abortion views reviewed as Alito vote nears. *Gallup News Service*, (January 20).

Sarat, A. (1977). Studying American legal culture: An assessment of survey evidence. *Law & Society Review*, *11*, 427.

Scheingold, S. A. (1989). Constitutional rights and social change: Civil rights in perspective. In: M. W. McCann & G. L. Houseman (Eds), *Judging the Constitution: Critical Essays on Judicial Lawmaking* (pp. 73–91). Glenview: Scott, Foresman.

Scheingold, S. A. (2004). *The politics of rights: Lawyers, public policy, and political change* (2nd ed.). New Haven: Yale University Press.

Schneider, E. M. (1986). The dialectic of rights and politics: Perspectives from the women's movement. *N.Y.U. L. Rev.*, *61*, 589.

Silverstein, H. (1996). *Unleashing rights: Law, meaning, and the animal rights movement.* Michigan: University of Michigan Press.

Sparer, Ed. (1984). Fundamental human rights, legal entitlements, and the social struggle: A friendly critique of the critical legal studies movement. *Stan. L. Rev.*, *36*, 509.

State of the First Amendment 1999. (1999). First amendment center. Available at http://www.freedomforum.org/templates/document.asp?documentID = 3971

State of the First Amendment 2007. (2007). First amendment center. Available at http://www.firstamendmentcenter.org/pdf/SOFA2007results.pdf

Sullivan, J. L., Pierson, J., & Marcus, G. E. (1979). An alternate conceptualization of political tolerance: Illusory increases 1950s–1970s. *American Political Science Review*, *73*, 781–794.

Survey by Freedom Forum and New England Survey Research Associates, August 16–26, 2007. iPOLL databank. The Roper Center for Public Opinion Research, University of Connecticut. Available at http://www.ropercenter.uconn.edu/ipoll.html

Survey by Hearst Corporation and Research & Forecasts, October 20 to November 2, 1986. iPOLL databank. The Roper Center for Public Opinion Research, University of Connecticut. Available at http://www.ropercenter.uconn.edu/ipoll.html

Survey by National Constitution Center and Shepardson Stern & Kaminsky, September, 1997. iPOLL databank. The Roper Center for Public Opinion Research, University of Connecticut. Available at http://www.ropercenter.uconn.edu/ipoll.html

Survey by Newsweek and Princeton Survey Research Associates, June 27–28, 2002. iPOLL databank. The Roper Center for Public Opinion Research, University of Connecticut. Available at http://www.ropercenter.uconn.edu/ipoll.html

Survey Research Consultants International, Inc. (Various Years).E. H. Hastings & P. K. Hastings (Eds), *Index to international public opinion*. New York: Greenwood.

Symposium. (1987). The constitution and American life: A special issue. *Journal of American History, 74*, 661–1178.

Texas v. Johnson, 491 U.S. 397 (1989).

Thelen, D. (1987). Introduction. *Journal of American History, 74*, 795–797.

Tushnet, M. (1984). An essay on rights. *Tex. L. Rev., 62*, 1363.

Tushnet, M. (1987). The politics of equality in constitutional law: The equal protection clause, Dr. Du Bois, and Charles Hamilton Houston. *Journal of American History, 74*, 884–903.

Waldron, J. (1987). *Nonsense upon stilts: Bentham, Burke and Marx on the rights of man.* London: Methuen.

Walker, S. (1998). *The rights revolution: Rights and community in modern America.* New York: Oxford University Press.

Wansink, B., & Peters, J. C. (2007). The food industry role in obesity prevention. In: S. Kumanyika & R. C. Brownson (Eds), *Handbook of obesity prevention: A resource for health professionals* (pp. 193–208). New York, NY: Springer.

Webster v. Reproductive Health Services, 492 U.S. 490 (1989).

Westen, P. (1986). The rueful rhetoric of 'Rights'. *U.C.L.A. L. Rev., 33*, 977.

White, J. B. (1992). Looking at our language: Glendon on rights. *Mich. L. Rev., 90*, 1267.

Williams, P. J. (1987). Alchemical notes: Reconstructing ideals from deconstructed rights. *Harv. C.R.-C.L. L. Rev., 22*, 401.

THE RIGHT'S REVOLUTION?: CONSERVATISM AND THE MEANING OF RIGHTS IN MODERN AMERICA

Thomas Hilbink

ABSTRACT

While many see the 1960s as the era of a "rights revolution" in American law, this article looks back from the present moment of conservative legal dominance to better understand the ways in which conservative ideas began to grow during the heyday of legal liberalism. Using recent histories of post-1945 grassroots conservatism, the author argues that conservative rights claims – while often legally questionable – constituted for many a powerful and persuasive understanding of the Constitution. Due to this popular conservative jurisprudence's endurance and influence, its existence in the 1960s forces reconsideration of understandings of the 1960s as the era of the "rights revolution."

INTRODUCTION

That the 1960s marked the era of the "rights revolution" is a widely accepted truth, in both American jurisprudence and sociolegal scholarship.

Revisiting Rights
Studies in Law, Politics, and Society, Volume 48, 43–67
Copyright © 2009 by Emerald Group Publishing Limited
All rights of reproduction in any form reserved
ISSN: 1059-4337/doi:10.1108/S1059-4337(2009)0000048005

Charles Epp's widely (and rightly) lauded book *The Rights Revolution* (1998) succinctly makes the case for this view. In the United States, during the 1960s, the Supreme Court devoted nearly 70 percent of its docket to individual rights claims. The court had "essentially, proclaimed itself the guardian of the individual rights of the ordinary citizen. In the process, the Court created or expanded a host of new constitutional rights, among them virtually all of the rights now regarded as essential to the Constitution: freedom of speech and the press, rights against discrimination on the basis of race or sex, and the right to due process in criminal and administrative procedures" (Epp, 1998, pp. 1–2). Epp carefully acknowledges that the extent of the change brought on by the Court's adopted role was limited by both erosion of those rights due to opposition and the limits of law's power in action. Yet, he holds that "the transformation has been real and it has had important effects" (Epp, 1998, pp. 1–2). Epp is correct. The "rights revolution" he describes has impacted American society in some important ways. But looking at the present landscape of American law, I can't help but wonder if what happened in the 1960s truly constituted a revolution.

The decade since Epp's book has seen a major change in the landscape of American law, changes that suggest the celebration of the 1960s as the era of a "rights revolution" needs to be reconciled with the fact that the era also saw the birth of what might be considered the "right's revolution." The end of the Cold War, the rise of a government dismissive of constitutional rights, and the arrival of a Supreme Court openly hostile to "the individual rights of the ordinary citizen" have all served to undermine the idea that the 1960s changed the nation to the extent once widely believed. More significantly, perhaps, recent events force us to ask whether it was the left or the right who left the 1960s on the rise. From today's perspective, it appears that the conservative conception of rights borne out of reaction and backlash to the era of Warren Court and civil rights represents a counter-revolution that must be accounted for in considering the long-term impact of the rights revolution (cf. Blasi, 1983; Schwartz, 1998).

June 2007 saw the Supreme Court hand down its decision in *Parents Involved in Community Schools v. Seattle School District No. 1* (2007), a decision that called into question whether the "rights revolution" has had the enduring power attributed to it in countless celebrations of the 50th anniversary of *Brown v. Board of Education* just four years ago. In that case, the Roberts Court all but overturned what can be considered the crowning achievement of the Warren Court's revolution: *Brown v. Board of Education* (1954, 1955). Writing for a plurality of the Court, Chief Justice Roberts ignored the realities of structural racism and enduring segregation when he wrote:

> Before *Brown*, schoolchildren were told where they could and could not go to school based on the color of their skin. The school districts in these cases have not carried the heavy burden of demonstrating that we should allow this once again – even for very different reasons. For schools that never segregated on the basis of race, such as Seattle, or that have removed the vestiges of past segregation, such as Jefferson County, the way "to achieve a system of determining admission to the public schools on a nonracial basis," is to stop assigning students on a racial basis. (*Parents Involved in Community Schools v. Seattle School District No. 1*, 2007, p. 40)

The deceptively simple language announced what may well turn out to be the beginning of the end of government-led school desegregation in American society, despite the fact that in the fifty years since the Warren Court decided *Brown*, the real effect of the decision has been undermined by massive resistance, legal interference, and private blockading of the ideas and intent of the Rights Revolution. In the larger political and social context of the past fifty years, and when read with recent cases like *Ledbetter v. Goodyear Tire* (2007) (employment discrimination), *Gonzales v. Carhart* (2007) (reproductive rights), and the multitude of decisions that have slowly eviscerated the Fourth Amendment and criminal due process rights, *Parents Involved* reads like the victory parade of triumphant revolutionaries: the right's revolution.

This is not to say that the "rights revolution" either lacks enduring impact or, even more, has been completely rejected. Indeed, in the realms of gay rights, free expression, and other important pillars of the 1960s revolution, progress has been made beyond what was imaginable when Earl Warren left the bench in 1969. Rather, the point here is to attempt to understand the 1960s with greater complexity and to move away from a narrative of (legal) liberal triumph and begin to understand how as a nation – politically, socially, and legally – we arrived where we are today. The search for an answer leads directly back to the 1950s and 1960s when a conservative conception of rights was growing in plain sight of the rights revolution.

If we wish to understand what constitutes this "right's revolution," we need to understand how it came to pass and what it entailed. Was it led by conservative legal intellectuals, those who advocate the back-to-*Lochner* concept of a "constitution in exile" (Rosen, 2005)? Was it brought about by political leaders such as Barry Goldwater, George Wallace, and Ronald Reagan (Perlstein, 2001; Carter, 2000)? Perhaps. A series of recent histories, when read in combination, reveal a grassroots, popular constitutionalism that must be considered an essential piece of the movement that emerged from the 1960s with a full head of steam. This grassroots conservative constitutionalism is arguably as strong and significant as the other so-called constitutional moments (Ackerman, 1993; Ackerman, 2000). In the 1960s, these ideas were in conflict (if not in direct contradiction) with the legal liberalism of the Warren Court era (Kalman, 1996; Horwitz, 1998). Such contradiction was hardly fatal to the life of these rights. In the decades that followed, after germinating in the interstices of the conservative grassroots and growing in the incubators of conservative legal organizations (Teles, 2007), these rights concepts emerged as a powerful and, in certain sectors, dominant ideology of American law and politics, the hegemonic ideas against which other ideas were measured.

This article brings together the findings of a growing number of studies on the growth of grassroots conservatism in the 1960s and 1970s. Since historian Alan Brinkley's call over a decade ago for greater attention to the "problem" of American conservatism, scholars have combined the recent historiographical trend toward local studies with an eye to understanding the growth of conservatism in American society and politics at that level (Brinkley, 1994). Studies of the South generally and particular southern cities such as Atlanta, Georgia, and Charlotte, North Carolina, delineate the parameters of a conservatism rooted in opposition to the civil rights movement (Sokol, 2006; Kruse, 2005; Lassiter, 2006). But far from adopting as gospel truth George Wallace's observation in the 1970s that "the Whole United States is Southern!," a second group of books focused on northern and western locales such as Boston, Detroit, and Orange County, California demonstrates that the conservative movement was not a southern phenomenon either in its origins or its reach (Lukas, 1986; Formisano, 2004; Sugrue, 1995, 1998). Issues of civil rights *may* have "migrated from the South to the North," as Jason Sokol (2006, p. 237) observes (though this is debatable). However, because it was a broad-based movement with deep roots around the nation, the flow of ideas also traveled in other directions: north to south, west to east, east to west, and south to north (Kruse, 2005, p. 12). What fed the roots varied city to city and region to region, but the commonalities remained steady.

For a sociolegal scholar, what emerges from these books (sometimes explicitly, sometimes inadvertently on the part of the authors) is the beginnings of a new understanding of rights and constitutionalism in modern America, a qualification of and correction to the legal liberal narrative of the era. There emerged from the grassroots white population in the 1950s and 1960s a form of rights talk and ideology that would come to dominate American politics and law in the following decades. Evolving over the course of two decades, this ideology emphasized "freedom of choice," the rights of parents, and a right to make decisions free from government regulation and interference. These rights may have run counter to official constitutional interpretations at the time, but they resonated with people and echoed in politics and (eventually) the law itself. The concepts of rights did not always follow a consistent internal logic, and they were at times vague, but to a group of people who rightly or not had come to see themselves as the voiceless victims of a powerful federal government, they offered both comfort and power much as participants in other social movements then and since found a variety of uses for and value in rights (McCann, 1994; Silverstein, 1996; Poletta, 2000).

Counter-hegemonic to the "rights revolution," this "right's revolution" constituted the meaning of rights for a major segment (and perhaps a majority) of Americans in the 1960s and beyond. Understanding this much neglected conception of rights is important should we hope to capture an accurate picture of rights and rights talk in American society today. This understanding challenges the idea that it was the left's rights revolution that defined the meaning of the Constitution for most Americans and changed society accordingly. Particularly in light of the law and politics of the past decade, it was arguably popular, conservative conceptions of rights that emerged from the 1960s on the rise in social, political, and legal circles.

WHAT GRASSROOTS RIGHTS WERE NOT

To understand the development of a grassroots conservative conception of rights, it is important to begin by challenging some misconceptions about grassroots conservatism in the years after World War II. First, the grassroots conservatism *was* concerned with and focused on using rights. Up until the past few years, most historical and popular depictions of grassroots conservatism have painted a crude portrait of a lawless, racist population. Images from Little Rock in 1957, sit-ins in the 1960s, and the Freedom Rides in 1961 tend to depict an ugly, hateful violence that, despite it being condoned by those in power at the state and local level, was lawless. These images are not incorrect, to be sure. Violence was common, particularly surrounding issues of race and desegregation. And violence frequently went hand in hand with conservative rights talk (violence was justified that way, in fact). But it is important to note the commonplace nature of conservative rights talk.

The second prefatory point is that although the use of rights talk was central to grassroots conservatives' framing of the issues of the day, the talk was often vague in nature. A poem written in reaction to the "forced" integration of that Boston's public schools in the 1970s reflects this point.

"Twas on a dreary Thursday morn"; As the buses rolled along. They came up to our peaceful town; With orders from the law; Desegregate and integrate; Or you will pay the price; Of loss of pride, humility; And even your children's lives.

But Southie's spirit was so strong; They made us a barrack town. They took their horses, dogs, and guns; and set them on the crowd. The TPF,[1] their sticks did crack; On the young and old alike. But united still, our spirits high; *We'll fight for freedom's right.* (MacDonald, 1999, p. 79)

Rights are clearly central to the narrative here. Yet, it is hardly clear from the poem, or the context, what the right in question was. Was it the right to maintain segregated schools? The right of a community to maintain control over local institutions (note the reference to "our peaceful town")? The right of parents to protect their children? The right to human dignity? The right to protest? The right to majority rule? "Freedom's right" may have meant all of those things or, more likely, different things to different people. But as a rallying cry to the Southie community, "freedom's right" carried significance. For similar reasons, the primary anti-busing organization in Boston was ROAR: Restore Our Alienated Rights. White homeowners in Atlanta, policing the eroding border between black and white neighborhoods, used the phrase, "Whites have rights, too," finding meaning therein, however unclear it may seem to an outsider (Kruse, 2005, p. 5). The grassroots did not always appear concerned with clearly explaining what they meant by "rights." Rights talk of this sort followed Mary Ann Glendon's formula, carrying "a rich train of associations" for both speaker and his or her allies (Glendon, 1991, p. 9). It served to unify and dignify the beliefs of a group of people who felt left out of the political and legal processes that were impacting their daily lives.

The third preliminary point is that, contrary to most depictions of 1960s conservatism, grassroots conservatism in the era was not largely concerned with questions of "states' rights." This fact is evidenced in the extent to which the language of "states' rights" is generally absent from these bottom-up histories. One finds the concept of states' rights to be prevalent in histories of the civil rights movement where scholars have tended to reconstruct history from the vantage point of white elites: Southern political leaders such as George Wallace, Orval Faubus, or James Eastland. Official statements from the time support such a perspective. Barry Goldwater complained in *Conscience of a Conservative* that in 1960, neither party was committed to the principle of states' rights (Goldwater, 2007). That same year, Young Americans for Freedom listed as one of their core beliefs that the "genius of the Constitution – the division of powers – is summed up in the clause which reserves primacy to the several states ..." (Young Americans for Freedom, 2007; McGirr, 2001, p. 63). Yet, in these bottom-up histories, one finds few examples of such rhetoric amongst average southerners. A student council officer at Little Rock's Central High explained that if he had his way, "he would have said, 'Let's don't integrate, because it's the state's right to decide'" (Sokol, 2006, p. 117; see also Sokol, 2006, p. 156). But this was one of the only examples in the many books. States' rights rhetoric, it seems, reverberated with state leaders for it was their personal power that was being usurped. But for those not in power, it appears that community-centered or individual rights came more naturally and easily.

Questions of racial equality and integration – at the center of nearly all these books – were for most Americans questions of everyday life, of how quotidian issues impacted people's sense of self and community, rights, and privileges. The Federal government may have been far away from their everyday existence, but so too was the state government. Thus, people did not conceive of rights in terms of their state government. Instead, they saw things in terms of the loss of *their* rights to a series of increasingly distant powers. For instance, a high school student in Boston during the busing crisis complains that, "Democracy is slipping away. The federal government is taking over the power of the states, the state is taking over what the city should have, the city is taking what the family should have" (Lukas, 1986, p. 544; Formisano, 2004, p. 17). Orange County conservatives complained of "distant elites" doing what should have been controlled by "the 'people' and the locality" (McGirr, 2001, p. 166). Down at the grassroots, again and again, the language of rights emphasizes the loss of rights not at the state level but at the level of the community, the family, or the individual. States' rights lost out in the battle with the federal government, but that mattered little in the long term when other, more immediate rights were threatened.

FROM PRIVILEGE TO POWERLESSNESS: RIGHTS AND THE POLITICS OF VICTIMHOOD

People felt their control of their lives slipping away. The world they had known – not just in terms of race, but in terms of work, family, and community – were changing. The fear of social change was rooted in a concern about destabilization of a "natural organic order" and "familiar, secure, and comfortable ways" that had provided value to white conservatives (McGirr, 2001, p. 182). Change, whether involving racial equality, religion, or other factors, in the words of one right-winger in Anaheim, California, posed a threat: "Customs, traditions, and mores have too often been considered obsolete, old fashioned, and hence, discarded or minimized by a powerful faction of sincere but misguided Americans who have attempted to indoctrinate the American public through every possible media of communications and weapons of propaganda ... to the benefits of change and 'modernism' ... without ... an appreciation and understanding of the basic foundations of our country" (McGirr, 2001, p. 109).

But even when concern about change wasn't explicitly about race, it seemed to involve race nonetheless. Ronald Formisano explains the support for anti-busing leader Louise Day Hicks as coming from those who perceived in busing a threat to "familiar, secure, and comfortable ways." But one local's elaboration that the "fear that the old, good ways of life will change if Negroes move in" uncovers an important undercurrent (Formisano, 2004, p. 39).

Throughout America, whites' "way of life" had been supported by a structure of white privilege. The "wages of whiteness" recognized by David Roediger, Angela Harris, and others conferred benefits both quantifiable and unquantifiable upon whites around the nation (certainly not just in the South) (Roediger, 1999; Harris, 1993; Sokol, 2006, p. 217, 304). Jason Sokol stresses that the "Civil Rights Act did not so much heighten awareness of 'whiteness' as spur fears that 'whiteness' would stop paying wages" (Sokol, 2006, p. 224). To recognize rights for African-Americans was simultaneously to undermine the privileges of whiteness. Orange County conservatives were, as a result, against using state power to help lift up disenfranchised groups. "They feared that such changes would impinge on their affluent white havens and would undermine their prosperity and, as they saw it, their way of life," asserts Lisa McGirr (2001, p. 183).

Before and into the 1950s, the privileges of whiteness were enforced through both formal and informal law. Lynching represented the most disturbing example of such extralegal enforcement, allowing whites to maintain their status without legal ramifications. Atlanta streetcars stayed segregated in part due to the fact that courts showed great leniency toward drivers who shot "unruly" – read: those who challenged the color line – passengers (Kruse, 2005, p. 109). Through the 1940s and 1950s, whites in Detroit who committed acts of harassment or violence against black people who challenged residential segregation rarely found their lawless actions prosecuted (Sugrue, 1998). Yet as white privilege eroded, such extralegal enforcement was becoming less acceptable. As Sokol observes, "White southerners continued to use whatever means they wished to keep blacks in their 'place' in the 1940s, but their heinous crimes no longer occurred in a geographical vacuum" (Sokol, 2006, p. 37). Allies in the federal government and around the world (particularly in light of Cold War concerns, see Dudziak, 2000) no longer turned a blind eye to such policing of the color line, forcing whites to develop new ways to maintain their superiority.

Due to shifting sands of law and politics at the federal level from the 1950s through the 1970s – what Epp recognizes as the rights revolution – whites could not always count on the institutions that had once helped them maintain superiority and privilege. As recently as the 1940s, the federal government and the Democratic party had represented the interests of white middle- and working-class people. FDR had been a hero to whites in both the North and the South, with the New Deal's benefits falling disproportionately to them (Sugrue, 1998). Southern Democrats had dominated Congress, protecting Jim Crow. And the courts had turned a blind eye to violations of individual rights. Yet, briefly after World War II, the courts (particularly the Supreme Court) began taking up claims of constitutional rights. The executive branch was, however, reluctantly under Eisenhower and Kennedy, beginning to back civil rights laws with its power (Branch, 1988). By the 1970s in Boston, the sands had shifted even further. The city's white ethnic population – particularly the Irish – felt they had been abandoned "by the very institutions – City Hall, the Democratic Party, the Catholic Church, the popular press – that until recently had been their patrons and allies" (Lukas, 1986, p. 135). Indeed, they had long dominated and controlled those institutions. Yet now, the federal courts were ordering desegregation and city officials, party leaders in Washington, the *Boston Globe*, and the Cardinal of Boston were all telling people to heed the orders (Lukas, 1986; Formisano, 2004; Kruse, 2005). Rightly or not, white opponents of desegregation felt they had no say and no power in trying to stop the erosion of their privilege. They couldn't rely on informal laws to maintain their privileges, and government officials (more or less) told them that they had no recourse in the law either. But they still saw themselves as having rights.

Perceiving themselves as bearers of rights came more easily as whites also came to see themselves as powerless, as victims. Ronald Formisano (2004, p. 3) contends that whites in Boston during the 1970s were inhibited by "limited horizons" and people's "lack of faith rooted in a sense of powerlessness". With such a sense of powerlessness, the language of victimhood came easily. The institutions that once upheld white privilege were no longer so reliable. Thus, poor and middle-class whites had to stand by and watch their "wages" get cut. If freedom meant being able to "do as we please, when we please" (Glendon, 1991, p. 9), then it makes sense that many whites around the nation saw themselves as powerless, as losing something. From the perspective of whites around the country, the recognition of civil rights for black people instantly resituated them at the bottom of the power hierarchy. They became victims when they could not exclude black people from their businesses, schools, or neighborhoods (Kruse, 2005, p. 183). Thus, it should not have been surprising when whites in South Boston adopted James Brown's anthem, "Say it Loud, I'm Black and I'm Proud," as their own (MacDonald, 1999, p. 81).

At first, in response to their feelings of loss and powerlessness, whites simplistically challenged the legitimacy of civil rights claims. Southerners similarly complained that the Civil Rights Act of 1964 was, in fact, a "civil wrongs" bill. Business owners such as Ollie McClung in Birmingham, Alabama, similarly spoke of desegregation as a civil wrong against white, pro-segregationists (Sokol, 2006, p. 225). Whites in Detroit, who supported a pro-segregation "Homeowners' Rights Ordinance," "railed against 'the *Civil Wrongs* that are being forced on us more and more every day'" (Sugrue, 1995, p. 575 (emphasis added)). Yet, just as white privilege had lost much of its sociolegal value, complaining of "civil wrongs" did not carry much weight in the face of the positive message of civil rights. One poor white man seeming to notice that courts and the federal government were recognizing the rights of those who claimed them noted, "The negro are getting more help now than the poor white. Don't the poor whites have some rits? [*sic*]" (Sokol, 2006, p. 217). While many whites first reacted against civil rights by rejecting the concept, they eventually came to embrace the idea of rights, reappropriating the concept to advance their under-standing of law, society, the Constitution, and morality. Given the power that they saw stem from others' rights claims, this should come as no surprise. They, too, saw the rights revolution underway and developed a conception of rights to counter it.

The man's question alludes to a shift in white rhetoric about and understanding of rights. Unable to speak about white privilege and against the rights of others, whites began to speak in the positive language of rights for themselves: white rights. In Detroit, Thomas Sugrue observed that even while grudgingly acknowledging that racial equality was a fact, whites "believed that civil rights for blacks were won only at the expense of white rights" (Sugrue, 1995, p. 567). Lester Maddox, the ax handle wielding segregationist owner of Atlanta's Pickrick Restaurant, became a grassroots hero as the champion of "white rights," when he resisted laws requiring him to desegregate his business. For example, he thanked those who sent words of encouragement or came to his restaurant, seeing such acts as support of his family's effort to "remain FREE Americans and protect our 'Civil Rights'" (Sokol, 2006, p. 225). And in the Charlestown section of Boston, "Townies" shifted away from complaining about desegregation, "having moved beyond resentment of black demands to assertion of their own rights" (Lukas, 1986, p. 308).

Turning protection of white privilege into a defense of white "rights" transformed the discussion of racial equality, strengthening (rhetorically and politically, if not legally) the claims of white people while turning the question of equality into a zero-sum game (Glendon, 1991). The open housing movement in Detroit, opponents now argued, "elevated minority rights over the rights of the majority" (Sugrue, 1995, p. 576). White southerners believed the true goal of desegregation was "not to end the system of racial oppression in the South, but to install a new system that oppressed them instead" (Kruse, 2005, p. 9). A white resident of North Carolina saw civil rights "not as something to which blacks were entitled, but as an intrusion into white life: federal government seized freedoms from whites and redistributed them to blacks. Most whites saw civil rights not in terms of black liberties, but as a loss of white freedom" (Sokol, 2006, p. 216). "We should not sacrifice the rights of one group to the detriment of another," wrote a different southerner (Sokol, 2006, p. 217). "Our rights are as sacred as theirs," said another (Sokol, 2006, p. 223). With such a spin, "forced busing" was a "deprivation of rights" rather than enforcement of equality standards for all (Formisano, 2004, p. 172).

As a zero-sum game, the battle between white rights and civil rights put those in power in a more difficult position. Should a judge or politician recognize the civil rights of people of color, that action would quickly get framed as taking away "white rights" rather than representing an expansion of the basic rights already enjoyed by many. Thus, the power of rights rhetoric: it furthered the "us or them" dichotomy while allowing whites to claim (however, illegitimately) the mantle of the oppressed, the victim. In the "age of rights," rights claims, unlike privileges claims, gave conservatives – the "silent majority" – a voice "that would be heard by 'the system'" (Sokol, 2006, pp. 226–227; Formisano, 2004, p. 191). While privileges of whiteness were no longer enforceable under law, rights claims could still get you a hearing, either in court or in the public square.

Francesa Poletta, relying on Didi Herman, argues that "rights' meanings cannot simply be 're-invented' and disseminated at will."

> To be sure, people can assert anything as a "right," which can be defined as an "entitlement" without requiring that the entitlement be legally authorized or enforced. But we usually think of rights as claims backed up by the force of law – or *potentially* done so. This conception of rights allows for innovation, but not wild invention. (Poletta, 2000, p. 378)

Yet, here, the assertion of "white rights" and the more specific claims of the right to discriminate, the right to "freedom of association," and "freedom of choice" were, at the time they were made, just such wild inventions. From a legal point of view, the claims were without merit as demonstrated by one federal court after another in that era. However, over time, through repetition and political change, these "wild inventions" became mere innovations and the vanquished became the victors of a right-wing rights revolution. Conservatives found in rights claims some of the same benefits that their contemporaries in the civil rights movement did. In Francesca Poletta's words, "Rights-talk was the language of collective determination" (Poletta, 2000, p. 391). Such talk may not have carried legal weight, but it rallied the base and solidified their belief that they were right and the powers of the day were wrong.

And thus, the "right's revolution" was born. It adopted rights claims, accepting the dominant discourse of the day, while adapting them to their own view of American society. Rights claims took the unwritten cultural norms of white privilege and the written rules of segregation and, after a process of refinement, recast them in a new framework that masked their supremacist origins while still resonating in many white communities.

VARIATIONS ON RIGHTS

Conservatives did not rest their claims on claims of "white rights" for very long. Over the course of the 1960s and into the 1970s, they took the idea of white rights and refined it into a set of arguments that would eventually command respect and attention from a growing number of jurists and politicians who did not see themselves supporting white rights. They often took valid constitutional rights concepts and reconfigured them to serve a different end than intended. Claims of "freedom of association," "property rights" for business owners, and "freedom of choice" for parents in deciding where their children would go to school emerged as a bundle of rights that would come to be seen as the "property" of citizens, effacing the racialized nature of their origins, and seen as a birthright of Americans.

These deracialized conservative claims developed in both the North and the South in the years after World War II. African-Americans, empowered after the war to demand equal citizenship based on the fact that they had (once again) served the cause of freedom abroad only to be denied freedom at home, began challenging formal and informal color lines around the nation, whittling away at the privileges of whiteness by claiming to represent American values. (Weisbrot, 1990; Powledge, 1991; Milner, 2003).

Whites who were opposed to integration – whether of neighborhoods or of schools – responded in kind, relying on a different conception of the war and its relationship to rights and freedom. In 1964, a man in Charlotte, North Carolina, wrote, "Six brothers in my family including myself fought for our rights and freedom. Then why ... am I being forced to use the same wash-room and restrooms with negro[e]s. I highly resent this ... I'd be willing to fight and die for my rights, but can't say this any more for this country" (Sokol, 2006, p. 36). The writer suggested that World War II was fought to defend Jim Crow. Indeed, for him, that was the "American way of life." In the 1950s, a woman from Little Rock wrote *Atlanta Journal-Constitution* editor Ralph McGill regarding the desegregation of Central High School: "My son was in the Marine Corps during World War Two and spent 14 months in the South Pacific fighting, and for what? I can answer that one, to see Soldiers with rifles and Bayonets pointed to the backs of his children being forced to obey a DICTATOR instead of enjoying a FREE America and choosing their friends and associates" (Sokol, 2006, p. 36). And in Detroit in 1945, white residents rallied round the experience of World War Two to justify their belief in a right to racially homogenous neighborhoods. For instance, the head of an athletic club speaking against integrated public housing before the Detroit city council pointed to the stars on his jacket and said, "Those stars represent soldiers waiting to come back to the same neighborhood they left" (Sugrue, 1995, p. 565). He believed that fighting in the war gave white soldiers a "prior right to a neighborhood which we have built up through the years – a neighborhood which is entirely white and which we want kept white" (Sugrue, 1995, p. 565). Rooting these rights in patriotism and claiming them as American values demonstrated the extent to which segregation and white supremacy remained for many to be "as American as cherry pie" (Kunstler, 1994, p. 177 (quoting H. Rap Brown); Smith, 1997). Yet, for many, the patriotic wrapping made the rights claims more convincing, more palatable. Their comments reveal that, while they agreed that World War II was battle over democracy and freedom, their vision of democracy allowed majority rule on questions of race while simultaneously ignoring the Constitution's guarantees of rights for minorities. Freedom meant the freedom to choose your neighbors, your children's classmates, and your customers.

After World War II people mobilized rights claims to bolster claims related to neighborhood, property, and the maintenance of residential segregation. Before the Supreme Court's *Brown* decision regarding school desegregation in 1954, it dealt with the question of discrimination and segregation of private property in *Shelley v. Kraemer* (1948). *Shelley* held unconstitutional the enforcement of restrictive covenants that barred transfer of property for reasons of race or religion. The case's presence before the courts indicated that home ownership was an emerging battleground as the imaginary borders that divided white neighborhoods and non-white neighborhoods began to fade (Sugrue, 1998). White home-owners began pushing back against such progress, relying on the perceived "prior right to a neighborhood which we have built up through the years – a white neighborhood which is entirely white and which we want kept white" (Sugrue, 1995, p. 565). In Detroit, the placement of public housing garnered opposition. Whites opposed to such housing saw not only African-Americans as their enemies but also "acquiescent federal officials" who would ignore color lines and allow such housing to be built. The language of victimhood flowed easily after that, with the Greater Detroit Neighbors Association choosing as its slogan: "Help Stamp Out Oppression – Fight for Our Rights."

The use of the word "our" was significant. White segregationists in Detroit, Atlanta, and elsewhere were not typically seeking to prevent their own land from being sold to non-whites. Rather, they sought to prevent the private property of others from being sold to non-white people. Maintaining an all-white neighborhood required turning private property into communal property. Thus, one white Atlanta family brought a suit to stop real estate agents from listing for or selling to people of color, claiming "rights to the entire neighborhood, which they described as 'a completely developed and established section of long standing, with white schools, parks, churches, and shopping centers nearby'" (Kruse, 2005, p. 68). Others spoke the language of common rights, common ties, and common goals (Kruse, 2005, p. 68). Enforcement of such common rights often took the form of protest or extreme violence against whites who sold to black families or against the black families once they had moved in. But again and again, the justification for such action resided in the idea that the common rights of community members had been violated. The rights talk, while legally ineffective, carried weight in political debates while simultaneously serving as an organizing force in those white communities.

Kevin Kruse makes the argument in *White Flight* that while early resistance to desegregation came in the form of community rights claims, in the face of the history of property rights, parents, homeowners, and business owners slowly realized the weakness of their position and remade their claims in individual rights terms. In other words, they adopted (or co-opted) the dominant framework of rights discourse forged by the left, adapting it to the interests of the right.

Still, while Kruse is certainly correct and the Atlanta case shows a weakening of the community-based rights arguments in regard to property, the community-centered argument continued to resonate well into the 1970s in places like Boston, where neighborhoods such as South Boston and Charlestown used community identity as the foundation for their fight against school busing. At times, it was as simple as a chant – "Here we go Southie, Here we go!" – but that concept of community identity undergirded claims of rights to maintain and control public, neighborhood institutions. Louise Day Hicks, when running for Mayor of Boston in 1967, declared, "I will continue to defend the neighborhood school as long as I have a breath left in my body" (Lukas, 1986, p. 134). Anthony Lukas noted that by that time the phrase "neighborhood school" "had accumulated layers of other meanings – it was not just a school to which one's children could walk, a school which enshrined one's own values and attitudes, but a white school safe from black inundation. It had become a potent political slogan, loaded with subliminal connotations" (Lukas, 1986, p. 134).[2] The emphasis on community control and localism would persist and, while not always concerned with maintaining racial homogeneity, it nonetheless carried that subliminal message in politics and law into the 21st century. Thus, the coalition of plaintiffs challenging Seattle's voluntary desegregation plan named itself "Parents Involved in *Community* Schools." The concept of community might not have held legal weight, but it carried enduring political and social importance nonetheless.

Despite its continued resonance, community rights talk gave way to more individualized conceptions of rights such as the increasingly common mobilization of claims of "freedom of association." In legal terms, the Warren Court had recognized "freedom of association" in the civil rights context in 1958 when it held that the state of Alabama could not demand that the NAACP hand over its membership lists (*NAACP v. Alabama*, 1958). In that case, the right gave a group engaged in a legitimate, non-discriminatory activity protection from government interference.

Simultaneously, white segregationists were using claims of "freedom of association" to defend a right to attend all white schools, to maintain all white neighborhoods, and the right to run a segregated business. Though such claims did not hold up under legal scrutiny, they, again, carried political and rhetorical weight in the communities in whose defense they emerged. When Atlanta segregationist and restaurant owner Lester Maddox ran for Mayor in 1961, he echoed the arguments of white parents who claimed their "'freedom of association' had been trampled upon by school integration" (Kruse, 2005, p. 200). Maddox saw a similar infringement of the rights of businessmen by the sit-ins. "If there is a right to integrate, there is a right to segregate," claimed Maddox (Kruse, 2005, p. 201). Just as Detroit homeowners wrapped their segregationist arguments in patriotism, so did Maddox and others situate their arguments in the Constitution. Rather than rejecting or running from the Constitution and the rights revolution, they infiltrated it (in a way), embracing its language, twisting its meanings, and using rights to advance an agenda that ran counter to the goals of legal liberalism.

This agenda did not find success at the epicenter of the rights revolution: in the federal courts. When Maddox challenged the constitutionality of the public accommodations section of the Civil Rights Act of 1964, despite the lack of precedent, his attorney pointed to the Constitution to defend his conception of freedom of association when arguing in federal court.

> The Constitution of the United States was designed to preserve the freedom of man to discriminate ... When you talk about rights and freedom, what is a greater freedom that the right to select your own associates; the right not to serve anyone that you don't wish to serve? That's real freedom ... and that's what we are battling to preserve in this country. (Kruse, 2005, p. 225)

The Supreme Court rejected such legal interpretations of the Constitution in *Katzenbach v. McClung* (1964) and *Heart of Atlanta Motel v. United States* (1964). But winning their constitutional rights claim in court was not necessarily the only goal at that stage. Rather, making the rights claim on behalf of segregationists served to weaken the claims of civil rights advocates in the public arena. It made judges appear to be picking favorites and harming one group to benefit another. Such a "wild innovation" and interpretation of the right to free association also provided a rallying cry for a far-flung group of conservatives.

In California, opponents of the Rumford Act, a fair housing measure challenged in a ballot initiative in the fall of 1964, found Barry Goldwater on their side when he evoked home owners' "freedom of association"

(McGirr, 2001, p. 133). Here again, by claiming a right to freedom of association, white conservatives set up a conflict between the civil rights of people of color and white people. The head of an Atlanta homeowners association put it succinctly:

> My views on the "school crisis," the "sit-ins," "kneel-ins," etc., remain summarized in the phrase "freedom of association." ... It is perfectly alright if people who want integration have all the integration they want, provided those who feel otherwise (including me, of course) are granted the same "freedom of choice" to do otherwise. (Kruse, 2005, p. 163)

While reinforcing the argument that "freedom of association" was a potent idea for conservatives, the above quote also shows the evolution of rights talk when a legal rights concept such as "freedom of association" began to weaken. For it was the "right to choose" that eventually came to dominate southern white expressions of what was at stake in the battle against the civil rights movement. And in adopting "freedom of choice" rhetoric, conservatives were tapping into a rich vein in American rights talk where "choice" was for many the very essence of freedom. "Choice" resonated on the left, right, and center. Whether in commercial advertising or at reproductive rights rallies, "choice" was seen as a basic tenet of individual freedom.

In 1960s conservative grassroots circles, "right to choose" rhetoric emerged in debates about school desegregation after *Brown*. Again, it was not a right made up out of whole cloth. Rather, it represents a twist on established constitutional rights. Conservatives were using rights concepts established in decisions such as *Pierce v. Society of Sisters* (1925) and *Meyer v. Nebraska* (1923). *Meyer* held unconstitutional a law barring the teaching of non-English modern languages on grounds that it violated substantive due process rights under the 14th Amendment, including a right to "establish a home and bring up children" (*Meyer v. Nebraska*, 1923, p. 399). *Pierce* struck down a law mandating that all children attend public (rather than private or religious schools), reasoning, "The child is not the mere creature of the State; those who nurture him and direct his destiny have the right, coupled with the high duty, to recognize and prepare him for additional obligations" (*Pierce v. Society of Sisters*, 1925, p. 535). As perceived by anti-integrationist parents, the right to choose in the education context rested in the parent's power to decide where their child should be educated and how.

It only required a minor leap of logic (easy for those unconcerned with logic) to argue that the right of a parent to direct a child's destiny also granted them the right to choose the members of their child's classroom.

"Is it not every father's and mother's inalienable right and duty to choose, for their children, associates and companions for life?" one Atlanta parent asked in 1956 (Kruse, 2005, p. 163). A Mississippi parent asserted that she and her fellow (white) parents, "wanted the freedom to choose who our child would sit next to in school" (Sokol, 2006, p. 167). This was a small step from the more community-oriented concept of "freedom of association" (just as "freedom of association" was a small step from "community rights"), but freedom of choice remade the action into one that sounded wholly individual. Furthermore, "freedom of choice" recalled the most basic idea of freedom: free will, the ability to act at one's own discretion.

The idea of "freedom of choice" and the parental right to direct a child's education resonated in other desegregation battles. For instance, parents in Charlotte, North Carolina, rallied around the concept that the parental right to choose was violated by desegregating schools, particularly through busing. One local parent wrote Nixon of her resentment that "my children, who live three blocks from the school we chose to move near, may be bused to another section of town to attend a school not of my choice" (Sokol, 2006, p. 276). More succinctly, a Charlotte anti-busing group asked on one of its flyers, "Is freedom of choice dead?" (Lassiter, 2006, p. 155).

With its large Catholic population, many Boston parents similarly latched on to "choice" language. As Ronald Formisano observes, Catholic parents had been taught for decades that they had a "right in usage, if not a right in law, to control" and choose an educational path for their children (Formisano, 2004, p. 19). That the right did not legally extend to maintaining segregated, neighborhood schools was of little importance. The perceived parental right to choose empowered parents to fight against busing orders. Louise Day Hicks foresaw dark days ahead. "If under a court order a child can be forcibly taken from his parents into unfamiliar, often hostile neighborhoods … then we shall have opened a Pandora's box of new, unlimited government power" (Formisano, 2004, p. 192; Lukas, 1986, p. 130). A Charlestown parent more bluntly laid out her concerns (and priorities). "I want my freedom back. They took my freedom. They tell me where my kids have to go to school. This is like living in Russia. Next they'll tell me where to shop" (Formisano, 2004, p. 192). That the status of parenthood carried with it a bundle of rights, including a right to choose a segregated neighborhood school for one's child, is most clear in a photo from *Boston Against Busing*, where one protester carries a sign that reads: "We are not 'racists,' 'pigs,' 'animals' We are parents" (Formisano, 2004, p. 243). The sign suggests that parenthood carries with it a special, protected set of concerns that explain away the unequal effects of their "choices" while also excusing violent or otherwise distasteful behavior in defense of the "right to choose." Not surprisingly, the idea for school vouchers that persists in American politics today emerged from battles over school desegregation (Kruse, 2005), built on the idea that parents have a right to choose where to send their child to school: a public school, an all-white private school, a religious academy, or somewhere else.

But parenthood was hardly the only identity that carried with it the freedom of choice. In the 1960s, the "choice" concept spread to ideas about the rights of homeowners and business owners as well. In the context of homeownership, "freedom of Choice" rhetoric further expanded around the country in the early 1960s. In Detroit, a Homeowners' Rights Ordinance in 1963 promised homeowners the "right to choose his own friends and associates" and the "right to choose a real estate broker and tenants and home buyers 'for his own reasons'" (Sugrue, 1995, p. 576). A North Carolinian echoed that language in expressing concerns about how the proposed Civil Rights Act of 1964 would undermine residential segregation: "A person should have the freedom to decide whom he wants for neighbors" (Sokol, 2006, p. 216).

Freedom of choice received more attention from business owners, too, particularly in opposition to the Civil Rights Act of 1964. The Atlanta Restaurant Association, in a full-page ad, declared, "We still have the freedom of choice to operate our businesses as we see fit" (Kruse, 2005, p. 218). In the Supreme Court argument challenging the Act, Heart of Atlanta Motel owner Moreton Rolleston argued, "The fundamental question ... is whether or not Congress has the power to take away the liberty of an individual to run his business as he sees fit in the selection and choice of customers" (Kruse, 2005, p. 227).

In its decision in *Heart of Atlanta Motel v. United States* (1964), the Warren Court held that a business owner providing public accommodations has "no right, to select its guests as it sees fit, free from governmental regulation" (p. 259). Concurring in the decision, Justice Hugo Black specifically challenged the business owner's claims that the Civil Rights Act violated his rights under the Due Process Clause of the 14th Amendment. "[I]t would be highly ironical to use the guarantee of due process – a guarantee which plays so important a part in the Fourteenth Amendment, an amendment adopted with the predominant aim of protecting Negroes from discrimination – in order to strip Congress of power to protect Negroes from discrimination" (*Heart of Atlanta Motel v. United States*, 1964, p. 278). Yet, such official and blunt rejection of the rights claims of business owners did not blunt the ardor of conservatives in believing such ideas. In fact, the "right to choose" argument seems to presage the next thirty years of American politics: making politics a battle between the power of the central government and the individual. It echoes in arguments against business regulation, in claims that tax revenues are "your money," and in attacks on "big government."[3]

"Freedom of choice" language was not far from "freedom of association" rhetoric, but "choice" had a more acceptable ring to it. It appears to center on the individual and his or her private decision-making process devoid of the impact of that choice on others, even though that is not the case. The persistent segregation of Atlanta schools demonstrates that "freedom of choice" was not much different than "freedom of association," but it certainly carried less baggage (Kruse, 2005). Even erroneously perceived parental rights carried a seeming legitimacy. But "freedom of choice" also didn't necessarily recall segregationism. As *Atlanta Journal-Constitution* editor Ralph McGill noted in 1969, "There is all too often no freedom in the freedom of choice plan. It too frequently is freedom in reverse. It offers a segregationist, racist-dominated community or board an opportunity to proclaim a free choice while they covertly employ 'persuasions' to maintain segregation or meager tokenism" (Kruse, 2005, p. 238). McGill's point is echoed in the books on the rise of grassroots conservatism in the 1960s. As part of the larger move toward segregation through suburbanization, "freedom of choice" served to separate the idea from a direct connection to southern segregationists. As Kruse observes:

> Removed from their obviously racial origins, segregationist phrases, such as "freedom of choice" or "neighborhood schools," as well as segregationist identities, such as the angry taxpayer or concerned parent, could be easily shared by middle-class whites who had no [direct] connection to the segregationist past but who gladly took part in crafting the suburban future. (Kruse, 2005, p. 245)

By embracing the concept of "freedom of choice," modern conservatives found an ideal that, while having no fixed place in the Constitution, resonated as a political value while conservatives built their power over the course of the 1960s. But these political ideas – rallying cries to a significant and growing segment of the American population – through repetition and refinement would eventually serve as philosophical tenets of conservative politics and law in the 1980s and beyond. These ideas came to define the meaning of the Constitution in important ways for many people generally unfamiliar with the intricacies of the law and rights. They did know, however, that the Supreme Court, sometime in the past, had infringed on what they thought were their rights as Americans.

CONCLUSION

Kevin Kruse, in his book's final chapter, points out that in 1972, Richard Nixon named two justices to the U.S. Supreme Court. One, an Arizona lawyer named William Rehnquist, had begun his rise in Republican political circles working for Barry Goldwater. In 1964, he had opposed Phoenix's public accommodations law on grounds that business owners had a "right to choose" their customers. In 1967, he defended "neighborhood schools" while claiming that "we are no more dedicated to an 'integrated' society than we are to a 'segregated' society; we are instead dedicated to a free society ... in which each man is accorded the maximum amount of freedom of choice in his individual activities." Finally, in 1970, when he was Nixon's Assistant Attorney General, Rehnquist drafted a constitutional amendment creating a right to "freedom of choice" that would have barred busing as a remedy for school segregation (Kruse, 2005, p. 256).[4]

Rehnquist's rise suggests a line from the grassroots conservatism of the 1950s and 1960s to the conservative jurisprudence of the present. While without merit in the Warren Court era, the beliefs laid out by members of the conservative grassroots became increasingly accepted in American politics and, with the rise of lawyers such as Rehnquist to the bench, American law. That line was hardly straight and not consistently on the rise. The question raised by this current article is how the grassroots connected to the legal elite. Anecdotal and circumstantial evidence suggests a clear connection and it merits further attention from sociolegal researchers.

As recent scholarship on the growth of the conservative legal movement demonstrates though, it was the continuing power of legal liberalism that led conservative legal activists to begin to create organizations such as the Federalist Society in hopes of incubating conservative legal ideas as well as the lawyers and judges who would make those ideas into law (Teles, 2007; Hatcher, 2005). The conceptions of rights and interpretations of law that conservatives understood to be true were not seen as such by the Warren and then the Burger Court. What connections are there between popular conservative jurisprudence at the grassroots and elite legal conservatism from the 1970s to the present?

Recent analyses of conservative constitutionalism stress that its leaders believe that they are representing a "constitution in exile" (Rosen, 2005). That movement sees the Supreme Court's economic and property jurisprudence – starting with post-1936 decisions upholding aspects of the

New Deal – as a departure from the true meaning of the Constitution. What the recent series of books on the growth of conservatism suggest is that there was another group supporting the idea of a "constitution in exile," a group that would not necessarily have understood rights and the Constitution in the same terms laid out by today's legal scholars (that may be reserved for the highly educated elites). Rather, this group of grassroots conservatives preserved in their heads a set of beliefs about their rights – as parents, as business owners, as homeowners, as white people – that endured and spread around the nation at the same time that legal liberalism dominated the courts and academy.[5] This set of rights claims found its basis sometimes in court decisions, but often in a broader set of understandings of the Constitution, the rights of parents, the meaning of American values, and the concept of human freedom. The rights claims grew in reaction to the liberal rights revolution. But in their ascendance and endurance offer an important counter-narrative to our understanding of the 1960s legal culture and its legacy.

NOTES

1. TPF is the Tactical Police Force, an anti-riot squad within the Boston Police Department.
2. Thus, Charlestown residents felt justified in demanding that anti-busing organization Powder Keg be permitted access to Charlestown High to "act as spokesmen for the white student body" and "negotiate white student grievances" (Lukas, 1986, p. 309).
3. As mentioned earlier, the concept of choice also continues to resonate on the left in discussions of marriage, reproduction, artistic freedom, and so on. The "culture of choice" is hardly the sole domain of the right.
4. In the early 1970s, it was Rehnquist's fellow nominee Lewis Powell who first urged the creation of legal think tanks and law firms that could translate conservative principles into legal tenets (Teles, 2007).
5. This is a group that remains deeply concerned with the Constitution and the courts, as events such as "Justice Sunday" (a conservative evangelical event about the importance of the federal courts) and the campaigns of Republican presidential candidates have shown.

ACKNOWLEDGMENTS

I wish to thank Austin Sarat and Eve Darian-Smith for their help in thinking through the subject of this paper as well as for their years of mentorship. I appreciate the useful comments provided by members of the York University Law & Society Program, where I presented a version of this paper. I also thank the students in my course "Law and Lawlessness in the Busing Crisis" – particularly Arianne Waldron, Jennifer Jean-Baptiste, and Susan Allen – for their interest in the issues involved in that class and this paper. Their enthusiasm and passion were contagious. Finally, thanks to Susan Holmberg who offered needed support and valued proofreading during the incubation and writing of this paper.

REFERENCES

Ackerman, B. (1993). *We the people: Foundations.* Cambridge: Belknap Press.
Ackerman, B. (2000). *We the people: Transformations.* Cambridge: Harvard University Press.
Blasi, V. (Ed.) (1983). *The Burger Court: The counter revolution that wasn't.* New Haven: Yale University Press.
Branch, T. (1988). *Parting the waters: America in the king years: 1954–63.* New York: Simon and Schuster.
Brinkley, A. (1994). The problem of American conservatism. *American Historical Review, 99,* 409–429.
Carter, D. T. (2000). *The politics of rage: George Wallace, the origins of the new conservatism, and the transformation of American politics* (2nd ed.). Baton Rouge: LSU Press.
Dudziak, M. L. (2000). *Cold war civil rights: Race and the image of American democracy.* Princeton: Princeton University Press.
Epp, C. (1998). *The rights revolution: Lawyers, activists, and supreme courts in comparative perspective.* Chicago: University of Chicago Press.
Formisano, R. P. (2004). *Boston against busing: Race, class, and ethnicity in the 1960s and 1970s.* Chapel Hill: University of North Carolina Press.
Glendon, M. A. (1991). *Rights talk: The impoverishment of political discourse.* New York: Free Press.
Goldwater, B. (2007). Conscience of a conservative. In: R. Story & B. Laurie (Eds), *The rise of conservatism in America, 1945–2000* (pp. 59–63). Boston: Bedford/St. Martins.
Harris, C. I. (1993). Whiteness as property. *Harvard Law Review, 106,* 1707–1791.
Hatcher, L. (2005). Economic libertarians, property, and institutions: Linking activism, ideas, and identities among property rights advocates. In: A. Sarat & S. Scheingold (Eds), *The worlds cause lawyers make: Structure and agency in legal practice* (pp. 112–146). Palo Alto: Stanford University Press.
Horwitz, M. (1998). *The warren court and the pursuit of justice.* New York: Hill and Wang.
Kalman, L. (1996). *The strange career of legal liberalism.* New Haven: Yale University Press.
Kruse, K. (2005). *White flight: Atlanta and the making of modern conservatism.* Princeton: Princeton University Press.
Kunstler, W. M. (1994). *My life as a radical lawyer.* New York: Birch Lane Press.
Lassiter, M. (2006). *The silent majority: Suburban politics in the sunbelt south.* Princeton: Princeton University Press.

Lukas, A. (1986). *Common ground: A turbulent decade in the lives of three American families*. New York: Vintage.
MacDonald, M. P. (1999). *All souls: A family story from Southie*. New York: Ballantine Books.
McCann, M. W. (1994). *Rights at work: Pay equity reform and the politics of legal mobilization*. Chicago: University of Chicago Press.
McGirr, L. (2001). *Suburban warriors: The origins of the new American right*. Princeton: Princeton University Press.
Milner, L. B. (2003). Jim Crow in the army. In: *Reporting civil rights, part one: American journalism, 1941–1963* (pp. 52–61). New York: Library of America.
Perlstein, R. (2001). *Before the storm: Barry Goldwater and the unmaking of the American consensus*. New York: Hill and Wang.
Poletta, F. (2000). The structural context of novel rights claims: Southern civil rights organizing, 1961–1966. *Law & Society Review, 34*, 367–406.
Powledge, F. (1991). *Free at last? The civil rights movement and the people who made it*. New York: Harper Perennial.
Roediger, D. (1999). *The wages of whiteness*. New York: Verso.
Rosen, J. (2005). The unregulated offensive. *Times Magazine, New York*, April 17, 2005.
Schwartz, B. (Ed.) (1998). *The Burger Court: Counter-revolution or confirmation?* New York: Oxford University Press.
Silverstein, H. (1996). *Unleashing rights: Law, meaning, and the animal rights movement*. Ann Arbor: University of Michigan Press.
Smith, R. (1997). *Civic ideals: Conflicting visions of citizenship in U.S. history*. New Haven: Yale University Press.
Sokol, J. (2006). *There goes my everything: White southerners in the age of civil rights, 1945–1975*. New York: Vintage.
Sugrue, T. J. (1995). Crabgrass-roots politics: Race, rights, and the reaction against liberalism in the urban north, 1940–1964. *Journal of American History, 82*, 551–578.
Sugrue, T. J. (1998). *The origins of the urban crisis: Race and inequality in postwar Detroit*. Princeton: Princeton University Press.
Teles, S. M. (2007). *The rise of the conservative legal movement: The battle for control of the law*. Princeton: Princeton University Press.
Weisbrot, R. (1990). *Freedom bound: A history of America's civil rights movement*. New York: Plume.
Young Americans for Freedom. (2007). The Sharon statement. In: R. Story & B. Laurie (Eds), *The rise of conservatism in America, 1945–2000* (pp. 64–65). Boston: Bedford/St. Martins.

Cases Cited:

Brown v. Board of Education, (1954). 347 U.S. 483.
Brown v. Board of Education, (1955). 349 U.S. 294.
Gonzales v. Carhart, (2007). 550 U.S. ___ (slip opinion).
Heart of Atlanta Motel v. United States, (1964). 379 U.S. 241.
Katzenbach v. McClung, (1964). 379 U.S. 294.

Ledbetter v. Goodyear Tire, (2007), 550 U.S. ___ (slip opinion).
Meyer v. Nebraska, (1923). 262 U.S. 390.
NAACP v. Alabama, (1958). 357 U.S. 449.
Parents Involved in Community Schools v. Seattle School District No. 1, (2007). 551 U.S. ___
    (slip opinion).
Pierce v. Society of Sisters, (1925). 268 U.S. 510.
Shelley v. Kraemer, (1948). 334 U.S. 1.

IS THERE AN EMPIRICAL LITERATURE ON RIGHTS?

Thomas F. Burke and Jeb Barnes

ABSTRACT

The empirical literature that attempts to study rights is at an impasse. It can demonstrate that big claims about how some rights structure politics are overblown, but it has struggled to go beyond this step. This is in large part because studying rights is much more difficult than is commonly appreciated. A study of rights promises implicitly to be a study of how rights politics differs from other kinds of politics. But rights are so ubiquitous and so diverse in form that it is often unclear what the excluded other is. We examine three books on rights that we admire: two by political scientists, Gerald Rosenberg's The Hollow Hope *and Michael McCann's* Rights at Work, *and one by an anthropologist, Sally Merry's* Human Rights and Gender Violence. *These books conceptualize rights in diverse ways, in diverse settings, using diverse methodologies; yet they run up against similar difficulties in trying to think beyond the cases they study. At the conclusion, we make some humble suggestions for how researchers might try to overcome these problems.*

Revisiting Rights
Studies in Law, Politics, and Society, Volume 48, 69–91
Copyright © 2009 by Emerald Group Publishing Limited
All rights of reproduction in any form reserved
ISSN: 1059-4337/doi:10.1108/S1059-4337(2009)0000048006

INTRODUCTION

Rights are a central subject of sociolegal studies. Many books and articles use "rights" in their titles and thus seem to promise an understanding of this topic. We are avid readers of these books and articles, and we often find them provocative and useful in our own thinking about law and politics. Nevertheless, we are not at all sure that there is an empirical literature on rights.

This is because studying rights and their effects turns out to be much more difficult than is often appreciated. Like all concepts, a "right" is defined in large part by what it excludes. A study of rights politics promises implicitly to be a study of how rights politics differs from other kinds of politics. But rights are so ubiquitous, and so diverse in form, that it is often unclear what the excluded other is. The opposition between rights and non-rights is often left shadowy and unexplored. Rights studies are haunted by this other.

As a result, the empirical literature that attempts to study rights is at an impasse. It can demonstrate that big claims about how some rights structure politics – that they unilaterally deliver social goods or demobilize citizens – are overblown. But it has struggled to go beyond this step, to say anything more general about rights. In fact, we detect great ambivalence among sociolegal scholars in even attempting to cumulate knowledge about rights, developing general frameworks about rights consciousness and rights mobilization. Yet, without this, it is not at all clear what service empirical researchers can provide, other than to remind us (against some overstated theories) that rights politics is more complex, varied and fluid than is sometimes supposed. As currently composed, the sociolegal literature can give us wonderful portraits of particular instances of rights at work (or not at work), but little to link these studies other than the word "rights." They are merely studies of politics.

The struggles of rights researchers in part reflect developments in sociolegal studies that have radically decentered and so complicated our understanding of law. If law is conceived as a force that arises out of formal institutions – courts, agencies and legislatures – then the effects of law can be studied straightforwardly as top-down (or "center-out") implementation. One measures the effect of law by comparing legal commands, "law on the books" with the implementation process, "law on the streets," and the behavior that results. But as sociolegal researchers have long understood, people interpret legal commands in strikingly varied ways, and their interpretations have social effects that are just as significant as those of judges and legislators. Once this is recognized, and the formal institutions are decertified as the authoritative custodians of law, complications ensue, and sites of research far away from courts and legislatures gain prominence. There is, for example, added weight to studying how individuals think about law, "legal consciousness," because individuals, drawing on social understandings, are the first movers of the disputing process, and through their decisions help make the law. There is interest in how organizations that are the target of the law translate and construct it, because they too "make" law, both within the organization and sometimes in the larger society. In the newly decentered perspective of sociolegal research, the law is "all around" (Sarat, 1990) and so becomes hard to pin down; "cause" and "effect" models seem overly simplistic and difficult to specify. Studying the effect of law becomes a bewildering exercise, like trying to spot a friend in a hall of mirrors.[1]

In the study of rights, these developments in sociolegal studies were presaged by the publication of Stuart Scheingold's classic, *The Politics of Rights*. The first part of Scheingold's book takes aim at the "myth of rights," the view that the recognition of rights by courts can authoritatively resolve all political and ethical conflicts (Scheingold, 2004, p. 5). Scheingold, drawing on the work of Clifford Geertz and Murray Edelman, analyzed how rights function as symbols in American politics (Scheingold, 2004, pp. 14–17, 205–207). In the second part of his book, Scheingold urged a study "the politics of rights," in which activists, taking advantage of the symbolic power of rights, use that power to advance their goals. As Scheingold (2004) notes in his more recent preface to the book, *The Politics of Rights* reflected the decentering of law within sociolegal studies because it urged attention to the ways in which individuals, social movements, and intermediate organizations constructed rights claims. More subtly, *The Politics of Right* pointed the way to a less unified and more specialized study of rights. Rights, Scheingold suggested, had different functions and different mechanisms in different settings – as resources for social movement, as weapons of cause lawyers, as mechanisms of policy implementation, and as part of the everyday life of individuals. Rights were "all around" but not necessarily all one thing, an observation that should make researchers be wary of grand unified statements about rights.

Scheingold's call to study the politics of rights has been answered by a bevy of researchers in the past three decades, prominent among them his own students.[2] They have produced a body of work that has been influential within the Law and Society Association and that occasionally gains notice within anthropology, sociology, and political science. Yet, for all its successes, this field is still struggling with the challenges posed by a decentered, more highly contextualized conception of law, raising questions about the whole enterprise of rights research. The rest of this chapter is an attempt to explain what we mean when we wonder if there is an empirical literature on rights. We will focus particularly on three books on rights that we admire, two by political scientists, Gerald Rosenberg's *The Hollow Hope* and Michael McCann's *Rights at Work*, and one by an anthropologist, Sally Merry's *Human Rights and Gender Violence*. These books consider diverse forms of rights in diverse settings, using diverse methodologies; yet they run up against similar difficulties in trying to think beyond the cases they study. We certainly make no claim that these books can represent all works in the sociolegal literature – our selection is biased, for one thing, toward political science – but we do think they reflect divergent (and recurring) approaches to studying rights and thus illustrate some of the central difficulties that rights researchers find themselves in. Rights research as currently constituted is a field in which the whole is much less than the sum of its often wonderful parts.

At the conclusion, we make some humble suggestions for researchers as to how they could address these problems. In particular, we argue for more attention to concept formation, and more explicit comparisons between rights and non-rights forms of politics, or at least between different types of rights claims.

ROSENBERG'S *THE HOLLOW HOPE*

Gerald Rosenberg's *The Hollow Hope* is a classic in the field of rights studies. Whether one agrees or disagrees with its conclusions, *The Hollow Hope* synthesized an impressive array of literature, amassed reams of data, and in so doing helped to re-energize studies of rights-based litigation in political science. Soon after *The Hollow Hope* appeared, there was a flurry of scholarship on rights by leading sociolegal scholars such as McCann (1993) and Feeley (1993) and an entire volume devoted to assessing Rosenberg's conclusions (Schultz, 1998).

For our purposes, *The Hollow Hope* is particularly interesting because, at first blush, it makes very strong and controversial claims about rights. With characteristic punch, Rosenberg contends that rights-based litigation is almost always unable to produce significant social reform and thus offers a "hollow hope" for change. Rosenberg adds that the "fault lies not merely with the message but the messenger itself" (Rosenberg, 1991, p. 213), suggesting that courts are intrinsically weak agents of change.

Rosenberg argues that pursuing rights is a waste of scarce resources, diverting activists from more productive actions such as grassroots organizing and lobbying. Rosenberg concludes that courts "act as 'fly-paper' for reformers who succumb to the 'lure of litigation'" (p. 341).

Rosenberg's study uses a top-down approach to the politics of rights. He locates law straightforwardly within the courts – there is no "decentering" here, no sense of competing conceptions of law. In that respect, *The Hollow Hope* is a very traditional study of judicial implementation. Rosenberg's goal is to understand the conditions under which courts produce "significant" social change at the national level (p. 4). According to his "Constrained Court Model," Rosenberg hypothesizes that judicial decisions will be most effective when there is (1) ample precedent for judicial decisions; (2) congressional and executive support for change; (3) some public support (or at least low opposition); and (4) one of the following: (a) positive incentives for compliance; (b) costs for non-compliance; (c) market incentives for compliance; or (d) extra-judicial actors who seek to use judicial rulings as cover for implementing their own reform agendas.

Rosenberg examines his model through an analysis of some of the most celebrated social change decisions of the Warren and Burger courts, starting with *Brown v. Board of Education* and *Roe v. Wade*. He culls through primary and secondary sources looking for signs of direct or indirect influence. He finds time and again that these famous decisions generally had limited effects on policy, public opinion, and social behavior.

Rosenberg's conclusions are forcefully stated, but are not as sweeping, or as controversial, as they first appear. Part of the reason is that a significant portion of the analysis is geared toward debunking very strong – or, less charitably, very naïve – claims about the power of rights-based litigation and judicial policymaking. In discussing *Brown v. Board*, for example, Rosenberg begins with various quotes from leading civil rights advocates and law professors, who see *Brown* as "a revolutionary statement of race relations law," "nothing short of a reconsecration of American ideals," and the "most important political, social, and legal event in America's twentieth-century history." As Rosenberg argues, these views are not plucked from thin air; they were articulated by leading activists. Using the stated goals of activists is a standard strategy for avoiding observer bias in policy studies. Yet, by relying on these types of statements as his analytic baseline, Rosenberg tested an extreme set of beliefs about the efficacy of rights, one that few sociolegal scholars believed even at the time (Schuck, 1993; McCann, 1993; Feeley, 1993). From this vantage,

Rosenberg's findings are not surprising; they simply confirm Scheingold's analysis of the myth of rights.

Of course, Rosenberg does not merely seek to challenge the most extreme statements about the influence of courts; he also uses the cases to examine his contingent model of judicial influence. Here too, the sheer bulk of the analysis is impressive, but its scope is limited. From the outset, Rosenberg focuses on whether courts acting by themselves foster significant change at the national level. This is a high bar. It is hard to imagine any institution in the American system of shared powers that can be expected to produce unilateral national change. Thus, what seems at first to be a sweeping indictment of rights litigation can instead be seen as a restatement of the status quo orientation of the fragmented American policymaking process.

Moreover, *The Hollow Hope* does not provide much insight into how rights politics differ from alternative routes to social change. Rosenberg concludes that judicial decisions will be implemented when they receive support from the other branches and from the public and when they create incentives for others to implement them. These conditions, however, would likely apply to any mode of implementation, whether supervised by courts or other bodies. Presumably congressional initiatives too would flourish when they are supported by the other branches and by the public, when they create positive incentives for others to go along (and costs for them to ignore), and when local officials are happy to implement them. Rosenberg cites only one condition, ample legal precedent, that seems specific to rights, and even this has analogs, since precedent implies incrementalism, a mode that political scientists have long studied in legislatures and agencies. Because he does not fully consider rights against (implicit) counterfactuals of legislative or executive action, Rosenberg fails to identify the distinctive characteristics of rights politics.

Do Rosenberg's case studies support the claim that courts and rights serve as "fly-paper" for activists? Again, it depends on how one interprets the claim. If Rosenberg is merely arguing that activists should not focus all their efforts on one branch, in a polity in which power is shared among branches, his contention is clearly sound, but hardly controversial. The more provocative underlying claim, wrapped up in the metaphor of a "fly-paper" court, is that work that activists do through courts should be channeled toward other modes of politics. To justify this claim, the analysis must grapple with the counterfactual of what would happen in the absence of rights, or if the demands of activists had been framed outside the language of rights.

The Hollow Hope never does this in a systematic way. In a crucial passage in the analysis of the desegregation cases, which is the most well-developed of all the book's case studies, Rosenberg laments: "we can never know what would have happened if the Court had not acted as it did (if *Brown* had never been decided or had come out the other way)" (p. 157). Instead of grappling with this counterfactual, the book points to a whole host of factors that could have accounted for desegregation that are said to be independent of the court's decisions, especially actions of Congress and the executive branch that seem more proximately related to progress on the ground. This approach convincingly underscores that many factors potentially contributed to desegregation, but offers little purchase on their relative significance, the subtle ways in which these factors interact or, more importantly for our purposes, how rights-based strategies fundamentally differ from other reform strategies.

There are a whole host of methods for assessing counterfactual claims. One can use statistical controls to model the independent impact of formal rights. One can draw on comparative methods and contrast rights-based campaigns with those that do not rely on rights or rely less on rights. One can assess cases involving different types of rights, especially more or less qualified ones. As McCann (1993) notes in his insightful review of *The Hollow Hope*, by focusing on institutional constraints on the courts, the book leaves open the question of what would have happened if the Supreme Court had ruled more forcefully, especially at the implementation stages. As a result, it is not clear from the analysis whether the lack of results stems from some deep-seated limitations of rights politics or simply a lack of judicial follow-through in the particular cases at hand (McCann, 1993, p. 726).

In the end, *The Hollow Hope* is perhaps best understood as a salutary brush-clearing exercise. It helps dispose of the myth Scheingold identified, that rights are all-powerful, self-executing agents of national level change. It normalizes judicial implementation, suggesting that judicial effectiveness should vary depending on many of the same factors that affect the chances of successful implementation of legislation and agency rules. Yet, these insights leave many important issues unresolved. What would have happened if the courts had ruled more forcefully? What would have happened if activists had eschewed rights-based politics and turned to other means of pursuing their ambitious agendas? It is not difficult to imagine studies designed to take on these issues. However, by focusing on national level change involving prominent rights-based litigation, *The Hollow Hope* leaves them to others.

MCCANN ON *RIGHTS AT WORK*

Michael McCann's *Rights at Work* is among the most influential sociolegal studies of rights, particularly among political scientists. It is sometimes cast as a foil to Rosenberg's book, a "pro-rights" book to Rosenberg's more negative conclusions, and a "bottom-up" book to Rosenberg's "top-down" approach. Rather than focusing on judicial outcomes and the failure of courts to implement them, the typical stuff of "gap" research, McCann concentrates on the ways in which activists and everyday actors caught up in a rights movement think about politics and secondarily on the degree to which their material fortunes were improved during a period of rights activism.

McCann's case, the comparable worth movement, gives the book its pun: In seeking to understand how rights work, he analyzes a struggle – really a series of connected struggles – over equal employment wages. The comparable worth movement contends that job categories overwhelmingly filled by women are systematically underpaid as compared to "male" jobs and that this systematic pattern is a form of sex discrimination. An administrative assistant who handles complex documents and supervises employees, for example, receives less pay than a painter or a carpenter. These systematic differences in compensation at the level of job category explain much of the wage gap between men and women. Beginning in the 1970s, unions and individual plaintiffs sued under federal civil rights laws, contending that wage differentials across comparable job categories constituted sex discrimination. The logic of their argument did not fit the conventional formula of sex discrimination, in which differential pay is provided for the same job. But in a few celebrated cases, including a narrow 5-4 Supreme Court decision (*County of Washington, Oregon v. Gunther* 452 U.S. 161 (1982)), some judges accepted arguments consistent with the comparable worth framework, and states, local governments, and some private employers implemented some wage restructuring. Victory in the courts, however, was short-lived, as the judicial tide turned, most famously in a 1985 decision, *AFCSME v. Washington* (770 F.2d 1401), authored by 9th Circuit Appeals Court Judge Anthony Kennedy, himself on the verge of a major job promotion. No court beyond the trial level, McCann notes, ever fully accepted the comparable worth argument.

At first glance, then, comparable worth seems to be a good example of the perils of a rights strategy. Even where they won in court, comparable worth advocates had difficulty implementing their decisions. Moreover, the judicial victories of the movement proved ephemeral, and by the time

McCann was writing, many considered the movement stalled (p. 85). Thus, McCann sets up comparable worth a kind of "least likely" case, in which one would be least likely to observe rights working effectively. (This is the converse of Rosenberg's handling of *Brown*: Rosenberg argues that though *Brown* at first glance looks like a powerful example of rights at work, a closer inspection of the aftermath of the decision vindicates critics of rights.)

The strongest claim McCann rebuts is that rights demobilize grassroots movements. McCann shows that rights claims in fact seemed to attract and energize supporters. Media coverage of the initial judicial victories, McCann shows, was widespread and was used by savvy activists as part of organizing campaigns, who employed slogans like "Raises, Rights and Respect" and "Help Defend Working Women's Rights" (p. 67). The victories raised expectations among rank-and-file women workers and gave them a familiar vocabulary for naming their discontents about work. Moreover, the judicial victories transformed public discourse about wage equity and struck fear into the hearts of employers, providing leverage at the bargaining table and in legislatures that far outweighed the heft of the judicial victories themselves.

McCann's study knocks out the strongest claims of rights critics. Clearly, rights do not always destroy grassroots movements, and they do not necessarily block more radical consciousness about hierarchy and oppression. His comparable worth activists are not taken in by the "myth of rights" as all-powerful commands; they understand that rights are indeterminate and subject to the whims of judges. Nonetheless, McCann's interviewees also realize that rights can be useful political resource, both for mobilizing support and for bargaining with employers. Similarly, at the individual level, consciousness about rights does not seem to squash other kinds of thinking about employment justice. McCann finds that everyday people are perfectly capable of thinking about comparable worth as right, but also as an issue of distributive justice, of family need, even of efficiency.

Rights claims thus emerge as just one of many strategies that activists use, another arrow in the quiver, another way to think about social justice, complementary rather than hegemonic. Similar to Rosenberg's analysis, the effect of McCann's book is to normalize rights claims and legal strategies. This is a useful corrective to super-strong claims about the limits of rights and to the isolation of law within political science, a segregation that has impoverished both fields. But this normalization has a strange effect, because it comes close to abolishing its subject. By the end of McCann's book, we must ask: Are rights in any way different from other forms of politics? How are rights at work different from other kinds of strategies at work? These are questions *Rights at Work* is not configured to answer.

The normalization of rights is apparent when McCann attempts to explain the success of the comparable worth movement. He provides a long list of factors that will be familiar to students of social movement literature. On the political structure side, he links the movement's successes to earlier movements that had established its institutional and conceptual foundations, politicians' concern about the gender gap and the female vote, openness to reform within state and local bureaucracies, and supportive state political cultures. On the organizational resources side, he notes solidarity among women workers, union organization, feminist groups, and strong, savvy leadership. As with Rosenberg's book, the identified factors are convincingly grounded in McCann's data, but also generic: they could apply just as easily to any social movement, whether rights-based or not. Indeed, McCann sums up his findings with a "process-based Path Model" of legal mobilization that builds on the "political process" model of Douglas McAdam simply by adding legal action and rights consciousness to McAdam's framework (p. 136). McCann concludes that rights are "neither just a resource nor just a constraint for political movement building, but rather vary in utility with the specific situations in which they are deployed" (p. 137).

McCann's emphasis on complexity and contingency does not stop him from considering aspects of the comparable worth struggle that might reflect the distinctive characteristics of rights politics. He observes, for example, that the logic of antidiscrimination law generally pushed disputants in his cases toward more formal, more systematic approaches to wage setting that were separated from traditional wage negotiations. More formalized processes such as these, he observes, can benefit "traditionally marginalized interests" who are disfavored by more discretionary, informal processes typically managed by those on top of traditional hierarchies (p. 182). Does that mean that rights have a formalizing tilt that, *on average*, aids "outsiders" in their struggles with insiders? McCann avoids making such a strong claim, concluding that only his study reveals "the creative potential" of mobilizing legal norms and so demonstrates the "ambiguous and shifting role of law as a constitutive force." In fact, McCann agrees with radical scholars that "legal conventions do generally tend to sustain status quo relations"(p. 193). Yet, at the same time, McCann maintains that rights are a useful weapon for those on the bottom, one that has distinctive properties and advantages in political conflicts. By linking the local and personal with the abstract and universal, rights seem to call those in power to attention in a way that claims of needs or proclamations of interest do not. Rights, McCann says, "Provide at least some grounds for winning what Minow calls an 'equality of attention' in public debate."[3]

These are intriguing hypotheses about the politics of rights, generalizations whose adequacy we hope other researchers will pursue. McCann, however, is limited in his ability to probe them because of his research design, which limits his ability to compare rights mobilization with other forms of politics: He does not have a fully developed "other" to which he could compare rights politics. One might imagine a comparable worth movement, or at least a "pay increase for women" movement that did not invoke rights claims or have a legal strategy. At points, McCann seems to be considering this counterfactual, particularly in his discussion of the more technical job evaluation side of the movement. But a social movement based solely on such a technical discourse seems so implausible that McCann never fully considers it as a counterfactual. Similarly, while McCann observes a range of discourses around wage equity – family need, distributional justice, and workplace efficiency – he does not attempt to imagine a movement shorn of the discourse of rights.

McCann does has some variation across the 28 comparable worth struggles he analyses, and at points, he draws on this, again to upset overstated generalizations about rights. For example, in his discussion of mobilization, he compares more grassroots comparable worth struggles to more elite, less participatory campaigns. Across the 28 cases, he concludes, there seems to be no difference between the cases in which proponents brought a legal complaint and those in which they used other strategies exclusively. (Indeed, four of the five cases without legal action were among the least participatory – Fig. 3.4, pp. 79, 82.) But McCann undermines his comparison by noting that the cases are not independent of each other; activists in them all used the discourse of rights, and the threat of legal action, even where not taken up, loomed in the background (pp. 162–163). All of his cases, then, are treated as examples of rights at work, albeit in different formations. This makes it difficult for him to say what exactly is distinctive about rights politics.

An equally fundamental problem is that the scope of McCann's study is unclear. Are his conclusions limited to employment rights, antidiscrimination rights, or rights more generally? Even McCann's title is slyly ambiguous on this point: Is it merely *Rights at Work* – rights in the employment field – he is studying, or is he more generally concerned with how all rights "work"? Throughout the book, McCann sticks closely to fairly narrow conclusions drawn from the data in his study, which are confined entirely to comparable worth struggles. Yet, in his encounters with critics of rights, he does not similarly narrow the scope of his argument; he does not say that the critics are wrong *in the case of employment antidiscrimination rights*, he says they are wrong about rights. But what are "rights"? The only thing approaching a formal definition of "rights" appears at the outset of the book, when McCann says that rights "designate the proper distribution of social burdens and benefits among citizens," a very broad statement (p. 7). It would seem a prerequisite to any body of scholarship to have some common sense of what one is studying; yet, it is unclear whether McCann's conclusions are about rights in the broadest sense (concepts of the "proper distribution of social burdens and benefits"), antidiscrimination rights, or more narrowly, antidiscrimination rights at work.

This is not an immediate problem for *Rights at Work* because its aims are negative: it does a wonderful job of showing that rights, however defined, are not inevitably any of the things theorists sometimes claim – hegemonic, deradicalizing, or demobilizing. McCann and Rosenberg's analyses can be seen as mirror images. Where Rosenberg clears away overstated claims about the transformative value of rights, McCann clears out overstated claims about the demobilizing effects of rights politics. The problem for rights researchers lies in the next step.

The strange result of Rosenberg's and McCann's books is that by normalizing rights, they make them much less interesting as a subject. On their account, mobilization and implementation using rights looks a lot like mobilizing and implementing using other tactics, and theories about social movements and policy implementation generally work well for rights movements too. There is no body of scholarship about the role of pens in politics because we assume that pens can be used in so many ways, in so many contexts, that there is nothing that would unite their various uses, and thus, there would be nothing interesting to say about them. No social scientist would write *Pens at Work*, or *Pens in Politics*. If rights are like pens, then perhaps, there is an empirical literature on rights, but Rosenberg's and McCann's books are the beginning and end of it.

Are rights like pens? Marshall McLuhan famously argued that seemingly neutral media have effects, have tilt. Social context and contingency affect how media are employed – Soviet television programs were different from the CBS evening news – but McLuhan still argued that there were similarities across context. One could use a television simply to light up a room, but most people watched the screen, and McLuhan claimed, in similar ways across radically different societies. The strongest formulation was that "the medium is the message," a radical assertion that the technology itself had a meaning over and above the particular content of the medium (McLuhan, 1962, 2003). With rights, as with television, it is hard to escape the notion that the medium has a message, that a politics of rights looks different from another kind of politics, that *Rights at Work* are different in some way from *Non-Rights at Work*.

One could imagine an empirical literature on rights that tries to tease this out, but the emphasis in sociolegal scholarship on complexity and contingency can make one despair at the project. If even the subject of the study is decentered and fluid, difficult to pin down, what hope is there for comparing across cases? Empirical rights scholarship sometimes seems a chorus of Babel, with researchers condemned to talk past one another, and no larger goal then to pile up the number of myriad formations in which rights claims are invoked. At least scholars of pens in politics could be assured they were roughly talking about the same thing.

MERRY'S *HUMAN RIGHTS AND GENDER VIOLENCE*

Sally Merry's *Human Rights and Gender Violence* provides a useful contrast to the ways in which McCann and Rosenberg study rights. Merry's study is at the transnational rather than American level, and there is little in her book about courts or formal law. Instead, the main institutions she studies are the United Nations (UN) and its associated organizations, conferences, and committees, entities that argue over human rights norms and attempt to diffuse them. Perhaps, most importantly, unlike Rosenberg or McCann, Merry is not out to debunk inflated claims (positive or negative) about rights. Indeed, though rights appear in her title, Merry spends much of her book on another target, "culture," and the way this term is deployed in controversies over human rights. Finally, though Merry comes to the study of rights from anthropology, a discipline seemingly more steeped in context and contingency than political science, she is much more willing than McCann to generalize from her cases about how the rights she studies work.

This may be because Merry does not struggle as much as McCann and Rosenberg with the problem of "the other," the thing to which rights are being compared. For Rosenberg, the other is the spectral counterfactual of a civil rights politics without *Brown* and an abortion politics without *Roe*; for McCann, it is either a comparable worth movement that never filed a legal action or a pay equity movement uninfected by the language of rights. These are all rather shadowy apparitions. For Merry, by contrast, the other is at the center of her book. It is the local practices and institutions against which human rights covenants are aimed – rules and laws governing marriage, family, and sexuality that treat women as second-class citizens. These practices and institutions are both criticized and defended as vital components of "traditional culture," and one of Merry's primary ambitions is to show how that common framing gets culture wrong.

Through interviews, documents, and observation, Merry analyzes the process by which international organizations reach consensus on the language of conventions relating to gender equality, most prominently CEDAW, the Convention for the Elimination of All Forms of Discrimination Against Women. Merry and her assistants then document the processes by which the norms generated at the international level filter down to national and local settings – the transnational version of "rights at work." The fieldwork for the book is unusually, and admirably, wide-ranging, including India, Fiji, Hong Kong, China more generally, and the United States. Within these diverse locations, Merry analyzes the role of "translators," those who take the international discourse of human rights back to their countries and apply it to local conditions. She interviews local activists and service workers about the diffusion of programmatic innovations such as domestic violence centers. She analyzes controversies involving gender to see the extent to which human rights language and concepts play a role. Like McCann, Merry finds that human rights discourse, even where it takes root, is far from hegemonic: Her actors are perfectly able to talk the language of human rights, yet also locate themselves within other moral orderings such as kinship obligations. But Merry also finds that human rights concepts, though fitted by national actors to local contexts, are not fundamentally altered in the journey from global to local. Although they may be packaged to appeal to local sensibilities, they remain "part of a distinctive modernist vision of the good and just society that emphasizes autonomy, choice, equality, secularism and protection of the body" (Merry, 2006, p. 120). Thus, for Merry, human rights do have a tilt; they are not merely creatures of context and contingency, whose meaning and effect depend on the circumstances in which they are deployed.

Merry argues that to frame human rights as disrupting "traditional cultures" is misleading, not because rights are not disruptive but because the idea of a "traditional culture" is more confused than commonly supposed. She documents this claim through her observations of how human rights work in UN forums. UN conventions are said to be binding on the nations that sign them, but the UN has no enforcement power against countries that fail to live up to their commitments. UN committees attempt to monitor implementation of covenants by asking nations to report on their progress.

Merry observes the delivery of these country reports at UN committee meetings and notes that "traditional culture" is often used as an excuse for not living up to human rights norms. Culture, Merry shows, is often treated in these international forums as an unchanging, irrational set of practices sealed off from outside influence and generally associated with the rural "backwards" sectors of a developing nation. As any anthropologist knows, and Merry demonstrates, this way of talking conceals the dynamism, hybridity, and complexity of cultures. Practices advertised as ancient and endemic are often much more recent and partial – and claims to "tradition" are often politically strategic.

For example, when a Fijian national report noted that punishment of rape is sometimes diverted through the practice of "bulubulu," in which the offender offers a gift in apology to the victim's family, the UN committee harshly criticized the practice as a human rights violation – and Fijian officials angrily defended what they described as a practice central to their culture. But Merry concludes, based on several months of fieldwork in Fiji and research by other anthropologists, that bulubulu is a much more fluid tradition than the UN committee understood. Once used to smooth over tensions in village life, the tradition morphed as Fiji became urbanized. Indeed, the "tradition" of using bulubulu to divert punishment for rape seems to have arisen in just the past few years, as a response to increasing sentences for sex crimes (p. 118). Moreover, the valorization of bulubulu is one small part of a cultural conflict within Fiji, in which claims about the peacefulness and communalism of village life are used by ethnic Fijians in their struggle against Indo-Fijians, who are portrayed as greedy individualists. All of this, Merry notes, was missed by the UN committee, which instead of criticizing a particular (and apparently new) manifestation of bulubulu, bumbled into a "rights versus culture" conflict by criticizing the entire practice.

Merry argues that culture should be seen not as a "barrier to human rights mobilization but as a context that defines relationships and meanings and constructs the possibilities of action" (p. 9). Merry notes that more savvy human rights advocates have this dynamic view of culture and look for resources within their own nations' institutions and practices with which to overcome the oppression of women. Yet, Merry observes that international organizations strongly favor human rights norms over other approaches for improving the status of women. When, for example, an Egyptian national report argued for drawing on the progressive elements within Islam to promote gender equality, Merry notes that the UN committee reviewing the report was unimpressed, and reinforced the importance of human rights concepts (p. 97). Although Merry expresses ambivalence about some aspects of human rights discourse, she seems to agree that, in the end, it is "the best we have" for challenging the oppression of women (p. 231). She reaches this conclusion, it seems, simply from the logic of "rights at work" than from a formal comparison between different modes of cultural change: Human rights draw their strength, she argues, from their resistance to local context, to their universalism. If they were more adaptable to context, more pliable, they would also be less effective in challenging patriarchy.

Strangely enough, *Human Rights and Gender Violence* is much more careful and self-conscious about "culture" than it is about "human rights." Merry complains that "Although culture is a term on everyone's lips, people rarely talk about what they mean by it" (p. 10). The same, however, could be said just as accurately about rights. Like Rosenberg and McCann (and Stuart Scheingold before them), Merry in this book does not offer a formal definition of what she means by rights generally, or human rights in particular. It is not so clear, as a result, whether her claims are limited to CEDAW rights, to internationally created rights, or rights more broadly. Moreover, while Merry is careful in unearthing the many ways in which her subjects talk about culture and the puzzles this produces, she is not interested in analyzing the ways in which they talk about rights. Of course, this may be because, as she suggests at several points, human rights tend not to get pushed around the way culture does – on her account, rights travel undamaged, and are understood pretty much within Fiji, China, India, and Hong Kong the way they are at UN meetings. But even if human rights concepts are relatively unproblematic in the case of gender violence, conflicts about human rights are likely in other cases, and to the extent Merry wants to say something more general about the transmission of rights from the global to the national and local scenes, it would useful for her to be more explicit in conceptualizing rights in general and human rights in particular.

This leads to a second puzzle about Merry. She notes that culture is often identified as something that goes on "out there" amongst the primitives. But all places have cultures, even the UN, and one of Merry's tasks is to describe the culture that produces international human rights documents. Merry does not, however, consider the converse: Do the places "out there" have rights, or competing conceptions of human rights? The answer depends, of course, on how one conceptualizes "rights" and "human rights." At points, it almost seems as if Merry is holding off this question by considering "human rights" positively, as those rights that the international organizations declare as rights, or even more narrowly, as the particular rights in CEDAW. There are scattered passages in which Merry briefly raises the possibility of conflicts among rights claims. For example, in the struggle over Muslim personal laws in India, which have several discriminatory features, Merry notes that some Indian feminists defend the laws as part of a right against the "homogenization of communities" (Merry, p. 109). More humbly, Merry's examination of the conflict over female inheritance in Hong Kong contrasts the initial claim of women as part of a system of kinship rights, with their shift toward equality rights (pp. 195–204). Merry notes that the other side in the Hong Kong struggle also adopted the language of human rights (pp. 214–215). But these scattered acknowledgments do not lead her to open up the category "rights" and consider its various deployments; she instead keeps her category of "human rights" restricted to the rights she considers that are enshrined in international documents.

The upside of this is that Merry is willing to make much more strong claims than McCann about the tilt of rights. Rights on her account strengthen the state (because the state becomes the locus of their enforcement) and individualize, strengthening autonomy and equality at the expense of community and patriarchy (p. 137). She concludes that "human rights are ... based on a neoliberal privileging of choice rather than alternatives that could be more community-based or focused on socialist or religious conceptions of justice" (p. 102).[4] The downside of Merry's treatment of rights is that the reader cannot be sure exactly what she counts as part of the category. Moreover, it is not at all clear that her conclusions extend to fields other than gender, where there is likely to be much more conflict among competing conceptions of rights, even human rights.

More attention to conceptualizing rights would help with another puzzle: To what extent are Merry's claims about (human) rights at work rather than the process of applying international (and thus necessarily abstract and universal norms) to local circumstances? Merry seems to conflate the two (see, e.g., p. 104), and it is true that in the gender violence realm they are closely linked, so that it may be problematic to try to disentangle them. But one can imagine other realms (the environment, social welfare, labor, and education) in which international organizations attempt to impose norms that are not necessarily "human rights." Do these also individualize and empower the state? Conversely, would human rights have a different flavor if they were diffused in a less hierarchical, top-down manner? Because Merry does not explicitly conceptualize the features of human rights, she is not in a position to think about how much of her story is about the diffusion specifically of rights and how much about the particular structure of norm diffusion she observes. For example, one of her conclusions is that rights norms take root where institutions and the state recognize them (p. 223). But it is not clear why this is a feature of human rights, or just of norm diffusion more generally – presumably all norms are more likely to find a place in popular consciousness when they are institutionalized and state recognized. As with Rosenberg and McCann, the reader cannot be sure that Merry has identified anything specific about rights.

SOME RECOMMENDATIONS

All the three books are ostensibly about rights, and yet, all three fail to make clear how they bound their central concepts. As a result, it is hard to put them together because it is not at clear what they share. What, if anything, would be lost if we relabeled Rosenberg's book as study of judicial implementation, McCann's as a study of social movement mobilization, and Merry's as a study of conflict over transnational norms in national contexts?

The easy answer is to hold that these books illustrate the many different manifestations of "rights," that they show how context and contingency shape rights consciousness and claiming, and so offer a correction to simple, rigidified understandings of rights. Imposing sharper boundaries on the concepts of rights, from this perspective, creates significant drawbacks. In a recent review of the legal consciousness literature, McCann (2006) argues the boundlessness of the concept of law in that field of research is a necessary cost, the flip side of the virtues of a decentered approach to law. The research began, he notes, with a sense that "ostensibly more parsimonious, precise, positive conceptions of law" were oversimplified and misleading and that much could be gained "by recognizing the complex, expansive, dynamic and significant – if indeterminate – dimensions of legality" in studying legal consciousness (McCann, 2006, p. xix).

Nonetheless, McCann also concludes that boundlessness is only worthwhile if it generates new understandings of legality. He worries that focusing on the "plurality of legal meanings that citizens can construct" can obscure the important ways in which legal consciousness is tied to the acts and words of official institutions (p. xx) – arguably what makes legal consciousness "legal." In rights research, we are not convinced that boundlessness is a virtue or that greater conceptual clarity would come at a significant cost. We remain puzzled by the problems posed to rights researchers by a decentered understanding of law and are not sure yet how to resolve them. But based on our review of three very admirable and influential books, we suggest some tentative and humble recommendations for those who seek to contribute to a field of empirical rights scholarship.

First, we believe that whatever the virtues of boundlessness at an earlier stage, at this point, rights researchers need to be more self-conscious about the boundaries of their work. Once we move beyond debunking ("rights aren't always x"), empirical rights scholarship necessarily becomes concerned with tendencies and tilts, the stuff between 0% and 100% that characterizes most phenomena in social life. In that context, it is particularly important to create linkages between studies. But to link, say, McCann with Merry, one has to have a keen sense of the categories they are using. It is unclear to us how to integrate McCann's conclusions about the relative malleability and flexibility of rights with Merry's insistence that human rights are resistant to transformation and have certain characteristics that do not change with national or local context. Indeed, it is not clear that there *are* any connections between the studies. Are scholars in this field united only by the use of the word "rights"?

Doctrinal research on rights tends to emphasize typologies – to distinguish negative from positive rights, or social from political, or liberties from duties (Hohlfeld, 1923). Sociolegal scholarship, even where it is closely attentive to the connections among "law on the books," "law on the streets," and legal consciousness, tends to eschew typologies. Nevertheless, it is useful to make explicit distinctions within the broad category of "rights." It may be, for example, that studies of anti-discrimination rights at work are more about the particular logic of discrimination than about "rights."[5] The logic of privacy rights may share more with property rights than with discrimination. Merry's approach may reflect a particular focus on CEDAW or on international discourse about "human rights" that does not necessarily track with American conceptions of rights. Some of the problems of generalizing across the enormous category "rights" could be avoided if scholars were willing to create subcategories and be more explicit about the research that links most closely to them. In other words, we would urge scholars of rights to be more outward looking, more willing to link their works to similar studies, if only to distinguish the realm they study from the larger field. Sociolegal scholars might also distinguish more sharply across different spheres in which rights do their work. Studies of rights in social movements, for example, are likely to have more in common with each other than they will with studies that focus on everyday legal consciousness.

Second, given that so many rights studies make implicit claims about the distinctive (albeit diverse) nature of rights, we urge rights scholars to consider comparative research designs, particularly designs that match "non-rights" with rights. Many studies of rights are single-case studies that track changes over time in a particular field. Others, including the three studies reviewed here, examine how rights politics emerges in different settings. But there are few examples of studies that compare rights politics with non-rights politics or different types of rights politics. Because claims about the power or impotence of rights are implicitly comparative claims, it is very useful to think about what we have called "the other," the baseline to which rights are being compared. In the three studies reviewed here, "the other" is usually a counterfactual, a world that has not existed but must be conjured based on the author's imagination. Rights scholars who employ counterfactuals may want to take advantage of a methodological literature that is developed on their uses and their limits (see, e.g., Fearon, 1991). But an even better solution to the problem of the "other" is to consider a parallel case – another polity that dealt with the same problem using a different conceptual framework, a parallel issue in which rights consciousness failed to emerge, a social movement that rejected rights language or the use of a legal strategy. The parallel could be within the author's research or could be drawn from previous work by others. Silbey and Sarat (1989), for example, in their study of the conflict over alternative dispute resolution, assess the relationship between "rights" in judicial disputes and "interests" in mediation. Similarly, Burke (2001), in his analysis of the "rights revolution," compares rights-based to interest-based politics. Maynard-Moody and Musheno (2004) consider the differing ways in which social workers, teachers, and cops conceptualize social problems. Scholars could, following their example, compare how legal and non-legal (or at least, "less legal") professionals construct social issues.

None of these recommendations are to suggest that researchers in this field should give up their preference for in-depth, highly contextualized studies of (particular) rights at work. Our recommendations instead go to how the research is framed and how it is positioned within a larger body of work. Academic research gives scholars working on a common set of problems a chance to communicate and so learn from one another. Anyone who reads Rosenberg, McCann, or Merry, or many of the other wonderful books on rights politics, will see perceptive and fascinating accounts of particular cases and, more generally, of the interaction of law and politics. What they will not see – in these three books, and, we believe in the sociolegal literature as a whole – is a conversation about rights in which scholars consistently build on each other's efforts. Thus, we are not sure there is yet an empirical literature on rights, but we remain hopeful that such a literature is possible.

NOTES

1. Ewick and Silbey (1998) use the term "legality" to refer to the ways in which people construct legal meaning, thus distinguishing "legality" from "law."
2. See, for example, Bumiller (1988), Melnick (1994), McCann (1994), Greenhouse, Yngvesson, and Engel (1994), Silverstein (1996, 2007), Epp (1998), Gilliom (2001), Reed (2001), Engel and Munger (2003), Albiston (2005), and two collections of articles: Nielsen (2007) and Fleury-Steiner and Nielsen (2006).
3. McCann, p. 298, quoting Minow, M. (1990). *Making all the difference: Inclusion, exclusion and American Law* (p. 297). Ithaca: Cornell University Press.
4. This is fascinating because it suggests that Merry, like McCann, also confronts a spectral "other," alternative conceptions of justice that might more effectively raise the status of women.
5. See, for example, Anna Kirkland's study of "fat rights" (Kirkland, 2008) and David Engel and Frank Munger's related study of disability antidiscrimination rights (Engel & Munger, 2003).

ACKNOWLEDGMENTS

Our thanks to Michael Musheno, Susan Silbey, Michael McCann, Sally Merry, Brendan Swedlow, and the anonymous reviewer for the journal for helpful comments on previous versions of this manuscript.

REFERENCES

Albiston, C. (2005). Bargaining in the shadow of social institutions: Competing discourses and social change in the workplace mobilization of civil rights. *Law and Society Review, 39,* 11.

Bumiller, K. (1988). *The civil rights society: The social construction of victims.* Baltimore: Johns Hopkins University Press.

Burke, T. F. (2001). The rights revolution continues: Why new rights are born (and old rights rarely die). *University of Connecticut Law Review, 33,* 1259–1274.

Engel, D. M., & Munger, F. W. (2003). *Rights of inclusion: Law and identity in the life stories of Americans with disabilities.* Chicago: University of Chicago Press.

Epp, C. R. (1998). *The rights revolution: Lawyers, activists and supreme courts in comparative perspective*. Chicago: University of Chicago Press.

Ewick, P., & Silbey, S. (1998). *The common place of law: Stories from everyday life*. Chicago: University of Chicago Press.

Fearon, J. D. (1991). Counterfactuals and hypothesis testing in political science. *World Politics*, *43*(2), 169–195.

Feeley, M. (1993). Hollow hopes, flypaper, and metaphors. *Law and Social Inquiry*, *17*(4), 745–760.

Fleury-Steiner, B., & Nielsen, L. B. (2006). *The new civil rights research: A constitutive approach*. Burlington, VT: Ashgate Publishing.

Gilliom, J. (2001). *Overseers of the poor: Surveillance, resistance and the limits of privacy*. Chicago: University of Chicago Press.

Greenhouse, C. J., Yngvesson, B., & Engel, D. M. (1994). *Law and community in three American towns*. Ithaca: Cornell University Press.

Hohlfeld, W. N. (1923). In: W. W. Cook (Ed.), *Fundamental legal conceptions as applied in judicial and reasoning and other legal essays*. New Haven: Yale University Press.

Kirkland, A. (2008). *Fat rights: Dilemmas of difference and personhood*. New York: New York University Press.

Maynard-Moody, S., & Musheno, M. (2004). *Cops, teachers, counselors: Stories from the frontlines of public service*. Ann Arbor: University of Michigan Press.

McCann, M. W. (1993). Reform litigation on trial. *Law and Social Inquiry*, *17*(4), 715–743.

McCann, M. W. (1994). *Rights at work: Pay equity reform and the politics of legal mobilization*. Chicago: University of Chicago Press.

McCann, M. W. (2006). Preface: On legal rights consciousness: A challenging analytical tradition. In: B. Fleury-Steiner & L. B. Nielsen (Eds), *The new civil rights research: A constitutive approach* (pp. xi–xxx). Burlington, VT: Ashgate Press.

McLuhan, M. (1962). *The Gutenberg galaxy: The making of typographic man*. Toronto: University of Toronto Press.

McLuhan, M. (2003). *Understanding media: The extensions of man*. San Francisco: Gingko Press.

Melnick, R. S. (1994). *Between the lines: Interpreting welfare rights*. Washington, DC: Brookings Institution.

Merry, S. E. (2006). *Human rights & gender violence*. Chicago: University of Chicago Press.

Nielsen, L. B. (2007). *Theoretical and empirical studies of rights*. Burlington, VT: Ashgate Press.

Reed, D. (2001). *On equal terms: The constitutional politics of educational opportunity*. Princeton, NJ: Princeton University Press.

Rosenberg, G. N. (1991). *The hollow hope: Can courts bring about social change?* Chicago: The University of Chicago Press.

Sarat, A. (1990). 'The law is all over': Power resistance that legal consciousness of the welfare poor. *Yale Journal of Law and the Humanities*, *2*, 343.

Scheingold, S. A. (2004). *The politics of rights: Lawyers, public policy, and political change*. Ann Arbor: University of Michigan Press.

Schuck, P. (1993). Public law litigation and social reform. *Yale Law Journal*, *102*(7), 1763–1786.

Schultz, D. A. (1998). *Leveraging the law: Using the courts to achieve social change*. New York: Peter Lang.

Silbey, S., & Sarat, A. (1989). Dispute processing in law and legal scholarship: From institutional subject to the reconstruction of the juridical subject. *Denver University Law Review, 66,* 437–492.

Silverstein, H. (1996). *Unleashing rights: Law, meaning and the animal rights movement.* Ann Arbor: University of Michigan Press.

Silverstein, H. (2007). *Girls on the stand: How courts fail pregnant minors.* New York: New York University Press.

RIGHTS AT RISK: WHY THE RIGHT NOT TO BE TORTURED IS IMPORTANT TO *YOU*

Lisa Hajjar

A volume on the subject of "revisiting rights" offers a welcomed opportunity to reflect on my own claims about rights, especially the unique importance of the right not to be tortured. This right has been the subject of constant debate since 9/11, and even more so since mid-2004 when it was revealed that the Bush administration had "legalized" and utilized tactics that constitute torture and ill-treatment in the interrogation of people taken into custody in the "war on terror." The global power of the United States makes American torture more deleterious than torture by less powerful regimes because of its capacity to influence international legal norms and standards for the rights of prisoners (Hajjar, 2006). Moreover, because of the reliance on the torturing services of other regimes (e.g., Egypt, Syria, Morocco) as a feature of the Central Intelligence Agency's (CIA's) "extraordinary rendition" program, the United States was invested in the perpetuation of worse forms of torture elsewhere (Mayer, 2005). There are, however, certain "benefits" – in the form of unintended consequences – that derive from the fact that the US government claimed for itself a right to torture, which I elaborate in the last section of this chapter.

   The right not to be tortured *equals* the prohibition of torture, which poses a clear limit to what state agents can do to people who are in custody – unfree to fight back or protect themselves and imperiled by that incapacitation – but

Revisiting Rights
Studies in Law, Politics, and Society, Volume 48, 93–120
Copyright © 2009 by Emerald Group Publishing Limited
All rights of reproduction in any form reserved
ISSN: 1059-4337/doi:10.1108/S1059-4337(2009)0000048007

have not been found guilty of a crime. Any serious challenge to the legal and normative basis of the right not to be tortured is a rejection of the principle that state behavior can be limited by law, and this puts the rule of law, and thus rights writ large at risk. In this chapter, I explain why the right not to be tortured remains so important and why its violation, especially by the world's lone superpower, is so dangerous.

TORQUEMADA'S GHOST

Torture has been practiced for millennia, albeit the means, rationales, and objectives have changed. (For an extended discussion of torture's past, see Hajjar, 2009.) Starting in the 12th century, the rediscovery of Roman law in western Europe revived torture as an aspect of criminal legal processes, both ecclesiastical and secular. According to Edward Peters (1996, p. 41), "the inquisitorial procedure displaced the older accusatorial procedure. Instead of the confirmed and verified freeman's oath, confession was elevated to the top of the hierarchy of proofs...[T]he place of confession in legal procedure... explains the reappearance of torture in medieval and early modern law."

In the late 18th century, European governments began reforming national laws to abolish judicial torture as a means of gathering evidence and eliciting confessions, due to a combination of factors including changes in criminal procedure (Langbein, 2006), and a growing skepticism that pain was a good way to produce truth (DuBois, 1991) or was effective in governing well (Foucault, 1977). This legal abolition occurred in conjunction with the disallowance of some of the crueler forms of sanguinary punishment (i.e., penal torture) that cause protracted suffering and bodily disfigurement. In US law, the idea of forbidding torture traces back to the founding of the republic and was enshrined in the Constitution through the 8th Amendment prohibiting "cruel and unusual punishment." Along with habeas corpus and the separation of powers, the ban on unconstitutional cruel treatment served as a foundation of the modern rule of law because it was understood as essential for conditions of human dignity, liberty, limited government, and due process to thrive.

But in the 20th century, torture achieved a second revival. Militaries, security services and police forces instrumentalized torture to gather information and defeat "enemies" of one kind or another who were presumed to menace the security and power of the state. As Peters (1996, pp. 6–7) explains:

> Much of modern political history consists of extraordinary situations that twentieth-century governments have imagined themselves to face and the extraordinary measures

they have taken to protect themselves. Paradoxically, in an age of vast state strength, ability to mobilize resources, and possession of virtually infinite means of coercion, much of state policy has been based upon the concept of extreme state vulnerability to enemies, external or internal....It is in this sense that torture may be considered to have a history, and its history is part of...governmental exercises of power, whether officially or unofficially.

These "vulnerabilities" were used to justify the torture of rebellious colonized populations, militarily conquered (foreign) or ideologically suspect (domestic) enemies, or "racial inferiors" who were deemed to have no right not to be tortured. The *raisons d'etat* for modern torture include the elicitation of confessions to facilitate conviction and imprisonment (Hajjar, 2005a) or for the state-legitimating purpose of show trials (Abrahamian, 1999), for intelligence or military advantage (Feldman, 1991), or to terrorize populations into submission (Chandler, 2000; Klein, 2007; Weschler, 1998).

The rampancy of 20th century torture precipitated a new wave of legal prohibitions. In the decades after World War II, the passage of international and domestic laws prohibiting the practice expanded and reinforced its illegality. By the last decades of the 20th century, the right not to be tortured had clearly "ripened" into a universal norm (*jus cogens*) of customary international law. But this was also the period when odious innovations were devised to break the mind while leaving the body unscathed, including protracted sleep deprivation and isolation; sensory deprivation or overload; stress position abuses; temperature and light manipulation; degradation and humiliation (McCoy, 2006; Rejali, 2007). Although deniability was not the motivation that drove the CIA and other intelligence agencies to utilize tactics that attack the psyche and leave no long-lasting physical marks, so-called psychological, no touch, or stealthy torture had the added benefit of being easier to deny. After all, who but a prisoner and his interrogators and jailors could know "for sure" what had transpired in the clandestine cells of interrogation centers if there were no scars to confirm the former's allegations? The practice of "disappearing" prisoners had similar rationales.

By the end of the 20th century, the paradox of torture was that its illegality was universalized while it continued to be practiced by more states than those that did not (Forrest, 1996). The stealth tactics honed in the 1950s and 1960s were at least as harmful as beatings and burnings, but they had a certain aura of being more "humane," indisputably more easy to deny, and more resistant to the label of "torture" (Rejali, 2004, 2007; Wolfendale, 2009). By the 1970s and 1980s, the growing capacity of human rights organizations to investigate and publicize violations substantiated in abundant detail the amount and nature of torture around the world.

Every torturing regime, when allegations surfaced, denied that *it* engaged in the "dark arts" because torture was so categorically and universally illegitimate (Cohen, 2001; Hajjar, 2000).

For the United States, the prohibition of torture at home (Skolnick, 2004) and abroad was black letter law at the end of the 20th century. The 1949 Geneva Conventions, which prohibit torture and cruel, inhuman and degrading treatment of prisoners captured in war or abuse of civilians in occupied territories, were incorporated into the US Uniform Code of Military Justice. Federal anti-torture and war crimes statutes passed in the 1990s established criminal liability for violations in times of war or peace. Congress acknowledged the customary international law status of the prohibition by passing the Torture Victims Protection Act (TVPA) in 1992. Since 1983, US courts have acknowledged the universal prohibition, as evident in cases in which foreign plaintiffs successfully sued foreign torturers using the centuries-old Alien Torts Claim Act and the TVPA.

THE "NEW PARADIGM"

On September 11, 2001, millions of people around the world watched televised images of the World Trade Center towers collapsing from the impact of two hijacked commercial planes. Meanwhile another crashed into the Pentagon and a fourth was diverted from its course by passengers to crash in western Pennsylvania. These were the most devastating terrorist attacks perpetrated by a non-state group in history. That al-Qaeda successfully targeted the economic and military bastions of the most powerful nation on earth and killed thousands, and that President George W. Bush retaliated by launching a "global war on terror" intensified the sense that the world had entered a new phase of unprecedented danger and violence.

As is common in asymmetrical wars (i.e., wars between states and non-state groups), the lack of intelligence about al-Qaeda, and their unconventional tactics (e.g., targeting of civilians and civilian infrastructures) elevated the importance of intelligence gathering through interrogation. However, the authorization and use of unlawful methods was a choice, not a necessity. The oft-quoted phrase of Cofer Black, a US counter-terrorism expert, in testimony before Congress on September 26, 2001, that there "was a before 9/11 and an after 9/11, and after 9/11 the gloves came off," signaled rather succinctly (if crudely) that the Bush administration regarded respect for legal restrictions on violent interrogations unsuitable to the security imperatives of the new age.

In the months and years following 9/11, many rights – to privacy, association, due process – were eroded by new government policies (Cole & Lobel, 2007; Savage, 2007). The value of rights was thrown into sharp relief and subject to trenchant debates about how they should be protected or balanced against national security. To summarize, with the benefit of hindsight, what transpired was the development of a so-called new paradigm, shaped principally by Vice President Dick Cheney and his shadowy counsel David Addington (Mayer, 2006a), and varnished with legal opinions from the Justice Department's Office of Legal Counsel (OLC), most prominently by Berkeley law professor John Yoo, who served as deputy assistant attorney general from 2001 to 2003, and the Pentagon's General Counsel William J. Haynes (Benjamin, 2008; Mayerfeld, 2007; Streichler, 2008). The new paradigm expanded executive power at the expense of the courts and Congress, a direct assault on the separation of powers and official accountability. Yoo and his OLC colleagues produced memos opining that the president, as commander-in-chief, should have unfettered powers to wage war; that any efforts to constrain executive discretion in accordance with federal, military or treaty laws would be unconstitutional; that the laws restricting cruel, inhuman, and degrading treatment are unenforceable outside the United States; and that prisoners designated as terrorists by presidential fiat (rather than status review by a tribunal) could be denied the right of habeas corpus to contest their detention and any right not to be maltreated. These OLC opinions, by virtue of their institutional source within the government, were treated as "controlling legal authority" and were used to "legalize" the authorization of wiretapping without court orders, incommunicado and indefinite detention, brutal forms of interroga-tion, kidnapping and disappearance of persons suspected of being security threats or presumed to have valuable intelligence, and pre-emptive war (Danner, 2004; Danner & Rich, 2006; Grey, 2007; Greenberg & Dratel, 2005; Mayer, 2007; Risen, 2006; Sands, 2005, 2008; Yoo, 2006).

On February 7, 2002, the president secretly endorsed the new paradigm (over State Department dissent) that he had a constitutional right, as commander-in-chief, to disregard federal and treaty laws (including the Geneva Conventions) that might curb operational flexibility or infringe on executive discretion. The president asserted his right to regard anyone (including US citizens and legal residents) as "unlawful enemy combatants" with no rights to have their status reviewed by a tribunal. Without such a review, the mere fact of being in custody was equated with guilt. The assertion of a presidential "right" to capture people anywhere in the world, to classify them as "unlawful combatants," and to deprive them of the right

to habeas corpus along with the right not to be tortured were cornerstones
of the new paradigm (Hajjar, 2005b, 2006; Margulies, 2006). These prisoners
were characterized as the quintessential "outlaws" by virtue of assertions
that no laws applied to them, and thus, they had no legal rights in the official
view of the custodial state. Neither the policies nor the legal rationales
behind them were made public at the time.

LIGHTING UP THE DARK SIDE

The first significant illumination of the gap between the secretly "done" and
the publicly "known" was the publication of an article on December 26,
2002, in the *Washington Post* (Priest & Gellman, 2002) that quoted a
number of unnamed security officials who described how prisoners in
Afghanistan were subjected to "stress and duress" or mind-altering drugs
and that those who could not be broken by such means were shipped off for
interrogation to countries with well-established records of torture. That
article confirmed the fears and strengthened the resolve of anti-torture
activists, but its effect on broadening public opposition to the use of torture
in the "war on terror" was negligible.

In mid-2004, three watershed events did affect public perceptions about
interrogation and detention. The first and second were the publication of
photos from the Abu Ghraib prison in April 2004 (Hersch, 2004a, 2004b;
Salon.com, ND), and the declassification and leaking of "torture memos"
starting in June (ACLU, ND; Greenberg & Dratel, 2005; Danner, 2004).
The third was the June 2004 Supreme Court decision in *Rasul v. Bush*, which
opened the door for lawyers to access Guantánamo (GITMO) prisoners
who had been held incommunicado since 2002 (Ahmad, 2008; Ratner &
Ray, 2004; Stafford Smith, 2007; Wax, 2008). Hundreds of lawyers signed
on to represent detainees as habeas counsels, and the first-hand information
that they gleaned when they visited GITMO clients served to further expand
the anti-torture campaign within the legal community.

Following these public revelations and in response to the criticism they
evoked, Bush administration officials did what every torturing regime does:
First, deny allegations and condemn those making the allegations as
enemies of the state or, in the current context, "terrorist sympathizers."
Second, deny official responsibility by claiming that those engaging in
the torture and abuse of prisoners were violating, not following policy
(the "bad apple" argument). Third, engage in denial-through-euphemism
and redefinition – that is, branding torture "enhanced interrogation" and

claiming that "we don't torture" so therefore what we do cannot *be* "torture." Such doing-and-denying is an affront to the illegitimacy of torture and a flagrant disregard for the law (Human Rights Watch, 2006a; Lederman, 2005a).

By 2005, the ranks of torture policy critics included three powerful Republican "dissenters" in the Senate: John McCain, a torture survivor from the Vietnam war; Lindsay Graham, a Marine reservist in the Judge Advocate General (JAG) corps; and John Warner, a World War II veteran and chair of the Armed Services Committee. Their primary concern was the damage that torture was doing to the military and the risks it posed to people in uniform who might be liable to court martial (Human Rights Watch, 2006b; Lederman, 2005b). In a protracted tussle with Cheney (which earned him the nickname "vice president for torture"), the dissenters won the first round through the passage in October 2005 of the McCain Amendment to the 2006 Defense Authorization Act reasserting the applicability of federal and international laws. Its impact, however, was mitigated by the Detainee Treatment Act passed at the same time barring GITMO detainees from actually asserting their habeas rights in federal courts.

There was a brief moment of unbridled exhilaration among anti-torture lawyers and activists in June 2006, when the US Supreme Court in *Hamdan v. Bush* ruled that prisoners captured in the "war on terror" have rights under the Geneva Conventions (at minimum those designated in Common Article 3 that unequivocally prohibits torture and degradation), thus rebuking the administration's claim that they are rightless. The *Hamdan* ruling also declared the statute for the military commissions unconstitutional. Finally, the ruling raised the specter that those who had violated – or ordered the violation of – the Geneva Conventions could be prosecuted under the federal War Crimes Act (1996).

In response to *Hamdan*, President Bush criticized the Supreme Court and pushed Congress to pass new legislation for military commissions that would permit the use of evidence and confessions extracted through "enhanced interrogations." This legislative campaign was pursued using strong partisan pressure (easily heightened by the fact that 2006 was an election year) to rally Republican legislators who composed a majority in both houses, and a media campaign casting opponents of proposed legislation as "soft on terror." In October 2006, Congress passed the Military Commissions Act (MCA), which essentially gave back to the Bush administration everything prohibited by the *Hamdan* ruling, including a "CIA exception" for torture (Human Rights Watch, 2006C), and amended the War Crimes Act to provide retroactive immunity (i.e., impunity) for violations of Common Article 3. However, the legal fight continued, and in June 2008, the Supreme Court decision in *Boumediene v. Bush* ruled that the MCA unconstitutionally suspended prisoners' rights to habeas corpus and (re)granted GITMO prisoners access to federal courts.

THE ENDURING TORTURE SCANDAL

The illegitimacy of torture has proven quite resilient. The Bush administration had to contend with a gnarly mess of its own making, having authorized and utilized practices in secret that were difficult and contentious to defend when they became public. One vivid example was the predicament that Michael Mukasey faced during his October 2007 Senate Judiciary Committee confirmation hearing to become attorney general. He was asked repeatedly whether "waterboarding," a tactic used by the CIA on so-called high value targets, constitutes torture and thus is a criminal and prohibited practice. The rational and correct answer would have been, "Of course." But to say so would have put Mukasey at odds with the administration that nominated him and would potentially put in legal jeopardy those who had authorized and utilized waterboarding. It also would have impelled him to condemn a practice that Bush, Cheney, and others insisted produced "good information" and is "not torture" (Physicians for Human Rights and Human Rights First, 2007, pp. 17–19; Lederman, 2007). Mukasey resolved his own predicament by feigning ignorance about the practice and stating blandly that he would enforce the law (Blumenthal, 2007). A contrasting example was the experience of Acting Assistant Attorney General Daniel Levin who, when asked to write a legal opinion endorsing waterboarding, had himself waterboarded to understand first-hand what it involved, decided that it constituted torture, and was subsequently fired (Greenberg & de Vogue, 2007, 2008).

The Bush administration stubbornly refused to repudiate torture and fired or drove away military and civilian officials who were unwilling to go along with "the program" (Goldsmith, 2007). The logic of this refusal is the ill-founded perception that torture "works" and the corollary that some people are so exceptionally dangerous that they "need" to be tortured or have no right not to be. Torture, as a matter of fact, does not work if the work it is expected to do is produce truth. The life-saving truth of the "ticking bomb hypothetical," which undergirds torture-can-save-us rationales so popular among apologists for "enhanced interrogation," relies on dubious presumptions about security risks and effective recourse (Scheppele, 2005; Ginbar, 2008).

Darius Rejali's magnum opus, *Torture and Democracy* (2007), is the most detailed and comprehensive study to date on modern torture tactics. On the question of whether torture *ever* works to produce reliable information, his answer is complex but, given the scope and quality of his research, authoritative.

> [O]rganized torture yields poor information, sweeps up many innocents, degrades organizational capabilities, and destroys interrogators. Limited time during battle or emergency intensifies all these problems...Torture would work well when organizations remain coherent and well integrated, have highly professional interrogators available, receive strong public cooperation and intelligence from multiple independent sources, have no time pressures for information, possess enough resources to verify coerced information, and release innocents before they are tortured. In short, torture for information works best when one would need it least, peacetime, nonemergency conditions. (p. 478)

Rejali's conclusion, based on a global and comparative study, is an apt assessment of the US experience. There is now abundant evidence that torture has been ineffective in producing actionable intelligence, and its counter-productivity is the dominant view among experienced interrogators (Alexander & Bruning, 2008; Danner, 2009a, 2009b; Rose, 2008; Soufan 2009). Moreover, the absurdity of the ticking bomb scenario is demonstrated by the fact that there is not a single known incident of an *imminent* threat of an actual ticking bomb-sort in the world that was ever defused by torturing a person suspected of having information, the popular television series *24* notwithstanding. The CIA has not claimed to have defused any ticking bombs (i.e., disrupted imminent attacks) as a result of torture. The intelligence elicited through torture pertains, at best, to the structure of al-Qaeda, and there is no reason to presume that such information could not have been acquired by non-torturing means. (For a debunking of claims of actionable intelligence ostensibly elicited through torture that had direct disaster-averting effects, see Horton, 2009; Luban, 2008; Rose, 2008; Soufan, 2009; Suskind, 2006; see also Bell, 2008; Bufacchi & Arrigo, 2006; Danner, 2009a, 2009b; Mayerfeld, 2008.) "Apologists often assume that torture works, and all that is left is the moral justification. If torture does not work, then their apology is irrelevant" (Rejali, 2007, p. 447). But the importance of the right not to be tortured goes far beyond absurdist hypotheticals and false claims about efficacy.

DEFINING RIGHTS

The importance of the right not to be tortured must be assessed through a consideration of the work that rights do and, by extension, the work that law does. This explanation requires a very clear definition of rights – what rights *are* – for which I offer the following: *Rights are practices that are required, prohibited or otherwise regulated within the context of relationships governed by law.* I am, in this regard, a legal positivist because I endorse the view that rights only "exist" if they are enshrined in law. Thus, I would argue that, outside of coffee shops, philosophy classes or bible/qur'an/torah school, natural or divine rights are alchemical unless they have been enshrined in laws *made, interpreted and used by people.* On this basis, I am of the opinion that "human rights" as such did not exist prior to 1948 with the passage of the Universal Declaration of Human Rights (UDHR), and even a declaration is not, technically speaking, a law, albeit the UDHR was the starting point for a host of conventions (i.e., real laws), including the Convention on Civil and Political Rights (ICCPR), the Convention on Economic, Social and Cultural Rights (ICESCR), and the Convention Against Torture, and Cruel, Inhuman and Degrading Treatment or Punishment (CAT).

To be sure, human rights have a long pre-history (Hunt, 2007; Lauren, 1998), including 18th-century declarations such as the French Rights of Man and the Citizen, and the America Declaration of Independence stating that "all men" have certain "inalienable rights." But these historic legacies were neither global nor universal in their reach; their exclusion of the vast majority of humans even within their own jurisdictions negates any claim that they articulated human rights per se.

To unpack this definition of rights, we begin with the point that *rights are practices.* With a nod to Michel Foucault (1990, p. 94), rights, like "power," are *not things* "that one holds onto or allows to slip away," not "owned" but exercised through relations. As *practices*, rights work through the activities and relations among people and institutions. The right to vote, for example, is not the practice of voting. Rather, it is the practices that are required or prohibited of states to enable people to vote, including registering voters, creating polling places and preventing obstruction of voters' abilities to access those places on voting day, establishing impartial means for the counting of ballots, and so on.

What distinguishes rights from other types of practices is that they *are required, prohibited or otherwise regulated…by law.* Rights are created when there is a perceived need *and* conditions exist to pass laws to regulate practices in new ways or to extend rights to new subjects. For example, breathing is a practice but not a right. In circumstances when a person's ability to breathe may be purposefully thwarted – or example suffocation during interrogation – then the right to breathe is constituted through the laws regulating what practices are permissible and prohibited in interrogation. At present, there is no perceived need to pass laws providing a right to breathe because breathing as a routine human function is not at risk, albeit there are various laws prohibiting purposefully thwarting breathing (including laws against murder and attempted murder through suffocation or drowning, asphyxiating weapons, and so on).

Finally, rights are practices that are required, prohibited or otherwise regulated *in the context of relations governed by law*. This speaks to the scope of a law's jurisdiction, whether local, national, or international. Relations that are not regulated by law are not the subject of rights. History is full of examples of formerly unregulated relations being brought into the jurisdiction of laws to establish rights by regulating what practices are permissible or forbidden. For example, in the United States and elsewhere, it was not so long ago when the beating of a family member was legally unregulated, and thus, there was no "right" not to be beaten or abused by a spouse, parent, or sibling in the home. It was not that the law had nothing to say about such violence; rather, what it said was that it would not enter the house to intervene. The perceived need for new and different laws, championed by feminists and anti-violence activists, created pressure to that led to the criminalization of domestic violence. Such laws created rights for people to be safe from violence in domestic settings and provided rights to seek the aid of law if they are beaten or abused. The right not to be domestically abused obligates the state to engage in practices necessary to prevent such harms, to protect victims, and to punish perpetrators.

One of the common misperceptions is that if the laws are ignored, violated, or unenforced, then people do not "have" rights. We need to distinguish among "getting" rights (i.e., demands and mobilizations for new rights laws), "enjoying" rights (enjoying the protections, freedoms, and liberties that rights laws promise), and "having" rights (having a legal right to rights whether or not the laws are effectively or adequately enforced). To say that people only have the rights that they can enjoy is to presume that the law does not exist or serves no purpose if it is not respected and enforced. But this would be analogous to saying that criminal law does not exist or serve a purpose if crimes are committed and some go unpunished, an obvious absurdity. The same holds true for rights laws.

WHAT GOOD ARE RIGHTS?

The importance of *having* rights has been the subject of fascinating and wide ranging intellectual debates. Within the socio-legal literature, Scheingold's

(1974) work on the "myth of rights" and the dangerous "lure of litigation," and Bumiller's (1988) critique of the "civil rights society" for requiring people who have suffered discrimination to comport themselves as "victims" are compelling skeptical accounts of rights. The evolving critique of rights from the school of Critical Legal Studies and others (Gabel, 1981; Galanter, 1974; Glendon, 1991; Rosenberg, 1991) gave rise to the critique of the critique of rights by Critical Race Theorists (Williams, 1991; Crenshaw, 1995). Despite significant differences of opinion among socio-legal scholars (Nielsen, 2004), two common themes are the utility – or limits – of law for producing social change, justice, equality, protection from harms, and the effects of rights laws on society, especially on more marginalized and disadvantaged individuals and groups.

I would argue that having rights is important for at least three reasons, two of which are quite well developed in the literature: First, aspirations and demands for rights galvanize political mobilizations, whether the goal is new rights or respect for existing rights through the enforcement of law (McCann, 1994). The value of rights, as Kimberle Crenshaw (1995, p. 111) has aptly observed, "is precisely this legitimating function that has made law receptive to certain demands in this area." Second, laws that establish and define rights constitute standards against which actual conditions and relations can be measured. Hence, what was previously "bad" or "harmful" becomes either unlawful or obligatory (depending on the nature of the right) with the passage or reinterpretation of rights laws.

The third reason I would offer is more idiosyncratic in the sense that it is not well developed in the socio-legal literature. Rights are valuable not just because they have the capacity or promise to make the world a better place and help people, but because they have the capacity to hurt people, that is, to hurt people who hurt people (Dorfman, 2002). In regard to rights generally, and human rights especially, the violence of law is a *good* that is underappreciated and undertheorized by progressive scholars, although it commands serious attention among right-wing scholars and pundits who are exorcised about "lawfare" – the use of courts and legal processes to punish or restrain state agents and other powerful actors who engage in rights violations (Carter, 2005; Dunlap, 2007; Horton 2007b; Pearlstein, 2007). As I have argued in the pages of this journal (Hajjar, 2004), penalizing, punishing, disempowering, and delegitimizing rights violators; transforming the conditions in which impunity thrives; harvesting vengeful "law and order" sentiments to expose and oppose – and hurt – law violators should be centerpieces of rights scholarship and politics. One "revisiting rights" suggestion I propose, therefore, is to cultivate a perpetrator-centered legal violence-is-good approach to rights. Although I would not subscribe to the utopian notion that law is a panacea, I do believe that the law can do some very good harm. I also believe that in this era when hard fought and long-cherished rights are at risk, the standards of law provide public measures to assess the "real" against the "ideal" and to inspire political action to enforce legal standards.

FIRSTS AMONG EQUALS

The right not to be tortured, along with the right not to be enslaved and the right to self-determination constitute a troika of firsts-among-equals as the most important rights. The right not to be enslaved equals the prohibition of slavery. This means that no social, economic, or political system – whether public or private – can be legitimate and lawful if some people are deprived of the most fundamental liberty – freedom over one's "self." This right, like the right not to be tortured, is absolutely non-derogable: there are no legal exceptions. Thus, no one anywhere can lawfully demand of another – or submit to such demands – to be or become a slave, and there are no circumstances under which slavery can be lawful unless the laws (international and domestic) prohibiting slavery are overturned.

But anyone familiar with the history of plantation slavery and abolitionism, or contemporary bonded labor, human trafficking and capitalist sweatshops will know the challenges of articulating a universal baseline of human freedom and the raging contests over minimum conditions under which it can be said to exist. These challenges and contests are not marks against the right not to be enslaved. Rather, they enrich the importance of this right by fueling contemporary efforts to resist and combat certain conditions of "unfreedom" as paramount to slavery, and thus illegitimate and unlawful (Bales, 1999; Dayan, 2007; Patterson, 1982). To take one contemporary example, Article 3(a) of the Protocol to Prevent, Suppress, and Punish Trafficking in Persons, Especially Women and Children, which entered into force in December 2003, draws a connection between trafficking in persons and slavery:

> The recruitment, transportation, transfer, harboring or receipt of persons, by means of threat or use of force or other forms of coercion, of abduction, of fraud, of deception, of abuse of power or of position of vulnerability or of the giving or receiving of payments or benefits to achieve the consent of a person having control over another person, for the purpose of exploitation. Exploitation shall include, at a minimum, the exploitation of the prostitution of others or other forms of sexual exploitation, forced labor or services, slavery or practices similar to slavery, servitude or the removal of organs.

If slavery truly were a thing of the past, the right would have little relevance or resonance, and it certainly would not be the subject of a recently minted Protocol. The right not to be enslaved animates ongoing efforts to articulate that right in law, to enforce existing laws (i.e., to close the "gap" between laws in the books and laws in action), to frame assessments of deplorable conditions against legal standards of freedom, and to galvanize movements and actors with liberatory political and legal agendas.

Slavery, or rather anti-slavery holds pride of place in the development of a "universal" conception of people as humans. The 19th century transatlantic anti-slavery movement, along with transnational movements opposing the forms of enslavement in King Leopold's Belgian Congo birthed what has evolved into international humanitarianism – caring about "strangers" because of a sense of shared humanity and acting politically and purposefully to alter conditions that cause unacceptable human suffering, exploitation and repression. These movements, as Keck and Sikkink (1998) and Hochschild (1999) among others have persuasively demonstrated, were early and exemplary instances of transnational advocacy, precursors to the contemporary human rights movement that operates on a global scale.

The right to self-determination, though quite different, is equally important because it is integrally related state sovereignty which, for better or worse, is the one true universal (Pollis, 1996). Although many things escape, elude, or transcend the sovereign power of states, people are not among them. Whether a person's relation to the state that rules him/her is one of citizen, refugee, undocumented alien, militarily occupied civilian or whatever, the key issue is that states rule people. Hence, the right to self-determination provides a critical measure for *how* states rule people. Self-determination is available, in principle, to all people, as individuals and as members of groups (usually but not necessarily exclusively constituted as nations). I define self-determination as a right to see one's "self" (i.e., one's rights and interests) reflected in the policies and practices of the ruling state and to have some available means to determine the nature and goals of the state. The standard is not universal equality in *outcomes* (although that may be an ideal) but rather in *processes* of state rule that validate and enable *representative power*. Thus, the right of self-determination justifies resistance and refusal to tolerate colonial rule, political dictatorship, racist regimes, and foreign occupations, although there are legal limits to the methods that can be deployed to challenge and change a government.

State–society relations in the modern world take many forms (e.g., pluralist democracy, theocracy, ethnocracy, confessional balance, one-party rule), and the political contents and demographic parameters of a "people" deserving of and demanding the right of self-determination vary dramatically across time and place. But the "inalienable" right of self-determination establishes legal standards against which actual state–society relations can be evaluated. Even non-*national* rights claims – including women's rights, gay rights, dalit rights, immigrants' rights – can be construed as demands for the right of self-determination in contexts where states discriminate against and/or provide impunity for non-state actors who discriminate against classes of people on the basis of collective forms of identity (Coutin, 2007; Fiss, 1998). Because everyone is ruled by a state – the modern universal – the right to self-determination is important as a fluid, vibrant, and aspirational standard of representative rule.

Self-determination holds one additional importance in the larger scheme of rights: Not only are states obligated to represent the rights and interests of people that they rule, but people have an obligation to ensure that states rule "right." This is not limited to struggles of collective self-interest for a state to represent *them*, but extends responsibility when states violate the rights of "others" to the constituencies who regard the state as "theirs." Passivity, apathy, or ignorance about the rights-violating practices of a state are common in many societies and have many causes, some unavoidable (state secrecy being a prime example), but indifference is not normatively acceptable as long as the right of self-determination invests people with a right and a responsibility to determine how states rule. The more representative a state *claims* to be, and the more people believe themselves to be represented by the state that rules them, the greater their responsibility for the state's rights-violating practices. Torture by a military regime is deplorable, but torture by a democracy is inexcusable.

THE RIGHT NOT TO BE TORTURED

The right not to be tortured is the most important right of all because of the ways it speaks directly to the powers and limits of the modern state in its treatment of human beings. This is one of the classically negative rights: people *have* the right not to be tortured because there is *no right* to torture. This right prohibits state agents and anyone acting "under the color of law" (e.g., government-hired private contractors) to authorize or engage in practices to purposefully harm someone who is in custody, when the capacity to do harm is so available and tempting. An "authority" obviously includes states and their agents, but it does not exclude non-state groups. The prohibition of torture is not contingent on legitimacy, jurisdiction, or international recognition. Rather, it is contingent on an organized rather than individualized capacity to take people into custody and then harm them for a purpose that is public rather than personal.

Three factors make the right not to be tortured unique – and uniquely important. First, the prohibition of torture is absolutely non-derogable because the law recognizes no exceptions, including in times of war or national emergency. In the words of the UN Convention against Torture and Other Cruel, Inhuman or Degrading Treatment or Punishment (1984), "No exceptional circumstances whatsoever, whether a state of war or a threat of war, internal political instability or any other public emergency, may be invoked as a justification for torture." (The US Congress ratified CAT in 1994, but inserted reservations concerning the interpretation of cruel, inhuman, and degrading treatment or punishment that would inoculate the death penalty and other domestic penal practices such as protracted isolation.) In contrast, all other political and civil rights, under certain circumstances, can be suspended or abridged temporarily, and social, cultural, and economic rights are not legally enforceable in comparable ways. Indeed, many rights laws have abridgements and suspensions built into their language to anticipate emergencies or other temporary contingencies.

Second, the prohibition of torture is a *jus cogens* norm under customary international law, and its violation is a crime that attaches universal jurisdiction. The doctrine of universal jurisdiction was developed in the 18th century to combat and deter piracy and the slave trade. To compensate for the limitations of territorial and personal jurisdiction, under universal jurisdiction perpetrators were classified as "enemies of all mankind" (*hostis humani generis*) and were held to be prosecutable in any competent legal system anywhere in the world. The purpose was to deny sanctuary to perpetrators of gross crimes. Today, the crimes that attach universal jurisdiction have expanded to include torture, as well as war crimes and crimes against humanity (Macedo, 2003). The "Pinochet precedent" of 1999 was a universal jurisdiction watershed: A British court, acting on an indictment from Spain, held that a former head of state (i.e., Chilean dictator Augusto Pinochet) was prosecutable for the crime of torture, albeit, he avoided prosecution abroad when a doctor judged him to be demented, and the British government allowed him to return home. The promise of universal jurisdiction remains a work-in-progress (Feitlowitz, 2000; FIDH, ND; Ratner, 2008), but its ongoing development exemplifies the perpetrator-centered legal violence-is-good principle.

Third, the right not to be tortured extends to all people everywhere, making it an "ideal" right common to all human beings, regardless of their social status, political identity, or affiliations. In contrast, the right to life is highly circumscribed; there are many ways that people lawfully can be killed. For example, the right not to be deliberately killed in war hinges not on one's humanity but rather on one's status as a civilian or non-combatant, or a surrendered or captured soldier, and the non-deliberate killing of civilians (i.e., "collateral damage") is a legal contingency explicitly anticipated by the laws of war. The right of persons not to be exterminated through genocide hinges on a clear motivation by perpetrators to kill people because of a collective identity as members of a national, religious, or ethnic group; purposefully killing people because of their political identity or for other political reasons was excluded from the text of the Genocide Convention. Many criminal justice systems incorporate legal exceptions to the prohibition of killing through death penalty laws, necessity defense laws, so-called honor crimes laws, and so on.

There is no bright line empirically distinguishing torture from other forms of pain and suffering caused by state agents or people exercising some form of public authority. For example, being beaten while being arrested changes from "cruel treatment" or "excessive use of force" to torture only when custody has been achieved, obviously a blurry and contestable line (Parry, 2005). The combination of "torture" and "cruel, inhuman and degrading treatment" (CID), as well as physical and psychological pain and suffering in the same international laws contributes to this confusion, which is further compounded by the exclusion of painful – but lawful – punishments such as floggings, amputations, or the death penalty.

OFFICIAL TORTURE AND CRUELTY

The Bush administration based its torture policy on a narrowed definition of "torture" that would exclude any practices that cause pain less than that associated with "organ failure, impairment of bodily function, or even death." Any treatment that did not rise to this narrowly defined torture was deemed to be "not torture." These (ostensibly) lesser harms were deemed permissible for use on "unlawful combatants" on the grounds that, unlike torture, CID is not a criminal offense in US anti-torture laws and, moreover, that US laws do not apply to off-shore detention facilities.

The universally recognized baseline standard for "humane treatment" of prisoners in wartime is Geneva Convention Common Article 3, a *jus cogens* norm that extends to all detained persons regardless of their status, the violation of which is a grave breach punishable as a war crime. It states that prisoners "shall in all circumstances be treated humanely" and that "[t]o this end," certain specified acts "are and shall remain prohibited at any time and in any place whatsoever" including "cruel treatment and torture," and "outrages upon personal dignity, in particular humiliating and degrading treatment." To go below the baseline, as the Bush administration did – and justified doing – literally undermines the very concept of "humanity." If some people cannot claim any legal right to the minimum standards of treatment in Common Article 3, then they are, by extension, no longer legally recognized as "human." The 9/11 Commission, dissident military lawyers (Mayer, 2006b), and numerous others have declared that, even where Common Article 3 might not apply as a matter of treaty obligation, the standards must constitute the lawful treatment of prisoners.

The Bush administration's only concession on this matter was to state that prisoners would be treated humanely as a matter of policy, implying that some people had no legal right to their humanity. What this meant, in practice, can be deduced from the July 2005 report by Lt. Gen. Mark Schmidt who headed an investigation into FBI allegations of detainee abuse at Guantánamo. The report certified that some detainees were subjected to tactics that were clearly "abusive" (20-hour interrogations for 48 days in a row, short-shackling to the floor for extended periods) and "degrading" (being smeared with fake menstrual blood, being forced to bark like a dog and perform dog tricks). However, the report, hewing to the Bush administration's legal conjectures, concluded that these tactics were not "unlawful" because "abusive" tactics were not "inhumane," and nothing in US law prohibited degrading and humiliating treatment of "unlawful combatants."

On June 17, 2008, in testimony for the Senate Armed Services Committee on the roots and consequences of American torture during the "war on terror," former Navy general counsel Alberto Mora provided a devastating assessment (quoted from Democracy Now, 2008):

> To use so-called "harsh" interrogation techniques during the war on terror was a mistake of massive proportions. It damaged and continues to damage our nation. This policy, which may be aptly called a "policy of cruelty," violated our founding values, our constitutional system and the fabric of our laws, our overarching foreign policy interests and our national security. The net effect of this policy of cruelty has been to weaken our defenses, not to strengthen them…The choice of the adjectives "harsh" or "enhanced" to describe these interrogation techniques is euphemistic and misleading. The legally correct adjective is "cruel,"… and could, depending on their application, easily rise to the level of torture…. Our efforts should be focused not merely on banning torture, but on banning cruelty.

WHAT IS WRONG WITH TORTURE?

Let us begin with a consideration of what torture does "well": If the legitimacy of a legal system or a detention system depends on persuading domestic constituencies that the people in custody deserve to be there, then even flagrant lies elicited through torture in the form of confessions can have a validating effect. Israel, in its occupation of the West Bank and Gaza, has depended for decades on tortured confessions to legitimize both the military court system used to prosecute Palestinians and the imprisonment of hundreds of thousands of Palestinians as strategic measures to control and punish resistance to the occupation and nationalist aspirations and mobilizations for the right of self-determination (Hajjar, 2005a). Likewise, the Bush administration advanced the flagrantly false claim that people detained in GITMO were "the worst of the worst" and justified their continued detention on the basis of information and confessions elicited through torture (Lasseter, 2008; UN Commission on Human Rights, 2006; Worthington, 2007).

If accurate intelligence is the goal and torture is the means, the record is not just abysmal but catastrophic. The Bush administration persuaded the US public of the legitimacy of attacking Iraq in part because of a purported connection between Saddam Hussein's regime and al-Qaeda. This "information" was extracted by torture from a Libyan prisoner, Ibn al-Shaykh al-Libi, who subsequently recanted the lies he had told interrogators about such a connection (Priest, 2004). The Abu Ghraib debacle emanated from the desperate resort to torture for intelligence about the anti-American insurgency because the administration was suffering politically at home for the rising American death toll in Iraq. According to Matthew Alexander (pseudonym), a retired Air Force major who has extensive interrogation experience in Iraq, the number one reason foreign fighters gave for coming to Iraq was the torture and abuse at Abu Ghraib and Guantánamo. In light of this fact, Alexander offers a damning indictment: Because the majority of US casualties and injuries are the result of suicide bombings, the majority of which are carried out by foreign fighters, "at least hundreds but more likely thousands of American lives (not to count Iraqi civilian deaths) are linked directly to the policy decision to introduce the torture and abuse of prisoners as accepted tactics" (Horton, 2008a).

If legal justice is the goal, torture fouls the process and makes it difficult or even impossible to prosecute suspects. The Bush administration sought to skirt this problem by creating military commissions that would admit tortured evidence. As David Cole (2005) noted, "One probable reason for the military's reluctance [to charge and prosecute most detainees in US custody] is the real risk that any trial will turn into a trial of the United States' own interrogation practices." The inherent flaws and biases in the military commissions pitted principled military lawyers against the Pentagon; six prosecutors quit or insisted on reassignment rather than go along with a system that relies on torture (Horton, 2008b). In 2007, Lt. Col. V. Stuart Couch, a Marine lawyer, was invited by the House Judiciary Subcommittee to testify about how "enhanced interrogations" affected commission trials. According to Scott Horton (2007a),

> Couch was going to testify about the dilemma he faced as a prosecutor when he learned that a potential defendant against whom he was trying to build a case had been tortured. Couch was assured not to worry, the fact that the detainee had been tortured would be suppressed, so that the court would never learn about it....But Col. Couch didn't want to play that game....The problem is that he was prepared to testify honestly about the torture program, and that was a show-stopper.

Couch was prohibited by the Pentagon from appearing before Congress (Bravin, 2007).

In a May 21, 2009, speech to the nation, President Obama was blunt about the legal "mess" he inherited from the previous administration and the complicated problems of cleaning it up. There are, he explained, five categories and courses of action for GITMO prisoners: First, those who violated criminal laws will be prosecuted in federal courts. There is strong indication that these are people who can be charged for pre-9/11 crimes to avoid the problem of tortured evidence and to circumscribe defense lawyers' ability to make their mistreatment in GITMO and elsewhere part of the case. Second, those who violated the laws of war will be prosecuted in military commissions. Thus, Obama essentially rescinded his January 20 cancellation of this flawed system, but promised that the reformed commissions would not admit evidence elicited through torture or CID. The third and fourth categories are, respectively, people who can and must be released (e.g., the Chinese Uighurs), and those who can be transferred to other countries. Fifth, those posing the "toughest" problem are people who cannot be prosecuted yet are deemed too dangerous to release. Although vague about plans, Obama implied that some form of preventive detention was being considered. One obvious reason that people in this category – such as Muhammad al-Qahtani, suspected of being the "20th" hijacker" and for whom the "special measures" at GITMO were originally devised (Sands, 2008) – are unprosecutable is that they have been tortured. But the alternative, indefinite (possibly permanent) detention without trial is a far cry from the restoration of rule of law standards.

UNINTENDED BENEFITS OF AMERICAN TORTURE

The US torture policy has had significant consequences and complex ramifications domestically and globally. I would identify three unintended benefits to the fact that the Bush administration secretly authorized and then publicly justified the use of torture. The first pertains to domestic politics and the American intellectual/legal terrain. Revelations of American torture focused opposition to government policies in ways that transcend the parochial partisanship of "liberal versus conservative" politics. In the Abu Ghraib/torture memo era, strange bedfellow-type alliances were forged among long-time human rights activists and progressive lawyers, military lawyers, mainstream, and even conservative lawyers who were appalled by US interrogation and detention policies and practices that showed such disregard for law under the dubious premises of unfettered executive power. The common concern among disparate actors has fostered debates about the relationship between torture and the law *within* the anti-torture legal campaign. To generalize the fault lines, for some the compass is international law and the universal prohibition of torture. The elaboration of such views intensified the pre-9/11 fusion of human rights and humanitarian law (Meron, 2000; Teitel, 2002). For others, the compass is US law, including domestic interpretations of treaty obligations and US court rulings on how and where international laws apply. But the common opposition to torture, despite differences, has enriched discourse and debates about law and rights.

One example of the unintended benefit of the torture policy on American intellectual/political life is the formation of an anti-torture cyber community that includes lawyers, scholars, investigative journalists, and human rights activists who communicate through email about torture, interrogation, military justice, human rights, and all related matters. The electronic communications include messages from lawyers representing people imprisoned at Guantánamo or in Iraq or Afghanistan to solicit advice and share information; scholars and journalists offering or asking about historical facts and legal theories; and human rights activists alerting others to developments in investigations and newly uncovered facts about the whereabouts or treatment of prisoners. These electronic communications, so rich in opinions and analyses about military, federal, and international laws and the rights that derive, will provide an archive for the future (Sarat, 1996) when researchers seek to understand what our generation did in response to the US government's new lease on torture at the dawn of the 21st century.

The second unintended consequence of American torture has international implications. To the extent that, before 9/11, human rights was construed by some activists and intellectuals as a political tool in the neoliberal toolbox and by many around the world as a manifestation of Western neo-imperialism, then American torture is a rectifier to the erroneous notion that "Westerners" have a monopoly on the interpretation and enforcement of human rights. The international illegitimacy of the Bush administration's law-disregarding policies and practices has the paradoxical effect of relegitimizing and reinforcing the value of international law as the basis for judging the administration's treatment of prisoners as criminal. This is an example of a new critique of the critique of rights on an international scale.

Finally, executive branch disregard for the most universal and funda-mental legal right of all, the right not to be tortured, was the cornerstone – the "original sin" if you will – of the new paradigm, from which emanated all the other rights-violating law-disregarding practices that were instituted after 9/11. As more Americans experience the loss of rights, perhaps people will recognize that this trajectory traces back to torture, and thus will comprehend why the right not to be tortured is important. If you (and by "you" I mean anyone capable of producing a reflection in a mirror) assume that you would never wind up in a CIA "black site," Guantánamo, or an isolation cell in a Navy brig, statistically you are correct. But you would be naïve and incorrect to believe that your safety is guaranteed by your innocence, or that you have nothing in common with those who were subjected to such fates. Maher Arar, Khaled el-Masri, the "Tipton Three," Moazzam Begg, and James Yee are a few of the innocent people who were mistakenly arrested by the United States and subjected to awful treatment. Their experiences exemplify the dangerousness when a state accretes for itself the right to seize, isolate and torture people, and to deny them all cognizable rights that humans are supposed to enjoy. That these torture victims have found no justice in US courts adds to the risk that the embrace and "legalization" of torture poses to everyone.

According to former Maj. Gen. Antonio Taguba, who headed the 2004 investigation and authored the official report on prisoner abuse at Abu Ghraib, "After years of disclosures by government investigations, media accounts, and reports from human rights organizations, there is no longer any doubt as to whether the current administration has committed war crimes. The only question that remains to be answered is whether those who ordered the use of torture will be held to account" (Taguba, 2008; see also

Horton, 2008c). American citizens bear part of the responsibility for the illegal actions of their state, at least the responsibility to demand accountability. The Bush administration refused, and now apparently the Obama administration is refusing to prosecute or to institute any mechanism to hold accountable those top officials who authorized the torture policy.

When a state claims a "right" to torture anyone who might be suspicious, and when there is no retributive price to pay for this gross crime, then that state can get away with anything. It was such terrifying and tyrannical power that the prohibition against torture was – and is – intended to thwart.

REFERENCES

Abrahamian, E. (1999). *Tortured confessions: Prisons and public recantations in modern Iran.* Berkeley, CA: University of California Press.

ACLU. (ND). Torture documents released under freedom of information act. Available at http://www.aclu.org/safefree/torture/torturefoia.html

Ahmad, M. I. (2008). Resisting guantanamo: Rights at the brink of dehumanization. *Northwestern University Law Review* 103, 2009. Available at http://ssrn.com/abstract = 1268422

Alexander, M. (pseudo) & Bruning, J. (2008). *How to break a terrorist: The US interrogators who used brains, not brutality, to take down the deadliest man in Iraq.* New York: Free Press.

Bales, K. (1999). *Disposable people: New slavery in the global economy.* Berkeley, CA: University of California Press.

Bell, J. (2008). 'Behind this mortal bone': The (in)effectiveness of torture. *Indiana Law Journal,* *83*, 339–361.

Benjamin, M. (2008). A timeline to bush government torture. *Salon.com,* June 18. Available at http://www.salon.com/news/feature/2008/06/18/interrogation/

Blumenthal, S. (2007). The sad decline of Michael Mukasey. *Salon.com,* November 1. Available at http://www.salon.com/opinion/blumenthal/2007/11/01/mukasey/print.html

Bravin, J. (2007). Pentagon forbids marine to testify. *Wall Street Journal* (November 8), A9.

Bufacchi, V., & Arrigo, J. M. (2006). Torture, terrorism, and the state: A refutation of the ticking-bomb argument. *Journal of Applied Philosophy, 23*, 355–373.

Bumiller, K. (1988). *The civil rights society: The social construction of victims.* Baltimore, MD: Johns Hopkins University Press.

Carter, P. (2005). Legal combat: Are enemies waging war in our courts? *Slate,* April 4. Available at http://slate.com/id/2116169/

Chandler, D. (2000). *Voices from S-21: Terror and history in Pol Pot's secret prison.* Berkeley, CA: University of California Press.

Cohen, S. (2001). *States of denial: Knowing about atrocities and suffering.* Cambridge, UK: Polity Press.

Cole, D. (2005). Torture makes justice impossible. *Los Angeles Times,* December 3.

Cole, D., & Lobel, J. (2007). *Less safe, less free: Why America is losing the war on terror.* New York: The New Press.

Coutin, S. (2007). *Nations of emigrants: Shifting boundaries of citizenship in El Salvador and the United States.* Ithaca, NY: Cornell University Press.

Crenshaw, K. (1995). Race, reform and retrenchment: Transformation and legitimation in anti-discrimination law. In: K. Crenshaw, N. Gotanda, G. Peller & K. Thomas (Eds), *Critical race theory: The key writings that formed the movement* (pp. 103–122). New York: The New Press.

Danner, M. (2004). Torture and truth: America, Abu Ghraib and the war on terror. New York: New York Review of Books.

Danner, M. (2009a). US torture: Voices from the black sites. *New York Review of Books, 56*(April 9). Available at: http://www.nybooks.com/articles/22530

Danner, M. (2009b). The red cross report: What it means. *New York Review of Books, 56* (April 30). Available at: http://www.nybooks.com/articles/22614

Danner, M., & Rich, F. (2006). The secret way to war: The downing street memo and the Iraq war's buried history. New York: New York Review of Books.

Dayan, C. (2007). *The story of cruel and unusual.* Boston, MA: Boston Review.

Democracy Now. (2008). Congressional hearings shed new light on government's endorsement of torture. June 19. Available at http://www.democracynow.org/2008/6/19/congressional_hearings_sheds_new_light_on

Dorfman, A. (2002). *Exorcising terror: The incredible unending trial of general Augusto Pinochet.* New York: Seven Stories Press.

DuBois, P. (1991). *Torture and truth.* New York: Routledge.

Dunlap, Maj. Gen. Charles J., Jr. (2007). Lawfare today: A perspective. Available at http://www.yjia.org/node/74

Feitlowitz, M. (interviewer). (2000). The Pinochet precedent: Who could be arrested next? *Crimes of War Project.* Available at http://www.crimesofwar.org/expert/pinochet.html

Feldman, A. (1991). *Formations of violence: The narrative of the body and political terror in northern Ireland.* Chicago: University of Chicago Press.

FIDH. (ND). Universal jurisdiction. Available at http://www.fidh.org/spip.php?rubrique619

Fiss, O. (1998). The immigrant as pariah. *Boston Review.* Available at http://bostonreview.net/BR23.5/Fiss.html

Forrest, D. (Ed.) (1996). *A glimpse of hell: Reports on torture worldwide.* New York: Amnesty International and New York University Press.

Foucault, M. (1977). *Discipline and punish: The birth of the prison.* New York: Pantheon.

Foucault, M. (1990). *The history of sexuality: An introduction.* Vol. 1. New York: Vintage Books.

Gabel, P. (1981). Reification in legal reasoning. *Research in Law and Sociology, 3*, 25–52.

Galanter, M. (1974). Why the "haves" come out ahead: Speculations on the limits of legal change. *Law and Society Review, 9*, 95–160.

Ginbar, Y. (2008). *Why not torture terrorists? Moral, practical and legal aspects of the "Ticking Bomb" justification for torture.* New York: Oxford University Press.

Glendon, M. A. (1991). *Rights talk: The impoverishment of political discourse.* New York: The Free Press.

Goldsmith, J. (2007). *The terror presidency: Law and judgment inside the bush administration.* New York: W.W. Norton.

Greenberg, J. C., & de Vogue, A. (2007). Bush administration's internal waterboarding debate. *ABC News*, November 2. Available at http://abcnews.go.com/WN/DOJ/story?id = 3814076&page = 1

Greenberg, J. C., & de Vogue, A. (2008). Former AG accused of playing politics with justice. *ABC News*, June 19. Available at http://abcnews.go.com/print?id = 5202405.

Greenberg, K. J., & Dratel, J. L. (2005). *The torture papers: The road to Abu Ghraib*. New York: Cambridge University Press.

Grey, S. (2007). *Ghost plane: The true story of the CIA rendition and torture program*. New York: St. Martin's Press.

Hajjar, L. (2000). Sovereign bodies, sovereign states and the problem of torture. *Studies in Law, Politics and Society, 21*, 101–134.

Hajjar, L. (2004). Chaos as utopia: International criminal prosecutions as a challenge to state power. *Studies in Law, Politics, and Society, 31*, 3–23.

Hajjar, L. (2005a). *Courting conflict: The Israeli military court system in the west bank and Gaza*. Berkeley, CA: University of California Press.

Hajjar, L. (2005b). In the penal colony. *The Nation*, February 7.

Hajjar, L. (2006). International humanitarian law and "wars on terror": A comparative analysis of Israeli and American doctrines and policies. *Journal of Palestine Studies, 36*, 21–42.

Hajjar, L. (2009). Does torture work? A sociolegal assessment of the practice in historical and global perspective. *Annual Review of Law and Social Science, 5*, (in press).

Hersch, S. (2004a). Torture at Abu Ghraib. *New Yorker*, April 30.

Hersch, S. (2004b). *Chain of command: The road to Abu Ghraib*. New York: HarperCollins.

Hochschild, A. (1999). *King Leopold's ghost: A story of greed, terror and heroism in colonial Africa*. Mariner Books.

Horton, S. (2007a). Marine lawyer gagged by pentagon. No Comment, *Harper's Magazine*, November 8. Available at http://www.harpers.org/archive/2007/11/hbc-90001623

Horton, S. (2007b). State of exception: Bush's war on the rule of law. *Harper's Magazine*, July. Available at http://www.harpers.org/archive/2007/07/0081595

Horton, S. (2008a). The American public has a right to know that they do not have to choose between torture and terror: Six questions for Matthew Alexander, author of How To Break a Terrorist. *Harper's Magazine*, December 18. Available at http://www.harpers.org/archive/2008/12/hbc-90004036

Horton, S. (2008b). Jim Haynes's long twilight struggle. *Harper's Magazine*, February 8.

Horton, S. (2008c). Justice after bush: Prosecuting an outlaw administration. *Harper's Magazine*, December, pp. 49–60.

Horton, S. (2009). Busting the torture myths. *The Daily Beast*, April 27. Available at http://www.thedailybeast.com/blogs-and-stories/2009-04-27/myth-and-reality-about-torture/full/

Human Rights Watch. (2006a). By the numbers: Findings of the detainee abuse and accountability project. New York, April.

Human Rights Watch. (2006b). No blood, no foul: Soldiers' accounts of detainee abuse in Iraq. New York, July.

Human Rights Watch. (2006c). US: Vice President endorses torture: Cheney expresses approval of CIA's use of waterboarding. New York, October 26.

Hunt, L. (2007). *Inventing human rights: A history*. New York: W.W. Norton.

Keck, M., & Sikkink, K. (1998). *Advocates beyond borders: Advocacy networks in international politics*. Ithaca, NY: Cornell University Press.

Klein, N. (2007). *The shock doctrine: The rise of disaster capitalism*. New York: Metropolitan Books.

118   LISA HAJJAR

Langbein, J. H. (2006). *Torture and the law of proof: Europe and England in the ancien regime*. Chicago: University of Chicago Press.
Lasseter, T. (2008). Day 1: America's prison for terrorists often held the wrong men. *McClatchy Newspapers*, June 15. Available at http://www.mcclatchydc.com/detainees/story/38773. html
Lauren, P. G. (1998). *The evolution of international human rights: Visions seen*. Philadelphia, PA: University of Pennsylvania Press.
Lederman, M. (2005a). We do not torture. We abide by our treaty obligations. We treat detainees humanely. (Repeat as needed), September 21. Available at http://balkin.blogspot.com/2005/09/we-dont-torture-we-abide-by-our-treaty.html
Lederman, M. (2005b). Gitmo: Where was the law? Whither the UCMJ? June 14. Available at http://balkin.blogspot.com/2005/06/gtmo-where-was-law-whither-ucmj.html
Lederman, M. (2007). Waterboarding through the ages. November 4. Available at http://balkin. blogspot.com/2007/11/waterboarding-through-ages.html
Luban, D. (2008). Has torture saved innocent lives? The case for skepticism. June 18. Available at http://balkin.blogspot.com/2008/06/has-torture-saved-innocent-lives-case.html
Macedo, S. (Ed.) (2003). *Universal jurisdiction: National courts and the prosecution of serious crimes under international law*. Philadelphia, PA: University of Pennsylvania Press.
Margulies, J. (2006). *Guantánamo and the abuse of presidential power*. New York: Simon and Schuster.
Mayer, J. (2005). Outsourcing torture: The secret history of America's 'extraordinary rendition' program. *New Yorker*, February 14.
Mayer, J. (2006a). The hidden power: The legal mind behind the US's war on terror. *New Yorker*, July 3.
Mayer, J. (2006b). The memo: How an internal effort to ban the abuse and torture of detainees was thwarted. *New Yorker*, February 27.
Mayer, J. (2007). The black sites: A rare look inside the CIA's secret interrogation program. *New Yorker*, August 13.
Mayerfeld, J. (2007). Playing by our own rules: How US marginalization of international human rights law led to torture. *Harvard Human Rights Journal*, 20, 89–140.
Mayerfeld, J. (2008). In defense of the absolute prohibition of torture. *Public Affairs Quarterly*, 22, 109–128.
McCann, M. (1994). *Rights at work: Pay equity reform and the politics of legal mobilization*. Chicago: University of Chicago Press.
McCoy, A. (2006). *A question of torture: CIA interrogation, from the cold war to the war on terror*. New York: Holt Paperbacks.
Meron, T. (2000). The humanization of humanitarian law. *American Journal of International Law*, 94, 239–278.
Nielsen, L. B. (2004). The work of rights and the work rights do: A critical empirical approach. In: A. Sarat (Ed.), *The Blackwell companion to law and society* (pp. 64–79). Oxford, UK: Blackwell Publishing.
Parry, J. (2005). Just for fun: Understanding torture and understanding Abu Ghraib. *Journal of National Security Law and Policy*, 1, 253–284.
Patterson, O. (1982). *Slavery and social death*. Cambridge, MA: Harvard University Press.
Pearlstein, D. (2007). The 'Lawfare' scare. American Prospect (web edition), March 6. Available at http://www.prospect.org/cs/articles?article = the_lawfare_scare
Peters, E. (1996). *Torture* (Revised ed.). Philadelphia, PA: University of Pennsylvania Press.

Physicians for Human Rights, and Human Rights First. (2007). Leave no marks: Enhanced inter-
    rogation techniques and the risk of criminality. Available at http://www.humanrightsfirst.
    info/pdf/07801-etn-leave-no-marks.pdf
Pollis, A. (1996). Cultural relativism revisited: Through a state prism. *Human Rights Quarterly,*
    18, 316–344.
Priest, D. (2004). Al-Qaeda – Iraq link recanted. *Washington Post,* August 1.
Priest, D., & Gellman, B. (2002). US decries abuse but defends interrogations: 'Stress and
    Duress' tactics used on terrorism suspects in secret overseas facilities. *Washington Post,*
    December 26, p. A1.
Ratner, M. (2008). *The trial of Donald Rumsfeld: Prosecution by book.* New York: Center for
    Constitutional Rights and The New Press.
Ratner, M., & Ray, E. (2004). *Guantánamo: What the world should know.* New York: Chelsea
    Green.
Rejali, D. (2004). Torture's dark allure. *Salon.com,* June 18. Available at http://dir.salon.com/
    story/opinion/feature/2004/06/18/torture_1/index.html
Rejali, D. (2007). *Torture and democracy.* Princeton, NJ: Princeton University Press.
Risen, J. (2006). *State of war: The secret history of the CIA and the bush administration.* New
    York: Free Press.
Rose, D. (2008). Tortured reasoning. Vanity Fair (web exclusive), December 16.
Rosenberg, G. (1991). *The hollow hope: Can courts bring about social change?* Chicago:
    University of Chicago Press.
Salon.com. (ND). The Abu Ghraib files. Available at http://www.salon.com/news/abu_ghraib/
    2006/03/14/introduction/
Sands, P. (2005). *Lawless world: America and the making and breaking of global rules from
    FDR's Atlantic Charter to George W Bush's illegal war.* London: Viking.
Sands, P. (2008). *Torture team: Rumsfeld's memo and the betrayal of American values.*
    Hampshire, UK: Palgrave MacMillan.
Sarat, A. (1996). Narrative strategy and death penalty advocacy. *Harvard Civil Liberties-Civil
    Rights Law Review, 31,* 353–381.
Savage, C. (2007). *Takeover: The return of the imperial presidency and the subversion of
    American democracy.* Boston, MA: Little, Brown and Co.
Scheingold, S. (1974). *The politics of rights: Lawyers, public policy, and political change.* New
    Haven, CT: Yale University Press.
Scheppele, K. L. (2005). Hypothetical torture in the war on terrorism. *Journal of National
    Security Law and Policy, 1,* 285–340.
Skolnick, J. (2004). American interrogation: From torture to trickery. In: S. Levinson (Ed.),
    Torture: A collection (pp. 105–127). New York: Oxford University Press.
Soufan, A. (2009). My tortured decision. *New York Times,* April 23.
Stafford Smith, C. (2007). *Eight o'clock ferry to the windward side: Seeking justice in
    guantanamo bay.* Nation Books.
Streichler, S. (2008). Mad about Yoo, or why worry about the next unconstitutional war?
    Journal of Law and Politics, 24, 93–128.
Suskind, R. (2006). *The one percent doctrine: Deep inside America's pursuit of its enemies since
    9/11.* New York: Simon & Schuster.
Taguba, A. (2008). Preface to broken laws, broken lives. In: Broken laws, broken lives: Medical
    evidence of torture by the US. Physicians for Human Rights. Available at http://
    brokenlives.info/?page_id = 23

Teitel, R. (2002). Humanity's law: Rule of law for the new global politics. *Cornell International Law Journal, 35,* 355–387.

UN Commission on Human Rights. (2006). Situation of detainees at guantanamo bay. February 15. Available at http://www.globalsecurity.org/security/library/report/2006/guantanamo-detainees-report_un_060216.htm

Wax, S. T. (2008). *Kafka comes to America: Fighting for justice in the war on terror.* New York: Other Press.

Weschler, L. (1998). *A miracle, a universe: Settling accounts with torturers.* Chicago: University of Chicago Press.

Williams, P. (1991). *The alchemy of race and rights.* Cambridge, MA: Harvard University Press.

Wolfendale, J. (2009). The myth of 'torture lite'. *Ethics and International Affairs, 23,* 47–61.

Worthington, A. (2007). *The guantanamo files: The stories of the 759 detainees in America's illegal prison.* Pluto Press.

Yoo, J. (2006). *War by other means: An insider's account of the war on terror.* New York: Atlantic Monthly Press.

REVISITING RIGHTS ACROSS CONTEXTS: FAT, HEALTH, AND ANTIDISCRIMINATION LAW

Anna Kirkland

ABSTRACT

Doctors need to consider all kinds of traits and risk factors about a person in a treatment situation, while antidiscrimination law puts significant restrictions on what an employer can consider about a person in hiring. These two contexts – health care and the antidiscrimination-governed workplace – seem to adopt entirely incompatible conceptions of how to regard the person, and hence, what rights she is considered to deserve. Therefore, how can we make sense of the claim by fat acceptance advocates that doctors discriminate against them based on their weight? Even when little or no formal rights exist for fat citizens in either sphere, there are nonetheless transformative discourses available that cross-pollinate each context. Revisiting rights by bringing these two discordant contexts together helps illuminate problems of injustice that must be confronted in the future as we move toward a more universal and equitable health care system in which conceptions of rights must have some place.

Revisiting Rights
Studies in Law, Politics, and Society, Volume 48, 121–145
Copyright © 2009 by Emerald Group Publishing Limited
All rights of reproduction in any form reserved
ISSN: 1059-4337/doi:10.1108/S1059-4337(2009)0000048008

INTRODUCTION: ANTIDISCRIMINATION, RIGHTS, AND HEALTH

American antidiscrimination law tells employers how to treat (or not to treat) their employees based on certain protected traits, but no correlative law tells doctors how to treat patients. To many, it would seem very odd to apply antidiscrimination-type restrictions to doctors' decisions about patients. What is a protected identity trait to be ignored in antidiscrimination law – race or gender, for example – is an important factor to take into consideration about a patient. There is an entire competing edifice of the person in the realm of health care, in fact. We have seen a significant historical transformation over the past century from concern with infectious diseases to the management of chronic disease. The patient is often someone who is presently free of disease or infection, but who presents various "risk factors" for future conditions (Rothstein, 2003). Risk factors are commonly about genetic heritage and lifestyle, but quite often they are the same traits that we consider candidates for antidiscrimination protections. If we accept that health and health care are sites for significant and troubling problems of injustice in our society, then this tension between the presuppositions of health care and the principles of antidiscrimination law demands our attention.

Much discussion of rights and health has taken place in terms of resource distribution questions about health care (e.g., Daniels, 1985). Limiting examination of rights and health to distributive questions, however, has left untouched the myriad ways that health discourses are also descriptions of persons – as a patient, as ill, as a cluster of risk factors, as a costly burden on society, as dangerous to public health, as recovering, and so on. These accounts of the person often emerge in discursive relationships between doctors and patients, and intriguing yet relatively unexplored site for sociolegal studies. I propose to revisit rights by colliding these two realms hypothetically together: antidiscrimination law and health care, as exemplified by fat patients who feel doctors discriminate against them.[1] Are there any rights there, either formally or aspirationally?[2] Is becoming a patient the opposite, or somehow deeply in tension with, becoming a political subject of rights? Is contesting one's medical identity somehow linked to changes in feelings of entitlement to rights? When one's identity is stigmatized as unhealthy, can antidiscrimination norms (by which I mean specific legal rights as well as more broad expectations that antidiscrimination law does and should apply) assist in building an alternative vision of one's self?

This inquiry aims to revisit health as well as to revisit rights. I revisit health to move it from a question about distribution to a question about identity construction. I revisit rights to understand how the preconditions for rights claiming form and move across contexts, even when there are no formal rights protections yet and even articulating them is quite difficult to do. I hope to show that the intersections of health, law, identity, and power are potentially rich territory for sociolegal scholarship. Putting health and antidiscrimination rights together in this analysis fruitfully exposes both as productive discourses rather than things one can get. Talking about health care as something to be properly distributed runs the risk of reifying health into a certain kind of thing. It can become different things, though: an entitlement, a locus of shared humanity, or perhaps a moral practice to be achieved by the virtuous. We imagine our identity in relationship to it or to its lack. We make it into a potentially achievable thing for every person, like having enough to eat, when we call it a fundamental human right. We presume that we know what it is. Then we can only talk about how everyone ought to have more and better access to health, forgetting the politics of health and the social construction of it through racialization and gendering, lifestyle practices, care of the self, elite agenda-setting, market forces, bourgeois norms, and excessive optimism (Crawford, 1980, 2006; Metzl, 2003; Metzl & Poirier, 2005; Orbach, 2006; Roberts, 2006; Rose, 2001). These forces make what health is always in flux, always hierarchical, always imperfectly achieved. Health is the perfect cloak for ideology, then, because it excuses itself from the usual tussles of politics, moral criticism, or insult. Like the concept of rights, the concept of health benefits greatly from the assumption that it is just a good thing to have. Sociolegal scholars know perfectly well that rights are not only things one can either possess or be dispossessed of, however, and it is time to acknowledge what scholars doing critical work on health and medicine know (e.g., Armstrong, 2002; Conrad, 1992, 2007): health is not just something one possesses, either. Like rights, one can "have" it but also be produced, transformed, diminished, or empowered by it in ways that reach far beyond what the language of possession can describe. Imagining the introduction of antidiscrimination rights into health care gives us a chance to see how they might interact. This interaction will only become more important as we move toward some kind of national health plan. National health care will mean that health is part of citizenship, perhaps making it easier to make arguments for equality and dignity in explicitly political terms rather than deferring to medical expertise.

Antidiscrimination rights are rights to be recognized as a certain kind of person and thus to be treated and judged according to certain rules designed to alleviate subordination of the group to which one belongs. I will focus here on the example of fat acceptance advocates, who want an end to job discrimination, but also to the disparaging treatment they receive in health care settings (if they are not shut out altogether, say by not being able to purchase insurance at any price because of their weight). My legal training pushed me to imagine that the interviews with fat acceptance advocates analyzed here would focus heavily on workplace rights, since our antidiscrimination laws mostly govern the workplace rather than other settings (e.g., with a few exceptions for housing and voting). But luckily, my protocol did not mention law at all until the second half of the interview, before which interviewees were prompted to discuss their reasons for joining a fat rights group and "experiences of unfair treatment" (deliberately phrased to be as open-ended as possible). The question about experiences of unfair treatment triggered intensely meaningful and important stories about struggles over the very meaning of health and the identity of a fat person in health care settings. Many interviewees returned to discourses about health again and again despite the lack of any specific prompt or question about it in the interview protocol. Of course, I should have expected that a legal view of discrimination would be narrowed compared to an ordinary person's descriptions of all the myriad ways one can feel unfairly treated in various settings. It became clear that being a patient in the doctor–patient interaction was a critical point in developing a sense of entitlement to antidiscrimination rights, though I concluded that the tensions between the subject as patient and the subject as rights-bearer are never fully resolved for these women.

The fat acceptance movement is centrally concerned with transforming ideas about body fat and health, such that fat citizens can receive dignified health care but also so that they can achieve individuality in the eyes of health care providers, avoid scapegoating and harassment, and move into public spaces on equal footing with thinner people. This chapter traces how fat acceptance group members contest the dominant view of them as unhealthy. As I will explain, there are no laws for fat citizens to use to formally contest their treatment in health care settings in terms of non-discrimination on the basis of weight. [A few jurisdictions – Michigan, San Francisco, Santa Cruz, Washington, D.C., and Madison, WI – prohibit weight discrimination in employment (District of Columbia Human Rights Act 2007; Compliance Guidelines to Prohibit Weight and Height Discrimination 2007; Santa Cruz Municipal Code 2007; Elliot-Larsen Civil

Rights Act 2007; Madison Equal Opportunities Ordinance 2007), and there are a few cases of fat plaintiffs winning disability discrimination cases (Kirkland, 2006). But generally, fatness is not considered worthy of protection from discrimination]. We know, however, that fat bias and discrimination across many settings including health care is widespread and has clearly measurable economic and health consequences for fat people (Brownell, Puhl, Schwartz, & Rudd, 2005). These fat advocates' accounts of their struggles help us to understand whether making rights claims about health depletes or expands the political standing of those citizens who articulate them (even if those rights are not formally recognized) and in what ways. Political possibilities are opened up through the introduction of new vocabularies, senses of entitlement, social practices, opportunities for solidarity, cultural discourses, and accounts of personhood.

Sociolegal scholars already know that rights claiming does not simply spring up even when there is a law available to fit claims into; rather, the appropriateness of rights claiming requires not only a legal basis and material resources but also a sense of propriety in one's community for the claim (Engel, 1991), an accord with one's self-image as a claimant (Bumiller, 1988), and a set of cultural and discursive frameworks in which one's claim makes sense (Engel & Munger, 2003). Perhaps, when one's identity is so stigmatized and overdetermined by an account of its unhealthiness, becoming a person who deserves protection from ill treatment must first occur through contesting one's identity as an ill person. One site of this contestation is the doctor's office. If this hypothesis is correct, we would expect to see fat acceptance advocates try first to gain redescriptions of themselves from doctors rather than to make claims using the specific language of legal rights. By revisiting rights in the health context, I suggest that health discourses are becoming a crucial extralegal site in which new cultural and discursive frameworks can be born and grow. We may not see anything like rights invocations at first. But if we see the patient becoming the kind of person who can resist her pathologized identity and claim a new version of it, we may see that the new identity fits much better with rights claiming, even if those rights are only a vaguely articulated possibility now.

REVISITING RIGHTS: WHAT DO RIGHTS DO?

When we think of the incompatibility of rights and health in the United States as primarily a distributive justice problem, as many critics have, it is easy to see that the losers so far in this debate – leftists, liberals, and other advocates of health as a right – would agree that critical legal scholars were correct about the ruse of rights first articulated several decades ago. Perhaps, rights are abstract, unstable, indeterminate empty promises without corresponding entitlements that lull us into thinking we possess something (Tushnet, 1984). We have the right to get health care, but only if we can pay for it. Rights can be not only empty, but worse than empty if they only appear to enhance social welfare while actually undermining more progressive social change. Perhaps, because they are often granted by a dominant group to a minority, their extension will nonetheless preserve the basic power relations of inequality while delivering only surface-level social change (Crenshaw, 1988; Siegel, 1997). That is, of course, if the vulnerable people rights are meant to protect even manage to swallow their pride and go through the process of thinking of themselves as damaged and claiming redress through rights claims, which many are disinclined to do (Bumiller, 1988; Felstiner, Abel, & Sarat, 1980; Nielsen & Nelson, 2005).

Rights talk might help call forth and establish a new account of a person that deserves relief from subordinating practices currently justified by her identity (her fat as a cause of disease, therefore fatness as unworthy of status protection). This frame makes the classic critique of rights much less applicable and instead begins from recent discussions about how rights claiming transforms the people who engage in it (Brown, 1995; Engel & Munger, 2003; Halley, 2000; Hull, 2006; Jenness, 1999). On the more pessimistic view, rights claiming imposes an ill-fitting or unusable set of requirements about what kind of person to be. The lofty terms in which legal elites think about rights may not correspond at all to the ways that more marginalized people have worked out to get by in a world in which the state is often an intrusive regulatory force and not a source of protection, as many poor women experience the receipt of welfare benefits and social services, for example (Gilliom, 2001; Roberts, 1999, 2002). Or, as Sandra Levitsky's study of family members providing chronic care shows, there may be a pre-existing non-legal frame for thinking about how to handle a problem (such as family responsibility) that prevents a person from turning to law for help (Levitsky, 2008). Those caregivers often could not wrap their heads around the idea of having a right to assistance in giving long-term care to a loved one, reacting with "befuddled incomprehension" (*ibid.*, p. 576). Accepting rights as a solution to a social problem presumes a level of resources (which are not substantively granted in most cases) and a liberal legal rights consciousness, in other words, which must be solicited from the person if it is not already there. Sally Engle Merry has observed how establishing rights for women to be free of domestic violence elicits a "new subjectivity defined within the discourses and practices of law," which "depends on her experience trying to assert [rights]" (Merry, 2003, p. 347). The battered woman becomes legally entitled by "being the rational person who follows through, leaves the batterer, cooperates with prosecuting the case, and does not provoke violence, take drugs or drink, or abuse children" (*ibid.*, p. 353). Linking rights to anything related to health care in American society is even trickier than in these criminal justice or employment contexts where rights are at least solidly part of the framework. As Miriam Ticktin's work on the French policy of granting legal residency to *sans papiers* (immigrants without papers) with life-threatening diseases on humanitarian grounds shows, even a generous state policy meant to grant rights based on health status can mean that people considered unhealthy are treated with compassion but not with political and legal equality (Ticktin, 2006). That is, even when a person invokes rights related to health, they may be extended in terms of a personalized, individualized, and discretionary humanitarian compassion. The problem then is that inequalities become depoliticized and diverted into highly personalized stories.

Yet, sociolegal scholars have also learned that rights discourses remain open in fascinating ways, supplying opportunities for people to mobilize new descriptions of what they deserve in ways that increase credibility, widen recognition, and unsettle oppressive norms (McCann, 1994; Williams, 1991). In their in-depth study of the relationship of law and identity for people with disabilities, David Engel and Frank Munger outline a new direction for theories of law and identity. Future theorizing, they argue, should take better account of the minimal role of formal legal proceedings in identity development; the ways that rights can transform self-perceptions; the ways that cultural and discursive shifts can occur in ordinary life, such as in discussions at work that show acceptance of a new rights regime; and finally, the responses of institutions to changes in rights that in turn create new contexts for individuals to seize opportunities (Engel & Munger, 2003, pp. 94–96). Critically, Engel and Munger's study focuses on people with disabilities, a population that has been the target of Congressional legislation for many decades, most recently with the much-publicized Americans with Disabilities Act of 1990 (ADA). The transformational powers of rights they discover, then, depend on fairly significant cultural, institutional, and discursive shifts happening around a particular legal identity: a change in mass culture that supports rights, in some sense. Logics for deciphering that identity must become available and become sufficiently powerful that it is possible to include the trait and the person who bears it in the antidiscrimination pantheon.

Fat people are certainly a much less politically popular group than people
with disabilities, and as I noted, there are only the smallest pockets of rights
protections in the United States on the basis of weight. Therefore, while they
are a marginal group, fat advocates are nonetheless politically active and
organized in some parts of the country and are already well versed in using
rights language in more recognizable contexts. Unlike Levitksy's family
caregivers, then, these are advocates already engaged in public claiming; the
trick is that they are bringing an account of how to judge them as persons
forged in antidiscrimination norms into a setting in which it is very ill-fitting:
the moment of health assessment and diagnosis. Can rights invocations
transform a risk factor into an identity trait? One way to avoid the problem
of prefigured and narrow discourses based on rights is to have activists
themselves shape the terms of their identity in one context (here, health care)
and shift those accounts over to their understandings of legal rights.
Acknowledging this "cross-pollination" effect helps us see that people will
not necessarily just borrow a perspective of victimhood, as Brown worried
happens with identity politics, or walk into a set of expectations that are
foreign to their circumstances, as Merry found with the domestic violence
plaintiffs.

ANTIDISCRIMINATION IN HEALTH CARE:
THE CASE OF FAT ACCEPTANCE ADVOCACY

Methodological Background of the Study

The interviews analyzed here are part of a larger project on rights claiming
in the fat acceptance movement in the United States. Much of the
methodology and analysis is presented elsewhere (Kirkland, 2008b), but
I have reserved discussion of rights in health care for this piece. The
interviews were conducted in 2005 and 2006 with thirty-four members of
fat acceptance organizations (primarily, the National Association for the
Advancement of Fat Acceptance, or NAAFA) across the country. The
sample reflects the general membership of fat rights groups (Gimlin, 2001;
Saguy & Riley, 2005): overwhelmingly, female, middle-aged and middle-
class, white, heterosexual, and weighing about 250–400 pounds.[3] Interview
questions prompted respondents to reflect about the desirability of
antidiscrimination laws and asked how the person would defend fat people
as deserving inclusion in them. As I noted above, health emerged as a

primary topic again and again, and interviewees recounted connections between their struggles over their health status and their feelings of deserving better treatment as patients but also as citizens.

Are There Any Antidiscrimination Rights in Health Care?

Before moving into the interviews, it is worth pausing for a moment to reflect on the sparse legal terrain where health care and discrimination laws currently meet. Antidiscrimination laws like Title VII of the 1964 Civil Rights Act, the (ADA, the Age Discrimination in Employment Act (ADEA), and others stipulate a trait or list of traits that should not be taken into account when making employment decisions. The Fair Housing Act, part of the 1964 Civil Rights Act, does the same thing for housing and rental decisions. Voting rights are another classic area for antidiscrimination law as well. As I mentioned above, the 1964 Civil Rights Act does prohibit race discrimination in health care facilities (and any institution) receiving public funds. However, weight is not included in any of these federal laws. No civil rights-type law requires physicians to ignore a patient's weight. In fact, being overweight or obese is considered one of the most salient things about a patient that a health care provider should confront, making it a perfect opposite of a trait properly protected in antidiscrimination law. The first thing that happens at most doctor visits is a step on the scale. As Abigail Saguy's work has documented, the health implications of body fat are the epicenter of disputes between activists, obesity researchers, and doctors (2005) and the focus of much moralistic, sensationalized news coverage (2008). Research into the stigma of obesity clearly shows that medical professionals exhibit the same contemptuous distaste for fatness that is found throughout our society, with nurses admitting that they do not like to touch fat patients, for example, and doctors noting that they assume fat patients are non-compliant (Fabricatore, Wadden, & Foster, 2005). Though so much of the public attention to fatness is framed in terms of health, fat men and women are entirely on their own in securing non-discriminatory treatment in health care settings.[4]

Antidiscrimination norms seem to have very little traction because one's traits may have health implications and therefore should not be ignored on the classic "color-blind" model, for instance. A new drug for heart failure came out in 2005 marketed for African Americans, in distinct tension with the antidiscrimination norm that a historically stigmatized trait like race should not form the basis for decision-making about a person.

Some scholars expressed concern (Brody & Hunt, 2006; Roberts, 2006), but the public reaction did not otherwise suggest that the drug racially profiles in an undesirable way. Once again, these group-specific medical interventions raise the question, is health just different? Can doctors profile and "discriminate" (in the sense of treating patients differently based on a trait) when it would be illegal for employers to do so? Is their use of knowledge about persons fundamentally different and isolated from the bad impulses and outcomes we use antidiscrimination laws to thwart? The fat acceptance advocates maintain that doctors are not so different from biased employers and that indeed they should not be given the authority to impose categories ("morbid obesity") upon patients or to infer that a patient should be viewed first as fat.

It is not just that fat citizens lack civil rights in the sphere of health care; Americans have very few positive rights related to health at all.[5] The main mechanisms for regulating physicians and providing patient rights are the tort law system, appeals to state licensing boards, various "Patient's Bill of Rights" laws, the American Medical Association's (AMA) own internal regulatory processes and resolutions, and federal laws such as the Health Insurance Portability and Accountability Act (HIPAA). Some rights to treatment, as in emergency rooms or for women in active labor, have evolved from common law principles of reliance (if the facility had held itself open to providing care in the past) and are now rooted in hospital licensing rules and the Emergency Medical Treatment and Active Labor Act (EMTALA) (Epstein, 1997, pp. 82–91). None of these impose a duty upon physicians to ignore stigmatizing features like employment discrimination statutes do. The AMA's guidelines say patients have the right to "courtesy, respect, dignity, responsiveness, and timely attention to his or her needs" within an established doctor–patient relationship. The punishment is expulsion from AMA membership.[6] A physician cannot strand a patient she's caring for, in other words. Since there are no requirements that a doctor (outside of the ER) take on patients without regard to stigmatizing traits they have, a doctor could refuse to establish a doctor–patient relationship with anyone over a certain weight (or for a lot of other reasons, too, like refusing to vaccinate one's child) without violating AMA guidelines.

These limited rights govern the actual interaction and treatment in the provision of health care. Access to insurance is the other major area of concern, since it often determines whether a person can enter a care setting in the first place and on what terms. States have enacted protective legislation to prevent insurance companies and health care providers from discriminating against patients based on variable list of things like results of genetic testing and past domestic violence complaints. No state law mentions weight in this context. Perhaps, most importantly, insurance companies can refuse to insure a fat person because of her weight. Marilyn Wann, whom I interviewed for this project, explained how she had secured health insurance through a writer's guild, but after that arrangement ended she was rejected for health insurance because of her weight and could not buy any at all. She is self-employed as a writer, speaker and fat activist in the San Francisco Bay area, weighs about 270 pounds, and has no health problems besides having to go without health insurance. How can people claim to be so concerned about fat people's health, she asks, when some of the main problems faced by fat people are in access to care in the first place?

One interviewee was suing a doctor over the death of her mother after complications from surgery, and she felt that the doctor's lack of knowledge about the risks of operating on a fat person had directly caused her mother's death. In all other cases, however, interviewees described the kind of conduct that would be very hard to place within formal claims under any existing law or guideline. Likewise, the kind of treatment the members described would not seem to be grounds for taking away a doctor's license. None of the other interviewees had been involved in any kind of lawsuit or formal complaint against a doctor, though some described writing letters in response to ill treatment.

"But What About Your Health?": Battling over the Meaning of Fat

As I noted, no interview question specifically alluded to doctors or health care, but humiliation in the doctor's office was the most common experience the members brought up when asked about "unfair treatment." Some interviewees explicitly said that discriminatory treatment in health care settings was much worse than discriminatory treatment in employment. Renee, a 36-year-old Human Resources manager from Ohio, was particularly well-informed about employment discrimination law through her job.[7] She had experienced a glass ceiling for fat women at a previous job after her supervisor, also a fat woman, had been told she could not advance because of her weight. Renee then left that job knowing the same ceiling would hold her back. Despite her professional perspective and personal experience with employment discrimination, she asked early in the interview when there would be a chance to talk about problems in getting health care because she felt those issues were more pressing than employment discrimination. "I wonder if legislation addressing equality in healthcare," she said, "whether it's through the ADA or through other type of means wouldn't be something that, not to minimize discrimination based on size in employment, but if people of size in general would not benefit more from trying to advocate in the healthcare system."

Interviewees overwhelmingly recognized that as long as being fat is understood as a health risk determined by individual patterns of behavior, there would be scant grounds for claiming rights against discrimination. That is, it shares all the medical certitude behind the "risk factor" conception of public health as well as all the weight of a century's worth of moral condemnation of fat (Stearns, 1997). As Frannie, a 62-year-old fundraising purchaser from the San Francisco Bay Area, put it: "We have to address the issue of health, because so often people will say to you, 'Well, I can agree with you about discrimination against fat people is wrong when they're denying jobs. But what about your health?'" She continued, tying discrimination to health care cost containment and insurance:

> They say that we're not healthy, that's why we're not being hired or promoted, because we'll cause all sorts of insurance risk to their company. That's really bogus, because when you're in a large company, all sorts of health risks are applied across the company. When you are a fat person and you're being denied a job, or you're a woman who's being denied a promotion because you might get pregnant, how is that any different than any other kind of discrimination? And we don't ever talk about men who die of heart attacks suddenly, and this is not certainly something planned for, and certainly the care of somebody undergoing a heart attack or a bypass is pretty expensive.

For Frannie, being fat can be made suitable for antidiscrimination law, like being pregnant. (Pregnancy is protected under Title VII, and conditions like heart problems would be considered disabilities under the ADA and gain protection that way.) Fat is unfairly singled out using health rhetoric, she argues, with other groups enjoying protection from their health vulnerabilities. Even if fat people sometimes cost their employers money, her view of collective risk pooling means that we should view one another as all potentially vulnerable and politically connected. Even being a walking risk factor does not mean one is ineligible for antidiscrimination protections, she argues. Frannie sees risk factor arguments as simple blockers for rights, an ideological move that separates fat people from everyone else and renders them unintelligible for rights protections. The way to counteract it is to make analogies to other conditions.

Frannie spoke more directly about antidiscrimination rights than many interviewees. As the others described encounters with doctors, many made no mention of anything about rights. The fundamental disagreement between the dominant health professional view of fat and the fat advocates' view currently prevents development of a widely accessible new identity for fat people. The women here wanted doctors to ignore their fat because they did not see their presenting issues (a sinus infection, for instance) as related to it, just like an employer should ignore skin color in hiring. But for the doctors, the fat was directly relevant – more like skill level as a consideration in hiring.

The primary complaint was that physicians regard fat patients as first and foremost fat, and thus castigate them about their weight regardless of the presenting condition, assume that any medical problem is caused by the fat, and treat fat patients as non-compliant, lazy, and contemptible. My subjects' stories also suggest some particular techniques some doctors use in dealing with fat patients: withholding information and use of silence as well as verbal castigation. Kristin, a 43-year-old sales consultant from the Chicago area, tells a story that I heard over and over of a doctor intent on discussing weight no matter what the presenting condition was:

> What does fat have to do with a sinus infection? I had a doctor do that one time. I went to her for a sinus infection. I have terrible sinuses. You know, I live where the weather's crazy. Everybody has bad sinuses around here. The doctor said, "Well, what's your downfall?" And I said, "Well, what do you mean, what's my downfall?" I thought she meant I had to get rid of my cat. And she said, "Well, because of your weight. Look at you." And I was a size 22 at the time and I said, "What does that have to do with it?" Now that I did something about. I went to my benefits administrator where I was working at the time and I reported her. And [the benefits administrator] reported her to [the insurance company]. So I fought back on that one and I never went back to her again either.

Anna, a 43-year-old plus-size beauty pageant competitor from the Chicago area, explicitly describes both inattention (to whether she had "medical problems" and what those might be) and attention (of the wrong kind, to her looks) to her as discrimination:

> I needed hand surgery. I went in, the doctor didn't even do much of a history and he told me that because of my medical problems, he really thought it would be better if I did not have my surgery at [a particular hospital], that I should have it [at another hospital] where my primary care provider is. And then I went into no high cholesterol, blood glucose fine, blah, blah. And I don't think he heard because I got a message from him again saying the same thing. So of course I wouldn't go back to him. But if I had to do that over again, I guess I would confront him and say, "Doctor, what are you referring to?" Make him say it. He's discriminating against me. It's a tone, the attitude of doctors. I went in for a mammogram and the doctor and a resident came in to see me afterward and the doctor said that I was really an attractive person but I could get a lot of guys if I lost weight. And I just felt so ashamed and awful. I never went back to that group to have a mammogram again.

Martin, a 50-year-old woman from Indiana trained as a special education teacher, had a negative experience with the birth of her son:

> The OB/GYN that I had was just horrible. My blood pressure must've been going up each time I went into his office. It was really bad because I would go into him and say, "My feet are swollen." And he would say, "You need to quit eating salt." At the time, I happened to be a secretary for the American Medical Association. [My boss] had given me the whole list on what foods were high in sodium. So I said, "No, I'm not," and I pulled my list and started to go through it. All of a sudden, he shut up and wouldn't talk to me anymore. I ended up having my son by C-section. I had been in labor for almost 12 hours. I had been in labor all night. I had two student doctors that were wonderful. Thank God they were with me. My OB/GYN came in the morning around six o'clock to examine me and these were his words: "You're too fat, that's why you're going to have a C-section." He didn't mention toxemia. The student doctors who were working with me told me I had toxemia [also called preeclampsia]. He never ever told me that I had that. That would have explained what all was going on with me. I knew that my blood pressure was up and my legs were swelling and stuff like that. But he never explained why. He just gave me a hard time about being fat, which didn't make any sense at all. [She had gained 26 pounds over the course of that pregnancy from a pre-pregnancy weight of a little under 200 pounds].

Martin's attempts to contest her doctor's knowledge of her eating habits led to a power struggle. She felt that the doctor wanted to punish her for being fat. Martin's experience of trusting some doctors (here, the medical students) but feeling betrayed by others was shared by other interviewees, many of whom were quick to point out that not all doctors are awful. Foxglove says she "found a doctor that's a little bit chunky herself" and happily reports that "she has never mentioned my weight." Finding a good doctor who is not prejudiced against fat patients is a very popular topic on fat acceptance listservs and in other activist settings.

Tina, a 60-year-old nurse and public health advocate from the Bay Area, argues for individualized care for fat women that puts their fatness aside in the interest of their health. She explains:

> We did a study on barriers to gynecological cancer screening for large women. Large women tell us that, as your weight increases you're less likely to get a pap smear. The women who have dieted most are the most likely to delay care. We asked women, "What's the problem?" [*What did they say?*] Equipment that doesn't fit us, the negative portrayals by the healthcare system, punitive attitudes and negative attitudes by healthcare providers and support staff, tables that tip over, gowns that fit one side of our body, not our full body. Blood pressure cuffs that are too small, so that they get an inaccurate blood pressure measurement. And the assumption, on the side of providers that they are entitled to give you a weight loss lecture, regardless of why you were at the doctor.

Her health advocacy also has personal and painful roots in her own loss of her sister.

> One of our focus group questions was, if you went to the doctor and complained about weight gain, bloating, or low back pain, what do you think the advice you would get from the doctor? All the fat women's groups, of course, they laughed. Well, they'd tell us to lose weight, you know. In the not-fat women's group, they were kind of confused, like, well, wouldn't they ask me a little bit more about my symptoms? It was not their experience to have every single complaint based on their weight. And those are the symptoms of ovarian cancer. My sister went to the doctor with exactly those symptoms. They kept putting her on a diet. A year later, they finally diagnosed her with ovarian cancer and she fucking died!

Fat acceptance advocates articulated a view of non-discrimination that, even though it does not mention law or rights, shares important presumptions with well-known antidiscrimination principles. Advocates wanted doctors to shift paradigms about obesity and to treat them as a thin person would be treated. To echo the "but for" test for discrimination, a mistreated fat patient would ask how a thin person walking in with the same malady would have been treated. Would a thin woman with a sinus infection been asked what habit was her "downfall"? Would an obstetrician fail to mention pre-eclampsia, a potentially life-threatening complication, as the cause of high blood pressure and swelling in a thin pregnant woman and just do a C-section without explaining why? Would a thin patient showing symptoms of ovarian cancer be sent home with another round of diet advice? The fat should not obscure the individual situation of the person beneath it, in the advocates' view, and it should not be a proxy for evaluating health and wellness. This impulse obviously shares much with the notion that job applicants should be evaluated for their skills and not their externally appearing and irrelevant traits. The bid to ignore fat is like practice for a rights argument and vice versa: the kinds of reasons the women articulated would work in both contexts, and they become stronger as arguments and as accounts of a deserving self by being applied in both areas. The prevailing medical view, however, is that body fat is unhealthy and dangerous and thus is critically relevant to assessing a patient (Saguy & Riley, 2005). Doctors would likely say that while no one deserves to be treated rudely, it is their professional duty to express their opinion about the effects of weight on health. The terms of the debate between fat advocates and the prevailing medical view have certainly not yet come into productive discussion. Each is simply insisting the opposite of the other's position: ignore the fat or focus on it as a crucially important risk factor.

"Their Fat Little Word": Recasting Identity by Contesting
Medical Categorization

The ways fat advocates resist categorization open up a more productive route to a new account of health and personhood than the bid to ignore the fat can provide. In this section, I examine how their very strong objections to terms like "obesity" call forth an account of the person who may indeed have certain health problems, but who is still entitled to an unstigmatized identity. The women I spoke with understood that the account of who is outside of antidiscrimination norms is ideologically constructed as deviant, dysfunctional, and part of a group set aside from normal people by their indulgent or antisocial behaviors. They know that the "risk factor" analysis is never so clinically neat as it pretends, and therefore, they go right to confronting the fat hatred. Janice, a 42-year-old Latina working for Los Angeles County government, pitches fat people as simply biologically different but simultaneously variable as a group so that it is impossible to generalize about why any particular individual is fat. "I would really, really, really like to see people understand that it's biological, that our bodies are different and some of us will eat more than others, some of us will eat less than others, than people who are normal, average-size, per se. And that it's okay if we do. There's nothing wrong with that. That we're not a horrible drain on society." Alice, a 54-year-old teacher from the Chicago area, understands the power that a label as a member of the "obese" group has:

> Today, obesity is a physical disorder on the medical books and it should not be. I would like to see that word outlawed. Because they can label it a physical disorder, which it is not, they then can discriminate on the basis of that physical disorder for insurance, for all kinds of other things. And I think the word, "obesity," as a physical disorder and the word, "homosexual," as a mental disorder, are very similar on those two planes. If you want to say that a person has high blood pressure, fine. That's an actual fact. That a person has diabetes, fine. That a person has this or has that, fine. Those are physical things that people of all sizes get. But to make up a category and call that category, "obesity," and thereby put all kinds of restrictions on the individuals, all kinds of biases on the individual, all kinds of taboos and all kinds of negative things based on this artificial category that you've come up with because it doesn't fit your particular size parameters is wrong, is very, very wrong.

Alice continued, mounting a very strong critique of power of both the labeling and the interventions that come with it:

> What doctors have done in the name of saving these "poor, morbidly obese people" from themselves is criminal. They have experimented on us by operations which have caused undue harm and distress, long-term difficulties. They have taken people that have

no physical problems other than their weight and then they label their fat little word, "obesity," and done things to them with chemicals, with knives, with all kinds of things in the name of "health." It should be outlawed.

Like most fat advocates, Alice is deeply opposed to weight loss surgeries (even invoking "outlawed" and "criminal" to describe how she thinks those interventions should be regulated) because of their very high complication rates and because she does not believe that fat people need to be fixed in the first place. She traces the movement of the label "obese" toward interventions with chemicals and knives that, because a fat person is seen as either about to drop dead or living a life that is not worth living in its present form, seem like reasonable risks to take. More than one interviewee reported overhearing thinner women remark: "If I ever get that fat, just shoot me." There is an obvious parallel here to the arguments of disability rights activists like Harriet McBryde Johnson of the group Not Dead Yet, who opposes selective abortions for fetuses with disabilities and euthanizing of people who are disparagingly called "vegetables" or otherwise thought to be living lives not worth living. As I explain elsewhere (Kirkland, 2008b), fat advocates are extremely reluctant to draw on disability rights arguments because they do not want to be considered diseased or defective. But if the point of national policy is to make fat people disappear as fat people and where comments like the one my respondents overheard are socially acceptable, it is not so hard to see that they are in the same boat with Johnson and others making similar anti-eugenics arguments (Johnson, 2003; Wong, 2002).

Only a few interviewees agreed that being fat should be categorized as a medical problem in and of itself. Monique, a 35-year-old woman from Missouri who directs a program for people with intellectual disabilities, compares it to having incurable cancer.

If [being fat] is not curable, then your best bet is to accept it, to make peace with it just like you would a cancer. It's a curse. It doesn't make you a bad person. However, it is a medical problem just like psoriasis or cancer. And I'm not saying aesthetically, it is a debilitating illness, you know? I'm not saying I would be proud to be fat any more than I would say I'm proud to have cancer or have psoriasis. However, I don't think we need to be ashamed of it either because it isn't a weakness of character.

Monique lost 100 pounds as a teenager but has struggled since that time with bulimia, extreme dieting, and anorexia. She still considers herself a size acceptance activist despite no longer being fat because of the misery of her own battles with weight and eating. Even in her endorsement of a disease model of obesity, she still insists that being fat is not a character problem, but more like an unfortunate affliction that should provoke medicalized empathy, not discrimination.

The fat acceptance movement has its own alternative approach to health and weight, which was endorsed by nearly everyone I spoke with. Tina articulates the view of health and physical activity associated with the Health at Every Size (HAES) movement:

> Everybody needs more social support, more involvement in their community, not being ostracized, not being the target of discrimination. I think that will help health for everybody. The whole idea of making regular routine, enjoyable physical activity accessible to everybody. And, you know, my work had been devoted to that. I trained instructors to do that. We helped the National Institutes of Health develop and publish a booklet to help all really fat people have access to physical activities. A little bit of movement goes a long way towards functional capacity, our health, let alone managing insulin resistance, diabetes and hypertension, the three things that are most often related to, you know, higher weight.

Tina had quit smoking and trained to run the Bay to Breakers race in San Francisco, transforming herself from a 200-pound out-of-shape smoker to a 190-pound fit non-smoker. She exemplifies the HAES conviction that hassling fat people about weight loss only demoralizes them and drives them from care and that improved health is a reasonable goal for anyone even without weight loss (Aphramor, 2005; Bacon, Stern, Van Loan, & Keim, 2005; Ernsberger & Koletsky, 1999). Indeed, research suggests that while making fat people thin is not something we know how to achieve broadly or sustain over time, it does seem that even moderate exercise for people of any size has health benefits (Campos, Saguy, Ernsberger, Oliver, & Gaesser, 2006a, 2006b). The HAES philosophy presents a way for doctors to see fat people as possibly needing to improve their health but without prejudging them, and to still think of risk factors while also practicing nondiscrimination.

CONCLUSION: BEYOND THE POSSESSION METAPHOR FOR BOTH RIGHTS AND HEALTH

I have argued that we should take up the question of rights and health not only as a problem of distributive justice but also as a question of producing persons and identities. Such a turn only makes sense if we think of health not only as an objective state one can simply stand in a possessed or dispossessed state in relation to but as a construct that makes up the persons it describes. Admittedly, some claims analyzed here are put simply in terms of entitlement to possess greater access to health care, like in Tina's public health work. This approach remains almost entirely within the pre-existing health paradigm and uses a possession model of rights. Perhaps, the relatively mobilized nature of this group explains why they put health claims in terms of rights when other researchers have found more reluctance to do so. But advocates also supply a more nuanced and radical argument that antidiscrimination norms entitle them to resist the ways that ideas about their ill health construct them as deviant, overdetermine their identity, and render their lives less valuable than thin people's lives. These are not arguments in favor of gaining possession of something, but rather re-describe personhood.

Alice mustered explicitly legal language ("criminal" surgeries, "discrimination" through labeling) to resist fat people's production as deviant and sick. Like Janice's plea for recognition as "not a horrible drain on society," Alice invokes rights to healthy identities as a bid for a broader new identity for fat people. (These are not rights that anyone currently actually possesses, of course, but it is crucial that she selects rights language to sound as forceful as possible.) These invocations are mostly put in negative terms – "We are not all these awful things you say" – but in their strongest versions, they de-essentialize fat and make it impossible for it to have any one meaning (controlled in this case by health professionals). Alice and Janice are doing the opposite of taking on a prefigured account of their identities as rights claimants; they are emptying out the identity of "fat" of its strongest meaning, that of ill health. Tina enacted it in her own life, going from being a sedentary smoker to a fit runner but with the same basic shape and size. They are trying to make it impossible to predict just from looking at her whether a fat person one meets (say, in an exam room) is healthy or unhealthy. Alice admittedly tries to fill in fat identity with some virtuous content, but their basic move is to push a negative account of fatness – what it is not – rather than a positive account of what it is.[8]

But what about the fact that most of these women did not talk in terms of rights at all? I argued that we should still take note of the ways that contesting the doctor's account of their ill health gave the women I spoke with many of the same tools they would also need to make rights claims. The advocates needed to de-naturalize their pathology and come to see it as imposed by narrow-minded and often quite rude people in positions of power. Once people see their condition as unjustly imposed rather than simply bad luck or their own fault, they can feel entitled to something better. Because fat identity is currently overwhelmed by the account of it as unhealthy, it makes sense that this process would begin in a health context without much invocation of legal redress yet. Later on in the interviews, everyone agreed when asked that fat people should be protected by antidiscrimination laws, and their earlier arguments against the health critique were a critical underpinning to the subsequent affirmation of nondiscrimination rights.

I also suggested that it may be possible to avoid the problem of prefigured and narrow discourses based on rights if activists themselves shape the terms of their identity in one context (here, health care) and shift those accounts over to their understandings of legal rights. It may be quite fruitful that rights language is taking a second seat to contestations over medical judgment here because the resistance developed in the health context can pollinate new accounts of identities for antidiscrimination law, which would probably be vaguely written and open to interpretation by vigorous entrepreneurs of meaning. If and when formal legal rights become reality, the understanding of what to expect from them built up in these interactions will be ready and waiting. We do not yet know what that might look like, but to even begin to understand it as it unfolds we must pay as much attention to debates over health as we do to debates over workplace discrimination. This alternative context of the doctor's office, I noted, can also help us see how rights discourses can get started without any standard nondiscrimination rights in place. Struggles there may unsettle deference to medical authority, as happened with feminist activism around childbirth. Insisting that fat is not a proxy for health could supply the shift in self-perceptions and the discursive shifts in medical world that Engel and Munger describe in the post-ADA workplace context, as well as the possibility for formal invocation and changes in institutional practice (like not weighing people as part of a routine exam and no longer advising dieting, just as obstetricians no longer shave women in labor or whisk infants off to nurseries as standard practice).

Because obesity is now so firmly considered a health matter and not a matter for rights, any movement toward antidiscrimination on the basis of weight in health care would likely transform notions of health even more than notions of rights. At the very least, a mutual transformation would be necessary. The possibilities are quite intriguing. These fat acceptance advocates insist that health is something that people experience in both individuality and solidarity, that it is something that is done to them as well as something that may be achieved, that it is constituted by power relations, and that it exists within institutions, practices, expectations, embodied sensations, and in political rhetoric. Putting antidiscrimination rights into health can usefully collapse the question of health as an individual right and as a group right. Groups, particularly socially marginal ones, experience political and personal relationships to health and health institutions as group-based, yet maintain the sense that health is located in individual bodies as well as in communities. Their perspective may be politically rich as we move into considering what the right to health care will look like – or what we would want it to look like – under a new national plan. We will not just tackle distributive questions, but we will also need to understand how health care interactions make citizens, how citizens frame complaints about injustice arising from those interactions, and how those mobilizations contribute to rights-bearing identities.

NOTES

1. I deliberately use the term "fat" rather than overweight or obese, following my interviewees. Fat acceptance advocates want to make fat into an ordinary word like short or tall and resist the medicalizing and stigmatizing effects of terms like obesity. Some will also argue that there is no right to anything on the basis of weight since weight is a voluntary status. I do not grant that point here – and analyze that debate extensively elsewhere (Kirkland, 2008a) – but instead hope that the liminal and contested status of body weight as a protected trait will help illuminate taken-for-granted discourses about who deserves what and why.

2. Even if we could apply antidiscrimination norms fully to health settings, a robust tradition of law and society scholarship on the constitutive, practical, and political effects of rights claiming may give us pause about the desirability of doing so. There could be political backlash, the rights offered could be meager and not enforced, they could promote a victimized identity for citizens, which is enervating or alienating, or they could operate to discipline and monitor the poor. This chapter cannot reach these compelling reasons to pause over a proposal for a new kind of law, but rather focuses on the ways that doctor–patient interactions – even with no law at all – can still be a site for contestations that are necessary for rights development in other areas. The closest civil rights law comes now to imposing an antidiscrimination principle on health care provision is through Title VI of the 1964 Civil Rights Act, which prohibits any institution receiving federal funds from discriminating on the basis of race, color, or national origin. (Title VII's broader employment discrimination prohibition applies to race, color, national origin, religion, and sex.) Discrimination here means things like segregating patients by race and does not seem to have legal implications for race-specific pharmaceutical dispensing, for example. The funding link covers nearly all health care providers such as clinics, nursing homes, drug treatment centers, and hospitals.

3. I discuss implications of the sample extensively in "Think of the hippopotamus: Rights consciousness in the fat acceptance movement (Kirkland, 2008b)," hence the very brief account here.

4. Kaiser Permanente has recently started an online program to combat weight bias in its health care providers (Rabin, 2008). Researchers at Yale's Rudd Center for

Food Policy and Obesity developed the tool, available at http://www.yaleruddcenter. org/what/bias/toolkit/index.html.

5. Of course, this view is a thoroughly political one, and many conservatives argue that in fact American life is awash with restrictive rights and frivolous lawsuits, particularly in health care and personal injury (Epstein, 1997; Goodman, 2005; Haltom & McCann, 2004). We have, for example, rights not to be treated with negligence, rights to care in any emergency room regardless of ability to pay, rights to privacy of our health care information, rights to a certain level of adequacy in nursing home care, the right to expect regular and respectful care from a doctor with whom we have an established relationship, and the right not to be discriminated against on the basis of race, color, or national origin. Some of these are positive rights, even. Strong libertarian views notwithstanding, however, it is more than reasonable to characterize the American health care system as one that is notable for the absence of a sense of health care as a public right, particularly as compared to the Canadian or western European systems (Morone, 2000; Redden, 2002).

6. American Medical Association, http://www.ama-assn.org/ama/pub/physician-resources/medical-ethics/code-medical-ethics/opinion1001.shtml

7. All names are pseudonyms, some chosen by the interviewees themselves and others made up by me.

8. Some of the HAES rhetoric comes close to arguing that fat people who are virtuous eaters and exercisers but remain fat should not be discriminated against, but then what about those who fail to live up to that regime? As Kathleen LeBesco (2004) has pointed out, defending the "innocent" fat person may end up re-inscribing healthism. Like Merry's battered wife, one could gain control over one aspect of one's status (vulnerability to private violence) but only by giving up other aspects of it (being willing to sever connections with one's batterer). It will be critical to see if fat identity can maintain this contingent and emptied-out quality, or if the main route of defense will be to say that fat people do in fact exercise and eat lots of healthy foods.

ACKNOWLEDGMENTS

This work is only possible because many people were willing to take the time to be interviewed, and I thank each of them for their time and willingness to open up about sometimes painful experiences. I gratefully acknowledge the funding for this project from the University of Michigan Institute for Research on Women and Gender (IRWG). Miriam Ticktin and an anonymous reviewer for *Studies in Law Politics and Society* made excellent comments on previous drafts that greatly improved the final version. My graduate research assistant, Carla Pfeffer, did extensive interviewing as well as transcribing and site observation. I am grateful for those many hours as well as for her thoughtful feedback on the initial interview protocol and on previous drafts of this paper. Kathy Wood also provided excellent transcription services.

REFERENCES

Aphramor, L. (2005). Is a weight-centred health framework salutogenic? Some thoughts on unhinging certain dietary ideologies. *Social Theory & Health, 3*(4), 315–340.

Armstrong, D. (2002). *A new history of identity: A sociology of medical knowledge.* New York: Palgrave.

Bacon, L., Stern, J. S., Van Loan, M. D., & Keim, N. L. (2005). Size acceptance and intuitive eating improve health for obese, female chronic dieters. *Journal of the American Dietetic Association, 105*(6), 929–936.

Brody, H., & Hunt, L. M. (2006). Bidil: Assessing a race-based pharmaceutical. *Annals of Family Medicine, 4*(6), 482–483.

Brown, W. (1995). *States of injury: Power and freedom in late modernity.* Princeton, NJ: Princeton University Press.

Brownell, K. D., Puhl, R. M., Schwartz, M. B., & Rudd, L. (Eds). (2005). *Weight bias: Nature, consequences, and remedies.* New York: Guilford Press.

Bumiller, K. (1988). *The civil rights society: The social construction of victims.* Baltimore: Johns Hopkins University Press.

Campos, P., Saguy, A., Ernsberger, P., Oliver, E., & Gaesser, G. (2006a). Response: Lifestyle not weight should be the primary target. *International Journal of Epidemiology, 35*(1), 81–82.

Campos, P., Saguy, A., Ernsberger, P., Oliver, E., & Gaesser, G. (2006b). The epidemiology of overweight and obesity: Public health crisis or moral panic? *International Journal of Epidemiology, 35*(1), 55–60.

Conrad, P. (1992). Medicalization and social control. *Annual Review of Sociology, 18,* 209–232.

Conrad, P. (2007). *The medicalization of society: On the transformation of human conditions into treatable disorders.* Baltimore, MD: Johns Hopkins University Press.

Crawford, R. (1980). Healthism and the medicalization of everyday life. *International Journal of Health Services, 10*(3), 365–388.

Crawford, R. (2006). Health as a meaningful social practice. *Health, 10*(4), 401–420.

Crenshaw, K. W. (1988). Race, reform, and retrenchment: Transformation and legitimation in antidiscrimination law. *Harvard Law Review, 101*(7), 1331–1387.

Daniels, N. (1985). *Just health care.* New York: Cambridge University Press.

Engel, D. M. (1991). The oven bird's song: Insiders, outsiders, and personal injury in an American community. *Law and Society Review, 18*(55), 1–82.

Engel, D. M., & Munger, F. W. (2003). *Rights of inclusion: Law and identity in the life stories of Americans with disabilities.* Chicago: University of Chicago Press.

Epstein, R. A. (1997). *Mortal peril: Our inalienable right to health care?* Reading, MA: Addison-Wesley Pub. Co.

Ernsberger, P., & Koletsky, R. J. (1999). Biomedical rationale for a wellness approach to obesity: An alternative to a focus on weight loss. *Journal of Social Issues, 55*(2), 221–259.

Fabricatore, A. N., Wadden, T. A., & Foster, G. D. (2005). Bias in health care settings. In: K. D. Brownell, R. M. Puhl, M. B. Schwartz & L. Rudd (Eds), *Weight bias: Nature, consequences, and remedies* (pp. 29–41). New York: The Guilford Press.

Felstiner, W., Abel, R., & Sarat, A. (1980). The emergence and transformation of disputes: Naming, blaming, and claiming. *Law & Society Review, 15*, 631–654.

Gilliom, J. (2001). *Overseers of the poor: Surveillance, resistance, and the limits of privacy.* Chicago: University of Chicago Press.

Gimlin, D. L. (2001). *Body work: Beauty and self-image in American culture.* Berkeley: University of California Press.

Goodman, T. (2005). Is there a right to health? *Journal of Medicine and Philosophy, 30*(6), 643–662.

Halley, J. (2000). 'Like-race' arguments. In: J. Butler, J. Gillory & K. Thomas (Eds), *What's left of theory: New work on the politics of literary theory* (pp. 40–74). New York: Routledge.

Haltom, W., & McCann, M. (2004). *Distorting the law: Politics, media, and the litigation crisis.* Chicago: University of Chicago Press.

Hull, K. (2006). *Same-sex marriage: The cultural politics of love and law.* Cambridge, UK, New York: Cambridge University Press.

Jenness, V. (1999). Managing differences and making legislation: Social movements and the racialization, sexualization, and gendering of federal hate crime law in the U S, 1985–1998. *Social Problems, 46*(4), 548–571.

Johnson, H. M. (2003). Unspeakable conversations, or how I spent one day as a token cripple at Princeton University. *International Journal of Humanities and Peace, 19*(1), 90–96.

Kirkland, A. (2006). What's at stake in fatness as disability? *Disability Studies Quarterly, 26*, http://www.dsq-sds.org/2006_winter_toc.html

Kirkland, A. (2008a). *Fat rights: Dilemmas of difference and personhood.* New York: New York University Press.

Kirkland, A. (2008b). Think of the hippopotamus: Rights consciousness in the fat acceptance movement. *Law & Society Review, 42*(2), 397–431.

LeBesco, K. (2004). *Revolting bodies?: The struggle to redefine fat identity.* Amherst, MA: University of Massachusetts Press.

Levitsky, S. R. (2008). What rights? The construction of political claims to American health care entitlements. *Law & Society Review, 42*(3), 551–590.

McCann, M. (1994). *Rights at work: Pay equity reform and the politics of legal mobilization.* Chicago, IL: University of Chicago Press.

Merry, S. E. (2003). Rights talk and the experience of law: Implementing women's human rights to protection from violence. *Human Rights Quarterly, 25*(2), 343–381.

Metzl, J. M. (2003). Selling sanity through gender: The psychodynamics of psychotropic advertising. *Journal of Medical Humanities, 24*(1–2), 79–103.

Metzl, J. M., & Poirier, S. (Eds). (2005). *Difference and identity: A special issue of literature and medicine.* Baltimore: Johns Hopkins University Press.

Morone, J. (2000). Citizens or shoppers? Solidarity under siege. *Journal of Health Politics, Policy and Law, 25*(5), 959–968.

Nielsen, L. B., & Nelson, R. L. (2005). Scaling the pyramid: A sociolegal model of employment discrimination litigation. In: L. B. Nielsen & R. L. Nelson (Eds), *Handbook of employment discrimination research: Rights and realities* (pp. 3–34). Dorecht, The Netherlands: Springer.

Orbach, S. (2006). Commentary: There is a public health crisis – it's not fat on the body but fat in the mind and the fat of profits. *International Journal of Epidemiology*, *35*(1), 67–69.

Rabin, R. C. (2008). Weighty assumptions: Doctors too quick to blame obese patients' ills on fat, studies suggest. *The Washington Post* (January 29), HE01.

Redden, C. J. (2002). Health care as citizenship development: Examining social rights and entitlement. *Canadian Journal of Political Science*, *35*(1), 103–125.

Roberts, D. E. (1999). *Killing the black body: Race, reproduction, and the meaning of liberty*. New York: Vintage.

Roberts, D. E. (2002). *Shattered bonds: The color of child welfare*. New York: Basic Civitas Books.

Roberts, D. E. (2006). Legal constraints on the use of race in biomedical research: Toward a social justice framework. *The Journal of Law, Medicine & Ethics*, *34*(3), 526–534.

Rose, N. (2001). The politics of life itself. *Theory, Culture & Society*, *18*(6), 1–30.

Rothstein, W. G. (2003). *Public health and the risk factor: A history of an uneven medical revolution*. Rochester, NY: University of Rochester Press.

Saguy, A. C., & Riley, K. W. (2005). Weighing both sides: Morality, mortality, and framing contests over obesity. *Journal of Heath Politics, Policy and Law*, *30*(5), 869–921.

Siegel, R. (1997). Why equal protection no longer protects: The evolving forms of status-enforcing state action. *Stanford Law Review*, *49*(5), 1111–1148.

Stearns, P. N. (1997). *Fat history: Bodies and beauty in the modern west*. New York: New York University Press.

Ticktin, M. (2006). Where ethics and politics meet: The violence of humanitarianism in France. *American Ethnologist*, *33*(1), 33–49.

Tushnet, M. (1984). An essay on rights. *Texas Law Review*, *62*(8), 1363–1403.

Williams, P. J. (1991). *The alchemy of race and rights*. Cambridge, MA: Harvard University Press.

Wong, S. I. (2002). At home with Down syndrome and gender. *Hypatia*, *17*(3), 89–117.

STATUTES CITED

Age Discrimination in Employment Act of 1967 (ADEA), 29 U.S.C. § 621.

Americans with Disabilities Act of 1990 (ADA), 42 U.S.C. §§ 12101-12213.

Civil Rights Act of 1964, 42 U.S.C. § 2000e.

Compliance Guidelines to Prohibit Weight and Height Discrimination, San Francisco Administrative Code Chapters 12A, 12B and 12C.

District of Columbia Human Rights Act, D. C. Code § 2-1401.01 (2007).

Elliot-Larsen Civil Rights Act, Michigan Compiled Laws § 37.2202 (2007).

Emergency Medical Treatment and Active Labor Act (EMTALA), 42 U.S.C. § 1395dd.

Health Insurance Portability and Accountability Act (HIPAA), 42 U.S.C. § 1320d.

Madison Equal Opportunities Ordinance, § 39.03 (2007).

Santa Cruz Municipal Code, § 9.83.010 (2007).

GENOCIDAL RIGHTS

Ruth A. Miller

INTRODUCTION

This is an essay that will be misinterpreted. Before I even mention genocidal rights, I want to make clear what my argument is not. First, my argument is not that genocide has not happened or does not continue to happen. Second, I will not suggest that genocide is not a serious crime. Finally, I will not try to develop a theory of victimhood – to challenge the centrality of the victim in discussions of genocide. Rather, my interest here will be the uncomfortably intimate relationship between genocidal violence on the one hand and the elaboration of civil, sovereign, and human rights on the other.

Situating genocide within a history of rights and rights rhetoric is certainly nothing new. Indeed, defining genocide as an act of violence inextricably bound up in national, international, and universal rights granting has become commonplace in twentieth and twenty-first century political theory (Arendt, 1968, 1976, p. 279; Foucault, 1976, 2003, pp. 256, 260; Agamben, 1995, 1998, pp. 128–129). When I talk in this essay about what I will be calling the "right to commit genocide," I engage with a tradition of legal and political argument that is at least a half century old.

At the same time, I will try to push this argument a bit further than it has gone before – or at least draw conclusions from it that may at first glance seem counterintuitive. First of all, whereas a number of scholars have drawn attention to the apparently paradoxical relationship between rights-based political structures and genocidal violence, I will emphasize the *foundational*

Revisiting Rights
Studies in Law, Politics, and Society, Volume 48, 147–175
Copyright © 2009 by Emerald Group Publishing Limited
All rights of reproduction in any form reserved
ISSN: 1059-4337/doi:10.1108/S1059-4337(2009)0000048009

nature of this relationship. I will suggest, in other words, that rights are inherently genocidal and that the fundamental right that precedes and underlies all others is the civil, sovereign, and human right to commit genocide.

Second and related, whereas most theorists see the tension, competition, or balance among civil, sovereign, and human rights to be both the reason for genocide and a source of hope for preventing its occurrence, I will argue that there is in fact no tension or difference among the three and that rights assume their genocidal character precisely because these divisions are false ones. My position will thus be quite different from that taken by the legal scholars during and after the Nuremburg trials who argued that sovereign rights erode civil rights in the absence of international structures to prevent such occurrences and that genocide in turn happens (Lemkin, 1947a, pp. 145–146). It will likewise be different from the position taken by those who argue that the extension of human rights can balance or curtail the sovereign and civil rights that, left alone, might lead to genocidal violence (*Ibid.*). Rather, I try to argue that all of these rights are identical and that it is as a result of this *absence* of difference that acts of genocide continue to "mock" rights-based preventative structures.

Most critiques of the relationship between rights and genocide, that is, either fault the ineffective practical implementation of what is perceived to be a generally sound theory of rights as remedies or attempt to tweak the theory in such a way that it no longer leads to genocidal violence – condemning, for example, the historical linkage between state-based civil rights and human rights (Arendt, 1968, 1976, pp. 175–177) or suggesting that human rights advocates should focus on individual "humans" rather than on humanitarian "groups" (Yovel, 2007, p. 17). My position, on the contrary, is that both the theory and the practice of rights granting are inherently genocidal and that every system of rights is preceded by a foundational act of rights-based genocidal violence.

I emphasize that my purpose in making this case is not to argue that genocide is unavoidable. Rather, I examine the foundations upon which systems of rights have been built. If there is an implication to my argument, therefore, it is neither that genocide is inevitable, nor that states by their nature will commit genocide. Instead, it is that to the extent that we continue to speak a language of rights, to the extent that we grant individuals, peoples, and populations rights, and to the extent we understand genocidal violence only in terms of rights, genocide will happen with more frequency and with greater efficacy as time passes. That the twentieth century has been called both the "Age of Rights" (Kennedy, 2004, p. 278) and the "Century of Genocide" (Melson, 1996, p. 157) is not a coincidence. The two, I suggest, are in fact the same thing.

THE RIGHT TO COMMIT GENOCIDE: BLOOD, RACE, AND TIME

With that in mind, I start with an apparent irrelevancy to this argument – the "scrap of paper," the neglected treaty, that brought England and the British Empire into the First World War. Nicoletta F. Gullace has traced the rhetorical journey taken by this scrap of paper over the course of the war, and the way in which law gradually became embedded in the bodies of (in particular, women) citizens in England at that time. "In the eyes of the Oxford faculty of Modern History," she notes,

> Britain was at war because "we are a people in whose blood the cause of law is the vital element....[T]he war in which England is now engaged with Germany is fundamentally a war between two different principles...The one regards international covenants to which it has pledged its own word as 'scraps of paper'...the other regards the maintenance of such covenants as a grave inevitable obligation". (Gullace, 1997, p. 719)

Gullace situates this rhetoric within the usual story of nineteenth and twentieth century international law (pp. 742–743). There was a competition, so the story goes, between a state-based sovereign right linked to "legalism" that was privileged by German jurists and an international humanitarian right linked to the "spirit of the law" that was privileged by English jurists. In the years following the Second World War, the story concludes, this competition ended with the apparent triumph of human rights and the spirit of the law over sovereign rights and the privileging of legal texts (Kennedy, 2004, pp. 271–274).

I return to the problematic aspects of this narrative later on in this essay. For now, I discuss in more detail the Oxford History faculty's assumption that the cause of law can be the vital element in any people's blood. This is, first of all, a familiarly racist assumption – an assumption that underlies most post-eighteenth century interpretations of rights, rights granting, and citizenship. Hannah Arendt (1968, 1976, p. 176), for example, analyzes it in her discussion of Edmund Burke, when she argues that "the concept of inheritance, applied to the very nature of liberty, has been the ideological basis from which English nationalism received its...touch of race-feeling ever since the French Revolution." Giorgio Agamben likewise invokes it when he states that the slippage between *homme* and *citoyen* in various eighteenth century declarations of rights lent "Burke's *boutade* according to which he preferred his 'Rights of an Englishman' to the inalienable rights of man...an unsuspected profundity" (Agamben, 1995, 1998, p. 127). It is an assumption that suggests, as Arendt and Agamben make clear, the inevitably political nature of human identity – an assumption that insists upon linking biological existence to political existence, one of many racist and potentially genocidal manifestations of modern political systems.

What I do in this essay, however, is consider an alternative implication of the blood/law relationship. Again, the racist nature of post-eighteenth century politics has been effectively analyzed by a number of scholars of rights and genocide. My purpose here, therefore, is less to add to their existing work than it is to highlight what is, I think, an overlooked aspect of this rhetorical connection between blood and law. What makes rights-granting genocidal, I suggest, is not necessarily, or not only, the racism inherent in modern political thought – although this racism is obviously key to the violence that derives from it. Rather, it is the *temporal* requirements of the blood/law relationship. To be clear, the Oxford faculty of Modern History do not state that *law* is the vital element in English blood. It is the *cause of law* that is the vital element. The cause of law (or rule of law) is not the same thing as law. It is an idea, devoid of content, that is generally assumed – especially in liberal theory – to precede or make possible a *future* articulation of law and legal systems.[1]

By arguing that the cause of law courses through the blood of the people, the Oxford faculty of Modern History are, of course, making obvious their deeply held race-feeling. But more than that – and I think more important – they are making a statement about the temporal relationship between blood, race, or nation[2] on the one hand and law, state, or rights on the other. They are arguing that blood, race, and nation *precede* law, state, and rights and that this is the case because the potential for law, state, and rights – the cause of law – is squarely situated in racial or national blood. It is, I think, confusion about this *temporal* formulation that has produced the apparent inconsistencies in rights rhetoric and that has obscured the genocidal nature of rights systems and rights granting.

At the same time, these temporal requirements have not gone completely unnoticed. In *Society Must be Defended*, for example, in the pages leading up to his influential discussion of racism and the biopolitical sovereign right to make live and let die, Michel Foucault (1976, 2003) emphasizes two key temporal shifts that occur in modern rights rhetoric and state formation. Invoking the political theory of Sieyès, Foucault argues, first of all, that in a post-eighteenth century world, "a contract, a law, or a consensus can never really create a nation" (p. 220). Sovereign power, he continues, is "no longer articulated in the name of a past right that was established by either a consensus, a victory, or an invasion," but rather must be articulated

> in terms of a potentiality, a future, a future that is immediate, which is already present because it concerns a certain function of Statist universality that is already fulfilled by "a" nation within the social body, and which is therefore demanding that its status as a single nation must be effectively recognized, and recognized in the juridical form of the state. (p. 222)

What therefore "defines a nation," in these post-eighteenth century analyses, "is not its archaism, its ancestral nature, or its relationship with the past; it is its relationship with something else, with the state" (p. 223). As a result, he argues, "the nation is not essentially specified by its relations with other nations. What characterizes 'the' nation is not a horizontal relationship with other groups" (*Ibid.*). Instead, what characterizes "the nation is…a vertical relationship between a body of individuals who are capable of constituting a State, and the actual existence of the State itself. It is in terms of this vertical nation/State axis, or this Statist potentiality/Statist realization axis, that the nation is to be characterized and situated" (*Ibid.*).

In these passages of *Society Must be Defended*, Foucault is in no way making a normative claim. He is not saying that this temporal relationship between the nation and the juridical form of the state – between statist potential and statist realization – is good or desirable. Indeed, both his reading of Sieyès and his discussion of eighteenth and nineteenth century French race-feeling can easily be read as ironic. At the same time, however, I think his descriptive claim about the temporal complexity of states, nations, and social contracts – about precisely the biopolitical and genocidal[3] potential of these modern nation/states – is key to understanding the genocidal nature of rights.

According to Foucault's analysis, legal, political, and social contracts are not the pre-conditions for national existence. They represent instead the juridical *potential* of the nation, the imminent existence of a *future* state. Systems of rights are thus not only not situated in the past, they are not even situated in the present. Rights-based social contracts and the juridical form of the state that they define exist *only* in the future, even if the universality of the state demands that this future be always immediate. As a result, it is not in relation to other nations that national existence becomes meaningful. Rather, it is in relation to the state – the state whose temporal potential is always yet to be realized, and whose spatial potential is necessarily universal. It is, therefore, the relationship among the individual, the body of individuals (the nation), and the potential juridical form of a (universal) state that is central to modern politics.

This articulation of biopolitics, in other words, does not in any way require the one to one correspondence between human life and political life, between blood and law, which we see in many later interpretations of it. It does not, for example, require that declarations of rights turn "birth" into the moment at which "bare natural life" becomes "the immediate bearer of sovereignty" – it does not require that "rights [be] attributed to man...solely to the extent that man is the immediately vanishing ground...of the citizen" (Agamben, 1995, 1998, p. 128). Instead, it suggests that both sovereign and individual rights exist in the future and that they are predicated upon the potential for a "statist universality," which is in turn a juridical manifestation of a single nation. Likewise, this reading of biopolitics suggests that the key political relationships are vertical rather than horizontal – involve not nations among nations, individuals among individuals, or states among states, but rather the displacement of individuals onto nations onto states and, above all, onto universal systems.

The key to understand the biopolitical nature of rights granting, therefore, is not that blood and law are the same thing, not that "men" become "citizens" and thus cease to be "men" at the moment of birth, nor even that national borders and bodily borders collapse into one another as human rights are linked to sovereign rights. Rather it is that blood and the *rule* or law or the *cause* of law, vertically, are one and the same thing. It is that being both a "man" and a "citizen" is something that can occur only in the future. And finally, it is that bodily borders become irrelevant, collapse into nothing, in the presence of universal systems that have no borders at all.

I pause here to note that all of this may seem like something of a detour given that my particular interest is genocide and its relationship to rights granting. I suggest, however, that approaching nations, states, and rights in this way is the only means by which we can understand the genocidal violence that has occurred with rapidly increasing frequency over the past half century. If rights granting can only happen once political identity is situated in the future, if it assumes a potentially universal state/system absent any boundaries, then its relationship to genocide is far more intimate than it might initially appear. Indeed, we do not seem to be talking here about a situation in which rights are linked to citizenship, and in which, in certain dysfunctional situations, some groups are deprived of their citizenship and in turn their rights. Rather, blood and nation, tied to rights, *precede* the state. Rights thus cannot exist without *first* declaring the irrelevancy of those outside of the nation – without engaging in an effectively genocidal relationship with those non-people who never *had* and therefore never *will have* rights.

Although citizenship rights are granted at the moment of birth, therefore – for all intents and purposes the past – these citizens are politically meaningful only as a "body of individuals" capable of "constituting the state" in the future. Rights never exist in the present except to the extent that they are a manifestation of a potentially universal system. What we see in the nineteenth and early twentieth centuries is thus arguably less a situation in which universal rights granting is, unfortunately, confined to sovereign nation-states – human rights tied to citizenship rights because of various theoretical paradoxes. Rather, what we see is a quite effective process of rights-granting, a process that is just as universal as every state (potentially) is. What we see in turn after the Second World War is likewise not a process by which the excessive national-sovereign right to dispose of any and all citizens is curtailed by international legislation protecting these citizens as humans. There is no mid-twentieth century about-face. Rather, what has occurred since the Second World War is simply a continuation of the genocidal rights granting that brought about colonial and Nazi policy in the first place – the universality of a system becoming more and more real as it realizes its potential.

Indeed, what I argue in the next section is that the usual narrative of international law and human rights – the narrative of competitions and tensions among human rights, sovereign rights, and citizenship rights – is a problematic one, and one worth challenging. In fact, if we understand rights granting in the way that I have described it earlier, the apparent competitions and tensions, the apparent paradoxes, dissolve. Human rights, sovereign rights, and civil rights become the same thing and the model that pits each against the others, carving out public and private space, or spaces of emancipation and spaces of oppression, becomes, I suggest, a flawed one.

CIVIL, SOVEREIGN, AND HUMAN RIGHTS

The question of sovereign rights is one that appears in many discussions of genocide, particularly to the extent that the post-war Genocide Convention seemed to curtail a nation-state's domestic jurisdiction and to undermine national constitutions in favor of international law. This apparent assault on sovereign rights was a matter of some concern, for example, to the American Bar Association, which fought against US ratification of the Convention until 1976 (Leblanc, 1984, p. 374). What I argue over the following pages, however, is that although sovereign rights, civil rights, and human rights appear to clash with (or "balance") one another, although the narratives surrounding the extension of human rights systems reinforce the notion that sovereign power must be controlled and civil rights expanded into something more universal, in fact these rights are in many ways the same thing – all three resting on the same fundamental right (of the sovereign, the citizen, and the human) to commit genocide.

To make this case, I am going to turn first to the discussion of sovereign rights that we see in the work of Carl Schmitt and second to the discussion of human rights that we see in the work of Arendt. I am drawing on Schmitt and Arendt in this chapter less because their work is bound up in the genocidal violence of the Second World War, and more because each has been invoked repeatedly as the defender of, in Schmitt's case, sovereign rights, and in Arendt's case, human rights. The work of each is usually read as diametrically opposed to the work of the other – and thus together they represent the apparently unbridgeable historical and theoretical gulfs that divide sovereign, civil, and human rights. Again, however, what I argue in this section is that their work is not as dichotomous as it might seem – that Schmitt, in particular, is far more indebted to the liberalism he criticizes than he might initially appear to be.

Be that as it may, Schmitt is not known as a political theorist particularly interested in rights – except to the extent, again, that he critiques their importance to liberal ideology. Nonetheless, in *Political Theology, The Concept of the Political*, and *Legality and Legitimacy*, he outlines both explicitly and implicitly a theory of what are essentially sovereign rights in their relation to other rights. Like liberal theorists, Schmitt sees a tension between the rights of the human or the citizen and the rights of the sovereign, and like liberal theorists, he situates this tension in the relationship between political identity and the right to exist.

In the opening sentence of *Political Theology*, for example, he states that a sovereign is "he who decides on the exception" (Schmitt, 1922, 1985, p. 5). A few pages later he elaborates on this single defining characteristic of sovereignty, arguing furthermore that "if individual states[4]...no longer have the power to declare the exception...then they no longer enjoy the status of states" (p. 11). Deciding on the exception,[5] in other words, is more than just a sovereign prerogative in Schmitt's analysis. It is indicative of whether or not sovereignty and a state exist at all. It is thus a sovereign *right* in every sense of the term: not just something that a sovereign can do, but more than that – constituting the very identity and being of the sovereign. And it is for this reason, I think, that Schmitt articulates this notion in an explicit vocabulary of rights, stating, for instance, that "the state suspends law in the exception on the basis of its right of self-preservation, as one would say" (p. 12).

There are a number of implications that arise from this relationship between deciding on the exception and the sovereign's right to exist, but I want to focus on only two of them right now. The first concerns the *type* of sovereign existence that is assumed by Schmitt's theory of exceptionalism. As the title of the book suggests, this is a sovereignty that is above all "miraculous" – miraculous in the sense both that sovereign rights are irrelevant to "a jurisprudence concerned with ordering day-to-day questions" and that they require "the suspension of the entire existing order" (p. 12). More specifically, sovereign rights are miraculous just as the divine right to intervene in natural systems is miraculous (Marramao, 2000, p. 1571). This is a sovereignty that is the apparent opposite of (rational) liberalism, which rejects "not only the transgression of the laws of nature through an exception brought about by direct intervention...but also the sovereign's direct intervention in a valid legal order" (Schmitt, 1922, 1985, pp. 36–37).

Sovereign existence, in other words, the sovereign right to self-preservation, is predicated upon a) deciding on the exception and b) miraculously suspending the existing order when this exception occurs. The state of exception thus does not just prove the existence of – it also *constitutes*, as a right – both sovereignty and the rule of law. Moreover, like the right theorized by Sieyès and described by Foucault as the basis of biopolitics, this is not a right situated in the past, relevant by virtue of conquest, contract, or consensus. Rather, it is a right predicated upon the ever present *potential* for a state of exception, for a suspension of a jurisprudence of the "day-to-day" and for the *imminent* constitution of sovereign existence. It is a right that exists only in the future, a right that assumes the potential universality of a state system.

This is also a sovereign right that has been described – by Schmitt himself, as well as by commentators – as completely antithetical to civil rights or human rights. Schmitt, for example, in his critique of the notion of the "sovereignty of law" argues that in such a situation, the state "does nothing but ascertain the legal value of interests as it springs from the people's feeling a sense of right," which results in "a limitation on law, in contrast with interest or welfare" (p. 23). He states more explicitly in *The Concept of the Political* (Schmitt, 1932, 1996) that "for the purpose of protecting individual freedom and private property, liberalism provides a series of methods for hindering and controlling the state's and government's power"

(p. 57). With regard to the individual right to life or existence in particular, he argues that,

in case of need, the political entity must demand the sacrifice of life. Such a demand is in no way justifiable by the individualism of liberal thought. No consistent individualism can entrust to someone other than to the individual himself the right to dispose of the physical life of the individual. (Schmitt 1932, 1996, p. 71)

Indeed, according to Schmitt, any attempts to "subjugat[e] state and politics…into an individualistic domain of private law and morality…deprive state and politics of their specific meaning" (p. 72). Quite basically, in other words, civil rights – especially to the extent that they are articulated in the idea of a "sovereignty of law" – undermine the sovereign's own right to existence. State and sovereign have no political meaning in the presence of liberal individualism – in the face of non-sovereign rights. There is no sovereign decision, no potential exception, and thus sovereignty itself disappears.

This contrast between civil and sovereign rights, though, is not as stark as it might at first appear – indeed sovereign rights, civil rights, and human rights collapse into one another in this analysis even as they are articulated. To begin with, I look in more detail at Schmitt's discussion of sovereignty in *The Concept of the Political* – a book, again, that is not usually seen as favorable to civil rights or certainly to human rights. In fact, however, I think one can argue that this book is as much a plea for each and every human being's right to a political existence as Arendt's *Origins of Totalitarianism* is. Indeed, just as eighteenth century liberal theorists and twenty-first century human rights advocates have all, in different ways, attempted to determine and then grant political status to human beings regardless of national borders, so too did Schmitt in *The Concept of the Political*. Schmitt, however, took this advocacy to its logical conclusion.

According to Schmitt, a human being becomes political – takes on a rights based political identity – only when an enemy has been identified who exists outside of the basic political grouping. Sieyès understood this political grouping as the nation – and, like Schmitt, identified those outside of it as political non-people, humans who had never possessed rights and therefore never could possess rights. Schmitt speaks primarily in terms of the nation as well, but he does not *necessarily* limit himself to this analytical category, and certainly does not situate it territorially within the borders of any one nation-state. Positing war as the most overt example of the political nature of this friend/enemy grouping, for instance, Schmitt argues that "only in real combat is revealed the most extreme consequence of the political grouping of friend and enemy. From this most extreme possibility human life derives its specifically political character" (Schmitt, 1932, 1996, pp. 34–35). But, again, this war is not a war of nation-states and their boundaries alone. It is a *genocidal* war. As Schmitt concludes, "he is an enemy...who no longer must be compelled to retreat into his border only" (p. 36).

The tension between civil rights or human rights on the one hand and sovereign rights on the other is in this way resolved in *The Concept of the Political*. A citizen's political identity is the same as the sovereign's political identity. What this means in turn is that the citizen's right to exist, the human being's political life, is as much founded on the right to commit genocide as the sovereign's right to exist is. I want to make clear, however, that my point in emphasizing this aspect of the friend/enemy distinction is not to suggest that this collapse of sovereign into civil into human rights is the result solely of defining and destroying an Other. Again, my argument about genocidal violence is emphatically *not* that in certain dysfunctional situations, groups are deprived of their citizenship, their political identity, and thus their right to existence. Rather, I am arguing that the right to commit genocide is foundational in any process of rights granting. Like the racism inherent in eighteenth century political theory, in other words, the defining of the Other – the enemy – though necessary, is not the key to the genocidal potential of the friend/enemy distinction. The key to its genocidal potential is instead the temporal assumptions about the right to exist that underlie it. Again, a human being's right to a political existence in this formulation is predicated upon a *potential* sovereign decision. Like sovereign rights, therefore, human rights in this analysis exist in the future – in the potential universality of the juridical decision.

Indeed, the necessarily universal nature of both these rights and their foundations is made clear in Schmitt's work. Like Sieyès who suggested the potential universality of the state and like Foucault who analyzed the implications of this universality, Schmitt too sees the friend/enemy distinction – and *therefore* the right of each and every human being to a political identity – as something that exists beyond the borders of any single territorial nation-state, as something that by definition must move beyond these borders. *The Concept of the Political* can thus, I think, be read as an argument quite explicitly in support of universal human rights. It simply interrogates the nature of these rights more insistently than many other texts do.

At the same time, if I have shown thus far that sovereign, civil, and human rights in the work of Carl Schmitt are the same thing – and all three situated in the fundamental right to commit genocide – I have really only done so within the internally consistent universe defined by Schmitt's own parameters. What I would like to do now, therefore, is to move on to an

alternative analysis of human rights and civil rights – and to demonstrate
that these, too, are embedded in the potential for genocidal violence, that
these too collapse into one another and then into sovereign rights. In
particular, I want to address the work of Hannah Arendt, both because her
writing is usually read as a defense of universal human rights against the
exclusionary power of the sovereign and because it is in apparent diametric
opposition to the work of Schmitt.

Most obviously, Arendt does not situate a human being's political identity
within the creation and elaboration of a friend/enemy diction. Rather,
political identity, according to Arendt, is a function of being "recognized"
(Arendt, 1968, 1976, p. 287), and "the fundamental deprivation of human
rights is manifested first and above all in the deprivation of a place in the
world which makes opinions significant and actions effective" (p. 296). What
I will try to show, however, is that although it appears quite distinct from
Schmitt's argument, and although its normative legacy is without question
vastly different, Arendt's analysis of human rights and rights-based systems is
not as far removed from the work of Schmitt as it might at first appear.

Following her initial articulation of the meaning of rights, for example,
Arendt moves on to her influential notion that the most basic human right is
the right to have rights, that "the abstract nakedness of being nothing
but human was [the] greatest danger" faced by those deprived of their rights
(p. 300). Indeed, she continues,

> the paradox involved in the loss of human rights is that such loss coincides with the
> instant when a person becomes a human being in general – without a profession, without
> a citizenship, without an opinion, without a deed by which to identify and specify
> himself – *and* different in general, representing nothing but his own absolutely unique
> individuality which, deprived of expression within and active upon a common world,
> loses all significance. (p. 302)

Like Agamben, Arendt highlights the simultaneity of "man" appearing "as
a completely emancipated, completely isolated being who carried his dignity
within himself without reference to some larger encompassing order," and
the disappearance of this man "into a member of a people" (p. 291). In an
elaboration on the violent potential of this paradox, Arendt cites the
institution of the Nuremburg Laws in Nazi Germany, where, for instance,
foundlings were

> explicitly regarded as stateless until "an investigation of their racial characteristics
> [could] be made." Here the principle that every individual is born with inalienable rights
> guaranteed by his nationality has been deliberately reversed: every individual is born
> rightless, namely stateless, unless subsequently other conclusions are reached. (p. 288)

Unlike Schmitt's concern in other words – the conditions that give rise to the *creation* of political identities and the *granting* of rights – Arendt's concern in these passages is the conditions under which certain populations are *deprived* of their political identities and *denied* their rights. Moreover, unlike Schmitt, who situates a human being's political identity within his or her participation in the friend/enemy distinction – within the abstraction of the sovereign decision – Arendt associates a human being's lack of a political identity with his or her loss of a concrete and meaningful "place in the world." Finally, whereas the logical conclusion to Schmitt's interpretation of civil, sovereign, and human rights is precisely their elaboration in the Nuremburg Laws, the logical conclusion to Arendt's interpretation is that all human beings must possess the right to a political identity – even before they posses the right to life – if rights are going to have any meaning at all (Arendt, 1968, 1976, p. 296).

At the same time, I think that Arendt's and Schmitt's interpretations of sovereign, civil, and human rights are not as different as they might at first appear. First of all, each seems to be operating according to the same temporal assumptions. When Arendt talks about populations deprived of their political identity, for example, she is doing more than simply pointing out that minority groups have sometimes and unexpectedly been denied what appeared to be their inalienable rights. Indeed, one running theme in *Origins of Totalitarianism* is that those groups who lost their political identity in the first half of the twentieth century never truly had such an identity to begin with. This is made most obvious in the example of the Nuremburg laws, but it is also clear in her analysis of mass de-naturalization during times of crisis (pp. 283–286). Whereas Schmitt situates a human being's political identity in the future, Arendt situates a human being's lack of a political identity in the past. For each, rights represent nothing more nor less than the nation's juridical *future* situated in the non-human's non-existent *past*.

Second, both Schmitt and Arendt appear to agree about the universality of this statist potential. Arendt's discussion of the de-humanizing individuality of the rightless human being, for instance – of his or her inability to create meaning with the loss of a common world – draws from many of the same assumptions as Schmitt's point that human life can only become "specifically political" when it is framed within the common friend/ enemy distinction. Indeed, the major difference between the two is arguably that when Schmitt states that the friend/enemy distinction transcends borders, he does not attach any obvious moral value to the point, whereas when Arendt states that "only with a completely organized humanity could the loss of home and political status become identical with the expulsion from humanity altogether" (p. 297), she suggests that this is both undesirable and paradoxical.

Finally, Schmitt and Arendt likewise appear to agree that these temporal and spatial characteristics of rights granting result in the collapse of human into civil into sovereign rights. We can see this in a straightforward way in the counterintuitive statement in the "Universal" Declaration of Human Rights, inspired by the work of Arendt, that the most basic *human* right is the right to a *nationality* (Article 15). On a more theoretical level, though, I think we can likewise see it in the centrality of the state of exception in the writing of both. Arendt may not use the term "state of exception" in the same way that Schmitt does, but her discussion of the damning "innocence" of the stateless (and thus rightless) person – of the comparatively better situation of the criminal vis à vis the refugee (Arendt, 1968, 1976, p. 286) – is arguably a statement about the exceptional nature of rights and rights granting. When she suggests, for instance, that "innocence, in the sense of complete lack of responsibility, was the mark of [stateless people's] rightlessness as it was the seal of their lack of political status" (p. 295), what she is saying is that rights have meaning only in exceptional circumstances. The criminal, unlike the refugee, is a person defined by Schmitt's non-exceptional, "day-to-day jurisprudence" – an individual irrelevant to sovereign (according to Schmitt) and human (according to Arendt) rights. The refugee, contrarily, is a person defined by the state of exception. The refugee's very rightlessness is thus evidence of the simultaneity of sovereign, civil, and human rights.

Once again, therefore, although they have inspired vastly different normative and historical legacies, the work of Schmitt and the work of Arendt intersect in a number of key areas. Indeed, the primary difference between the two appears to be that whereas Schmitt does not find the genocidal foundation of civil rights, sovereign rights, and human rights morally problematic, Arendt sees this linkage between rights and genocide as "paradoxical" or "perplexing" at best and "calamitous" at worst. What I suggest, however, is that this close relationship between rights granting and genocide is only a paradox, only a calamity, if we take it on faith that rights are a *good* thing – that at some point in the hypothetical past, rights were not inherently genocidal and that then, at a later point, something went horribly wrong. If, however, we recognize that all rights are founded upon a potential genocide, we can approach both the apparent failure of legislation on genocide and the persistent repetition of genocidal violence in a more effective way. We can recognize that rights are situated in one specific type of community formation and that this type of community formation must be played out upon a wide, indeed universal, stage.

THE GENOCIDE CONVENTION

In the previous two sections, I drafted a schematic theoretical framework for understanding genocidal rights. I tried to show first of all that rights rhetoric shifts political identity into the future and that the granting of rights is predicated upon the existence of certain politically non-human people who never possessed rights in the past and therefore will never possess them in the future. Second, I argued that the apparent tension or balance among sovereign, civil, and human rights is a chimera, and that in many ways sovereign, civil, and human rights are the same thing. What I would like to do now is move my discussion to a more concrete level and analyze the way in which these theoretical claims have played out in the 1947 Genocide Convention itself.

I am not going to reprint the text of the 1947 Genocide Convention here because it has already been reproduced in countless contexts all over the world. Suffice it to say that the Genocide Convention is couched within a relentless rhetoric of rights and rights-granting and is predicated on the idea that genocidal violence is a) antithetical to systems of rights and b) can be prevented through a recourse to rights. Again, what I demonstrate in this section is that in fact the Genocide Convention – like all other rights-based legislation – is founded upon a fundamental right to *commit* genocide and that its rhetorical framework has made genocide the most obvious endpoint to politics. I suggest that it is a concrete example of the theoretical issues raised earlier – that it assumes the conflation of civil, sovereign, and human rights, that it situates political identity in the future, that it demands the realization of a potential statist universality, and that it is therefore in and of itself genocidal. To get at these points, I will examine an overlooked, but I think fundamental, aspect of the Convention – namely the persistence of piracy and barbarism as analogies for genocide in the rhetoric leading up to and surrounding it.

At first glance, the repeated invocation of pirates and barbarians by advocates of the Genocide Convention seems to be nothing more than a superficial rhetorical move. Various post-war governments feared that ratifying a document like the Genocide Convention would undermine their national sovereignty, and so the "pirate" analogy was brought into play to allay these concerns. The international scope of the new crime of genocide was in fact nothing new, so the argument went, in that it was couched in the same terms as the age old international crime of piracy. As Raphael Lemkin argued in 1947,

> if the destruction of human groups is a problem of international concern, then such acts should be treated as crimes under the law of nations, like piracy, and every state should be able to take jurisdiction over such acts irrespective of the nationality of the offender and of the place where the crime was committed. (Lemkin, 1947a, p. 146)

In a *New York Times* editorial written the same year, he elaborated on this notion, stating that,

> all civilized nations consider piracy as an international crime and a great number of them consider as international crimes also trading in slaves, women and children, the drug traffic, spreading of obscene publications, and forging of currency. If a pirate is apprehended in New York he will be tried by the court in New York irrespective of whether he is a Frenchman or a Turk and regardless of the place where he robbed the vessel. Such will be in the future also in the case of genocide. The ground will burn under the feet of such offenders and they will be unable to get refuge outside of their territory. (Lemkin, 1947b, p. 24)

In the years that followed, a number of other jurists supported Lemkin's position on genocide, likewise drawing on the pirate analogy to explain the international character of the crime (Kunz, 1949, p. 745; Kuhn, 1949, p. 500). The basic purpose of holding up piracy as a legal equivalent to genocide was thus seemingly a purely doctrinal one – having everything to do with defining sovereign jurisdiction vis à vis international law and little to do with the deeper meaning of genocidal violence.

In the years leading up to the ratification of the Convention, equating genocide with barbarism became almost as common as equating it with piracy. Lemkin himself initially conceived of what eventually came to be known as "genocide" as "barbarism," and proposed the following law to the League of Nations in 1933:

> Whosoever, out of hatred towards racial, religious, or social collectivity, or with a view of the extermination thereof, undertakes a punishable action against the life, bodily integrity, liberty, dignity, or economic existence of a person belonging to such a collectivity, is liable, for the crime of barbarity.... (Naimark, 2006, p. 15)

After the war, Lemkin continued to imagine the crime as "barbarism," even as the term "genocide" acquired the emotional and political weight that it carries today. He was, for example, clear about the fact that the Nazis "constituted a reversion to barbarism" and that "once there was barbarism, consisting of tribal wars of extermination. Then there was gradual progress toward civilization, manifested particularly in the international law of war" (Freeman, 1995, p. 209).

Like piracy, therefore, barbarism became a necessary reference point for understanding the new crime of genocide. Indeed, throughout the 1940s and 1950s, barbarism was as much a staple of journal and newspaper articles supporting, for instance, United States ratification of the Genocide Convention as piracy was – in some cases even overlapping with the pirate narrative. As one *New York Times* article stated in 1947,

> this is no idealistic convention made for moralizing purposes. It is a practical treaty, drawn by practical men, which would bind nations to act collectively against the evil wherever it showed up in the world. The term genocide—the "rebarbarization" process practiced by the Nazis and Japanese—means the annihilation of national, racial, religious or ethnical groups whether by massacre, deportations (such as slave labor) or cultural destruction. Simply stated, the treaty would guarantee the right to live. (Anonymous, August 23, 1947, p. 12)

Here, in other words, the "practical" tone of the discussions linking genocide to piracy is brought to bear on the idea that genocide is also the same as barbarism. There is indeed a slippage between piracy and barbarism as each is invoked as a means of defining genocide. Whereas initially genocide-as-piracy operated in the realm of doctrine, making possible the extension of international jurisdiction over the crime, and genocide-as-barbarism operated in the realm of theories of civilization, turning the crime into an assault on the abstraction that was universal rights, soon the two collapsed into one another. It was precisely the assault on universal rights inherent in barbarism that made it subject to the law of nations, and likewise precisely the international jurisdiction over piracy that made it an assault on a universalizing rights-based system.

At the same time, as early as the 1960s, both piracy and barbarism began to disappear in discussions of genocide – or to appear solely as examples of what genocide was not. In her discussion of the trial of Adolph Eichmann, for example, Arendt criticizes both the invocation of barbarism and the invocation of piracy in analyses of genocide. With regard to the former, she argues that "the very word 'barbarism,' today frequently applied by Germans to the Hitler period, is a distortion of reality; it is as though Jewish and non-Jewish intellectuals had fled a country that was no longer 'refined' enough for them" (Arendt, 1963, 1994, p. 55). She goes into more detail dismantling the connection between piracy and genocide, stating that

> the principle of universal jurisdiction, it was said, was applicable because crimes against humanity are similar to the old crime of piracy, and who commits them has become, like the pirate in traditional international law, *hostis humani generic*....[T]he pirate's exception to the territorial principle...is made not because he is the enemy of all, and hence can be judged by all, but because his crime is committed on the high seas, and the

high seas are no man's land. The pirate, moreover, "in defiance of all law,
acknowledging obedience to no flag whatsoever," is an outlaw because he has chosen
to put himself outside all organized communities....[S]urely no one will maintain that
Eichmann was in business for himself. (Arendt, 1963, 1994, p. 261)

A few pages later, Arendt further emphasizes what she sees as the farce of
placing the pirate and the perpetrator of genocide into the same analytical
category, arguing that "one can hardly call upon the whole world and gather
correspondents from the four corners of the earth in order to display
Bluebeard in the dock" (Arendt, 1963, 1994, p. 276). According to Arendt, in
other words, genocide has nothing to do with barbarism in that, unlike
barbarism, it is very much the product of a "refined" or "civilized" society.
More to the point, it has nothing to do with piracy given, first, the "territorial
principle" – the pirate becomes the enemy of mankind because of *where* he or
she commits a crime, not because of *what* crime he or she commits. Second,
Arendt suggests that the pirate "has chosen to put himself outside all
organized communities" – something that perpetrators of genocide, like
Eichmann, clearly did not.

In contemporary discussions of genocide, pirates and barbarians serve only
one purpose, and that is to explain how international jurisdiction operates.[6]
Divorced from this rhetorical purpose, each category seems absurdly
anachronistic – barbarism with its taint of imperial civilizing missions, and
piracy as an eighteenth century terror turned into a twentieth century legal
fiction. But there is more going on in this mid twentieth century rhetorical
link between piracy or barbarism on the one hand and genocide on the other
than might at first appear – the invocation of pirates and barbarians, or
pirates *as* barbarians, goes beyond simple questions of the scope of
international jurisdiction.

In fact, I think that Arendt makes a perhaps inadvertently fundamental
point when she argues that pirates *choose* to define themselves as the enemy of
all mankind, to position themselves beyond the borders of organized political
structures, whereas Eichmann did not. Indeed, this issue of choice and its
relation to political identity is at the heart of a more basic connection between
piracy/barbarism and genocide – a connection that plays up the simultaneity
of civil, sovereign, and human rights in the Convention, a connection that
situates political identity in the future and the lack of a political identity in
the past, and a connection that therefore shows the Convention to be one of
the most relentlessly genocidal acts of legislation of the twentieth century.

First of all, it is important to realize that piracy was not actually a
throwback to seventeenth and eighteenth century norms, rehabilitated in the
twentieth century as a device to make the Genocide Convention palatable.

In fact, piracy as an international crime had been revived with some force during and after the First World War, in particular as a means of condemning German submarine warfare (Genet, 1938, pp. 255–256). Although the English, French, and United States governments never succeeded in officially designating German submarines as "pirates," they did succeed in linking the two in the popular and scholarly imagination – and eventually the submarine-as-pirate ship metaphor expanded into a broader narrative of civilization, barbarity, and human rights. As one legal scholar writing in 1937 noted, even the President of the United States Woodrow Wilson, "in recommending to Congress on April 2, 1917, a declaration of a state of war with Germany...declared 'the present German submarine warfare is a warfare against mankind. It is a war against all nations.' *Hostis humani generic* is the phrase usually applied by jurists to pirates" (Finch, 1937, p. 665).

By the 1920s, the pirate had become an indispensable player in the new international law system, manifested especially in the League of Nations. The legal scholar Philip Marshall Brown, for instance, was explicit about the close relationship between the legal/political personality (or lack thereof) of the pirate and the interconnected interwar systems of civil, sovereign, and human rights that were quickly becoming the only framework in which politics could be discussed. In 1924, in an article on "the Individual and International Law," he stated that

> the pirate is the enemy of mankind. He may be summarily executed without any thought concerning his nationality. A slave bound in chains is entitled to his freedom the world over. No one for a moment would think to ask what his political allegiance might be. Piracy and slavery are both proscribed by the law of nations. (Brown, 1924, p. 533)

By 1941, Brown had shifted his focus away from the rights of the individual and toward the rights of the sovereign. In his analysis of "Sovereignty in Exile," for instance, he develops a sophisticated – if in some ways counterintuitive – theory of sovereignty in relation to piracy, downplaying the importance of territory to sovereign existence and emphasizing the importance of political status:

> The members of the family of nations cannot with honor abandon any independent free nation to international gangsters and pirates....[T]he right of prescription cannot be conceded to freebooters, even though they hold their illgotten territorial gains for years....[T]his sovereignty may be suspended, and in exile, a mere figment even of reality, derided and discouraged, and yet entitled to every respect. Ambassador Biddle in London therefore is not dealing with fictions: he speaks to those valiant standardbearers of sovereignty in England the language of faith and confidence as well as of inalienable, immutable rights. (Brown, 1941, pp. 667–668)

The pirates in this scenario are – as they were during the First World War – the German government. The exiled "standardbearers of sovereignty" are the ambassadors of Poland and Norway. What I want to highlight in these discussions, however, is not the validity or invalidity of interpreting international law in this way, but rather the intimate relationship that has been forged in the text between the pirate on the one hand and the bearer of human rights or sovereign rights on the other.

What Brown argues in 1924 is quite basically that *both* the slave *and* the pirate are denationalized – that never would you give "any thought concerning nationality" to either. But whereas the slave – by virtue of this denationalization – becomes a member of mankind, entitled to "freedom the world over," the pirate, by virtue of the same process, is denied his or her very right to have rights. At the same time, the only difference between the slave who is everywhere politically free and the pirate who is everywhere politically dead is that one is designated the "friend" and the other the "enemy" of mankind.

This requirement that the friend/enemy decision precede any articulation of civil, sovereign, or human rights becomes even more pronounced in Brown's discussion of sovereignty. Here, sovereign power is an "inalienable, immutable right," a right that – like the right of the slave – transcends political boundaries, a right that is simultaneously national and universal, and above all a right that is defined as the thing that the pirate *cannot* possess. But how do we know who is a "pirate" and who is not? We rely on the decision that includes within or excludes from the "family of nations." In each case, in other words, rights are embedded simultaneously in the individual, in the sovereign, and in the international "family of nations." Civil rights, sovereign rights, and human rights become the same thing. More to the point, in each case, the coming together of the human or the sovereign on the one hand and universal *systems* of rights on the other renders one individual politically existent and one individual politically non-existent. Finally, in each case it is the pirate – that signifier so fundamental to the Genocide Convention – that operates as the latter.

These theoretical analyses of the relationship between the pirate and the rights-bearing sovereign, citizen, or human became concrete when the League of Nations codified the status of pirates in 1926. Starting with the apparently straightforward issue of territorial jurisdiction, the report published by the "Committee of Experts for the Progressive Codification of International Law" states that "when pirates choose as the scene of their acts of sea-robbery a place common to all men and when they attack all nations indiscriminately, their practices become harmful to the international community of all States" (Matsuda & Committee of Experts for the Progressive Codification of International Law, 1926, p. 224). It ends, however, in much the same place that Brown did, designating pirates "the enemies of the human race and...outside the law of peaceful people" (Matsuda & Committee of Experts for the Progressive Codification of International Law, 1926, p. 224). Indeed, pirates are once again explicitly denationalized – a process, however, linked as much to the "reality" of territory as it is to the abstractions of civilization and (or *as*) sovereignty:

> by committing an act of piracy, the pirate and his vessel *ipso facto* lose the protection of the State whose flag they are otherwise entitled to fly. Persons engaged in the commission of such crimes obviously cannot have been authorized by any civilized State to do so. In this connection we should note that the commission of the crime of piracy does not involve as a preliminary condition that the ship in question should not have the right to fly a recognized flag. (p. 225)

This interpretation of piracy was later reified in discussions of "rebels" and "pirates" during the Spanish Civil War, where, for example, a rebel was defined as a not-pirate – as Arendt's "criminal" – by the act of rebellion, while the pirate was defined as a not-rebel – in effect, the same thing as Arendt's "innocent" – by his or her (lack of a) political status: "one does not become a pirate by mere intent alone; there is a strict status of piracy. Within its limits one is a pirate; outside of them he is not....[T]he pirate is 'the bandit of the sea'" (Genet, 1938, pp. 256–257).[7]

The pirate in these analyses is thus nothing more nor less than the fundamental "enemy" in what has now become a universal friend/enemy distinction; the pirate's status is representative of who can – and who *cannot* – possess civil, sovereign, and human rights. Whereas the slave, denationalized, the sovereign, denationalized, and even the rebel – former citizen and potential sovereign – can possess all three, the pirate, by virtue of his or her *status*, by virtue of the fact that a civilized and therefore[8] sovereign state could never *have* authorized piracy, cannot.

Once again, my purpose here is not to criticize the position of pirates within the international law system – nor is it to argue that perpetrators of genocide, as "pirates," should not be subject to universal jurisdiction. Likewise, my purpose is not merely to highlight the exclusionary aspects of international law, to talk solely of defining the Other. Rather, I want to look more carefully at the *temporal* assumptions about rights that manifest themselves in the vocabulary of piracy and barbarism surrounding the Genocide Convention – at the extent to which in this vocabulary, political identity is situated in the future and the lack thereof in the past.

Arendt argues that Eichmann is not a "pirate," that pirates choose to place themselves outside of all organized communities, and that Eichmann obviously did not. What I suggest, however, is that this analysis involves a misreading of both "choice" and "organized community," especially as they are expressed in the framework of rights rhetoric. "To choose," for example, is a meaningful act, as Arendt (1968, 1976, p. 296) herself notes, only within an existing political structure – individuals do not "choose" to opt out of the social contract. It is not, in other words, the pirates who apply to *themselves* the sobriquet "enemy of mankind;" this is a status that results from some variation on a universal sovereign decision. More to the point, actually being a member, as Eichmann was, of some sort of community – even being a citizen of a sovereign state in possession of territory – by no means preserves one from being designated a "pirate." As Brown has made clear, entire governments, in possession of territory, can be "pirates," whereas "sovereigns in exile," possessed of nothing but their *potential* political identity, their inalienable right to *become* sovereign, cannot. Likewise, flying the flag of a sovereign nation state means nothing according to the League of Nations commission, if a ship in the past has already been designated by the "family of nations" as a pirate. In this sense, therefore, Eichmann was very much a pirate, in every sense of the word.

What, though, does this designation mean? And in particular, what does this designation suggest about the nature of rights? What it means first of all is that the "organized community" within which Eichmann – or any perpetrator of genocide – was or is operating ceases to be a member of the family of nations, ceases to be civilized, and therefore ceases to be sovereign. More fundamentally, however, it also means that this organized community *never was* a member of the family of nations, civilized, or sovereign. If the perpetrator of genocide is a pirate, in other words, if he or she cannot, as the League of Nations document put it, "have been authorized by any civilized state" to commit the crimes that he or she committed, then a key temporal shift has occurred. It is not just that both the sovereign and civil rights of the perpetrator of genocide *now* do not exist – it is that they never existed to begin with. Just as the articulation of *civil* rights in the late eighteenth century required the prior non-existence of non-people, in other words, of people who never had rights and never would have rights, here too the articulation of *human* rights requires the prior non-existence of other groups, of other nation-state formations. The *potential* nature of political existence – the placement of rights into the future – thus takes on much greater meaning as the crime of genocide is articulated. The state and/or citizen that commits genocide may have seemed sovereign, may have seemed to have had a political existence, but the moment the designation "perpetrator of genocide" is brought into play, it becomes clear that in fact this state and sovereign never did exist politically. The further implication of this move is that this state and sovereign likewise will never exist. They are explicit non-entities.

In many ways, this seems not to raise any problems. Genocide, like piracy, is a terrible crime, and so why not destroy both the past and future political existence of its perpetrators? At the same time, however, I suggest that in fact the Convention is founded upon precisely this right to commit genocide – and to commit genocide precisely as it is defined in the Convention. It is based in a rhetoric of civilization that moves beyond the simple act of designating certain groups uncivilized and therefore not sovereign. More than that, it takes the eighteenth century nation/state's juridical potential to its logical conclusion.

Once again, the key to designating Eichmann – or any perpetrator of genocide – an enemy of mankind, a pirate, is denying the *past* sovereignty of the state under which he was acting, of placing that state outside of the family of nations. What this argument entails is thus not only denationalizing Eichmann, but denationalizing each and every citizen of what used to be that sovereign state. To the extent that civil rights are linked to – or the same as – sovereign rights, rendering the genocidal state not sovereign and never sovereign therefore renders each and every individual within that state not a citizen, never a citizen, and, paradoxically or not, subject to genocidal violence. Put another way, to the extent that defining and prosecuting the crime of genocide relies upon certain individuals, and *therefore* certain states, becoming "enemies of mankind"—becoming not sovereign and never sovereign – it relies upon the elimination of those enemies of mankind that, as a group, never in fact existed to begin with.

More to the point, unlike Brown's slave who becomes a member of mankind in general upon his or her denationalization, the non-citizens of the non-sovereign genocidal state have already been defined as uncivilized, pirates, and outside of the family of nations. In this sense, prosecuting genocide as it is defined by the Convention, reinforcing the right to existence of certain national groups, entails the potential for, if not the actuality of, the elimination of other politically non-existent national groups. The twentieth century right of a "people" to exist is thus no different from the eighteenth century right of a human/citizen to exist – founded upon the same potential right to commit genocide.

Lemkin's statement that the "ground will burn under the feet of such offenders and they will be unable to get refuge outside of their territory" in this way becomes more than a simple statement that perpetrators of genocide will be subject to universal jurisdiction. Likewise, the argument in the *New York Times* that Germany and Japan had undergone a process of "rebarbarization," a process that assaulted an abstract, universal "right to live," becomes more than just an invocation of vague categories of savage and civilized. In each case, the political non-existence of the perpetrator of genocide is predicated upon a conflation of civil, sovereign, and human rights. The only way in which Lemkin's individual offenders can take on the status he assigns them is if the sovereign states, groups, or territories in which they operate likewise become barbaric, enemies of mankind. Put another way, the only way to make the pirate analogy viable is to turn entire territories into "water" – to render what seemed like the sovereign state of, say, Japan not-sovereign and never-sovereign. The non-existence of the perpetrator of genocide is reliant, that is, upon the present, past, and future non-existence of the organized group in which he or she operated.

This may seem like a reasonable punishment for committing genocide. But, again, the key point to keep in mind here is that punishment has nothing to do with these relationships. Rendering an individual, state, or group politically non-existent is completely irrelevant to what Schmitt calls day-to-day jurisprudence, irrelevant to notions of innocence or criminality. As Arendt argues, being criminal, being punished, implies a political status, a secure position, that being politically non-existent emphatically does not. "Paradoxically," therefore, the Genocide Convention turns the perpetrators of genocide into Arendt's "innocents." The right to existence of national, ethnic, religious, and racial groups as it is articulated in the Genocide Convention, in other words, is directly reliant upon the elimination of other groups – just as the human/citizen's right to existence as it is articulated in the eighteenth century political theory of Sieyès is. Indeed, the only difference between the Genocide Convention and the "rights of man" is arguably that the Genocide Convention is far more inexorable about the *universal* nature of this process than even the French revolutionaries were.

CONCLUSIONS

I end with a return to Foucault's discussion of rights, social contracts, and biopolitics. In his analysis of modern political relationships, Foucault repeats his point that the early modern emphasis on consensus, victory, or invasion as a precursor to political formation – the emphasis on noble agreements and barbarian conquests – had become anachronistic by the beginning of the nineteenth century. In the modern period, he argues,

> what constitutes the strength of a nation is not so much its physical vigor its military aptitudes, or, so to speak, its barbarian intensity, which is what the noble historians of the early eighteenth century were trying to describe. What does constitute the strength of the nation is now something like its capacities, its potentialities, and they are all organized around the figure of the State: the greater a nation's Statist capacity, or the greater its potential, the stronger it will be. Which also means that the defining characteristic of a nation is not really its dominance over other nations. The essential function and historical role of a nation is…its ability to administer itself, to manage, govern, and guarantee the Constitution and workings of the figure of the State and State control. (Foucault, 1976, 2003, p. 223)

Barbarians, in other words, have little to do with contemporary forms of political association or, more importantly, political violence. At the same time, however, it is precisely the work of barbarians that the criminalization of genocide – that most contemporary of all forms of political violence – is trying to curb. There are two simple ways of getting around this apparent contradiction. The first is to assume that Lemkin's use of the term "barbarism," and its subsequent appearance in mid (but not late) twentieth century discussions of genocide, was misguided – that his fear of genocide was quite sensible, but that his fear of barbarians was less so. The second is to argue that Foucault's understanding of contemporary political violence is flawed – and that trying to analyze genocide in a framework of biopolitics is a doomed project.

Each of these approaches makes a great deal of sense and each does indeed resolve the conflict between defining genocide as an act of barbarism and defining genocide as a function of biopolitics. What I have tried to do in this essay, however, is suggest that these two definitions of genocide are not as contradictory as they might seem – that the appearance of barbarians in discussions of genocide is precisely what gives the legislation on the crime its biopolitical clout. What the criminalization of genocide rejects, in other words, is indeed barbarism – it rejects, in the name of rights, the domination of one nation over other nations. What it does *not* reject – what it cannot reject, given its recourse to civil, sovereign, and human rights systems – is biopolitical state formation. It is precisely in the name of stopping the barbarians, in the name of endowing all citizens, sovereigns, and humans with inalienable rights, divorced from conquest, that it insists upon the elaboration of Foucault's universal State. And this is a State predicated not upon domination, but upon the management of the life and death of populations, upon the guarantee of a Constitution, and above all upon on the necessity, I have tried to show, of rendering non-existent – if not necessarily killing – those individuals and groups that exist outside of its universality.

In Foucault's interpretation of Sieyès, rights are always potential, always situated in the future, but never in the present. Rights do not derive from citizenship, but rather citizenship derives from rights – those within the nation have rights, and are *therefore* potential citizens within a potential state. Those outside of the nation never had rights in the past and never can have rights in the future. This process is manifested concretely (if in reverse) in a quite spectacular way in legislation on genocide. There is first the denationalization of the perpetrator of genocide and then there is *consequently* the stripping away of sovereign rights – in both past and future – of the state in which he or she was operating. We do not have here the domination of one nation over another – an attack on a national group in the abstract leading to attacks on certain members of that group in practice. Rather we have biopolitical state formation occurring – the non-existence of one member of a national group leading to the non-existence of the past and future State implied by that nation.

This leads in turn to two other issues that intersect in important ways in legislation on genocide. The first is the spatial placement of rights within the blood of a people, and the second is the apparent tension among civil, sovereign, and human rights. Ordinarily these two points – the racism inherent in, say, blood-based English rights-rhetoric, turned hyperbolic in the "scrap of paper" metaphor that was mobilized during the First World War, and the contradictions involved in advocating civil rights concurrently with human rights – are seen as reasons to advance a policy of *universal* rights granting, as reasons to try to block the "paradoxical" racism that seems always to undermine such humanitarian impulses. What I suggest, however, is that there is no actual tension between civil and sovereign, or sovereign and human rights systems – and that in fact it is precisely the potential universality of such systems that renders them so uncompromisingly racist.

Again, in the legislation on genocide this connection becomes concrete. The perpetrator of genocide, the pirate, and the barbarian – or the perpetrator of genocide *as* the pirate *as* the barbarian – are enemies of mankind, not human, subject to "summary execution" precisely because they belong – and belonged – to no recognized nation. It is the universality of the law of nations that renders them without any race – without any blood in which the cause of law might flow. Whereas before the elaboration of the right to existence of groups was based upon the non-existence of other groups, that is, here the elaboration of a universal system of rights is based upon the denial not just of rights, but of blood, of national existence, to those placed outside of that system.

When I say that all civil, sovereign, and human rights are based on the fundamental or foundational right to commit genocide, therefore, I am doing so not in order to provoke some hypothetical thought experiment. My argument is situated firmly within histories of rights, theories of sovereignty, and the doctrine – in this case – of the Genocide Convention. Moreover, my reason for choosing the Genocide Convention as a particular illustration of this point is not that it is the only place in which this connection between rights rhetoric and genocidal violence plays out. Rather, since it is a document concerned explicitly with the protection of groups – with the right to existence of groups – it is more insistent on the non-existence of other groups. Indeed, I think this reading of the Convention, or of any legislation on genocide, is a necessary precursor to addressing the reality of genocidal violence in any sort of serious way.

NOTES

1. For a concrete example of this assumption, see the discussions on the "rule of law" in occupied Iraq and how it must precede any "effective" state-building process (Liebl, 2005).

2. I use the word "nation" broadly here and throughout the chapter. Whereas it is true that not all states are nation-states, I think a case can be made that most rights-based states produce a version of "national" rhetoric. An excellent example of "nationalism" of this sort in a self-consciously imperial, multinational state can be seen in the rights rhetoric of the late Ottoman Empire. The first declaration of modern political rights by the Ottoman state was the 1839 *Hatt-i Şerif* of Gülhane, which turned all Ottoman subjects, regardless of religion or ethnicity, into Ottoman citizens. By the time the Ottoman Constitution appeared in 1876, rights and citizenship had become linked to "national" feeling – even as the Empire itself continued to be defined as an inclusive, multinational state that could ideally withstand nationalist separatist movements. See, for example, article 3: "Zat-ı Hazret-i Padişahî, hin-i cülusunda Meclis-i Umumi'de ve Meclis müctemi' değilse, ilk ictima'ında şer'-i şerif ve Kanun-i Esasi ahkamına ria'yet ve vatan ve millete sadakat edeceğine yemin eder." "Upon his succession to the throne, His Imperial Majesty shall swear before Parliament, or, if Parliament is not in session, at its first meeting, to respect the provisions of *şeriat* and the Constitution, and to be loyal to the fatherland and nation" ("Kanun-i Esasi" in Kahraman, Galitekin, & Dadaş, 1998, art. 3, p. 21).

3. It is from this position that Foucault goes on to develop his theory of biopolitics, which he then associates with genocidal colonial violence and Nazi policy.

4. In this case within Germany.

5. And also, therefore, "deciding whether [the] normal situation actually exists," Schmitt, *Political Theology*, p. 13.

6. This becomes particularly apparent in discussions of universal jurisdiction over torturers and terrorists at the beginning of the twenty-first century.

7. For a relevant discussion of bandits and the state of exception, see Agamben (1995, 1998, pp. 104–105).

8. See Antony Anghie (1999), for an excellent discussion of "civilization" and sovereignty in modern international law.

REFERENCES

Agamben, G. (1995, 1998). *Homo sacer: Sovereign power and bare life*. Trans. Daniel Heller-Roazen.. Stanford: Stanford University Press.

Anghie, A. (1999). Finding the peripheries: Sovereignty and colonialism in nineteenth-century international law. *Harvard International Law Journal, 40*(1), 1–80.

Anonymous. (1947). For a "genocide" treaty. *New York Times*, August 23, p. 12.

Arendt, H. (1963, 1994). *Eichmann in Jerusalem: A report on the banality of evil*. New York: Penguin Books.

Arendt, H. (1968, 1976). *The origins of totalitarianism*. New York: Harcourt.

Brown, P. M. (1924). The individual and international law. *American Journal of International Law, 18*(3), 532–536.

Brown, P. M. (1941). Sovereignty in exile. *American Journal of International Law, 35*(4), 666–668.

Finch, G. A. (1937). Piracy in the Mediterranean. *American Journal of International Law, 31*(4), 659–665.

Foucault, M. (1976, 2003). *Society must be defended: Lectures at the Collège de France, 1975–1976*. Trans. David Macey. New York: Picador.

Freeman, M. (1995). Genocide, civilization, and modernity. *British Journal of Sociology, 46*(2), 207–223.

Genet, R. (1938). The charge of piracy in the Spanish Civil War. *American Journal of International Law, 32*(2), 255–256.

Gullace, N. F. (1997). Sexual violence and family honor: British propaganda and international law during the First World War. *American Historical Review, 102*(3), 714–747.

Kahraman, S. A., Galitekin, A. N., & Dadaş, C. (Eds). (1998). İlmiyye Salnamesi. Istanbul: İşaret Yayınları.

Kennedy, D. (2004). *The dark side of virtue: Reassessing international humanitarianism*. Princeton: Princeton University Press.

Kuhn, A. K. (1949). The Genocide Convention and state rights. *American Journal of International Law, 43*(3), 498–501.

Kunz, J. L. (1949). The United Nations Convention on Genocide. *American Journal of International Law, 43*(4), 738–746.

Leblanc, L. J. (1984). The intent to destroy groups in the genocide convention: The proposed U.S. understanding. *American Journal of International Law, 78*(2), 369–385.

Lemkin, R. (1947a). Genocide as a crime under international law. *The American Journal of International Law, 41*(1), 145–151.

Lemkin, R. (1947b). For punishment of genocide: Adoption of convention advocated as step to safeguard civilization. *New York Times*, June 12, p. 24.

Liebl, R. J. (2005). Rule of law in postwar Iraq: From Saddam Hussein to the American Soldiers involved in the Abu Ghraib prison scandal, what law governs whose actions? *Hamline Law Review, 28*, 91–134.

Marramao, G. (2000). Schmitt and the categories of the political: The exile of the nomos: For a critical profile of Carl Schmitt. *Cardozo Law Review, 21*, 1567–1587.

Matsuda, M.Committee of Experts for the Progressive Codification of International Law. (1926). Questionnaire no. 6: Piracy. *American Journal of International Law, 20*(3), 222–229.

Melson, R. (1996). Paradigms of genocide: The Holocaust, the Armenian genocide, and contemporary mass destructions. *Annals of the American Academy of Political and Social Science, 548*, 156–168.

Naimark, N. (2006). Totalitarian states and the history of genocide. *Telos, 136*, 10–25.

Schmitt, C. (1932, 1996). *The Concept of the political*. Trans. George Schwab. Chicago: University of Chicago Press.

Schmitt, C. (1922, 1985). *Political theology*. Trans. George Schwab. Chicago: University of Chicago Press.

Yovel, J. (2007). How can a crime be against humanity? Philosophical doubts concerning a useful concept. *UCLA Journal of International Law and Foreign Affairs, 11*, 1–21.